Television Courtroom Broadcasting

Television Courtroom Broadcasting
Distraction Effects and Eye-tracking

Paul Lambert

intellect Bristol, UK / Chicago, USA

First published in the UK in 2012 by
Intellect, The Mill, Parnall Road, Fishponds, Bristol, BS16 3JG, UK

First published in the USA in 2012 by
Intellect, The University of Chicago Press, 1427 E. 60th Street,
Chicago, IL 60637, USA

A catalogue record for this book is available from the British Library.

Cover designer: Holly Rose
Copy-editor: MPS Technologies
Production manager: Bethan Ball
Typesetting: Planman Technologies

ISBN 978-1-84150-647-0

Printed and bound by Bell & Bain Ltd UK

MIX
Paper from responsible sources
FSC® C007785

To SG

Contents

Preface

Television courtroom broadcasting (TCB) is as hotly debated today as it was in the *Estes* case in the US Supreme Court in 1965. The same arguments and concerns that arose in 1965 exist today as they did then. For various reasons, the empirical research required to confirm and validate the respective effects which judges, policy makers and society have been concerned about has not been carried out.

It is unfortunate, therefore, that the debate surrounding television courtroom broadcasting still frequently rests upon hot air and personal opinions.

One of the central concerns in relation to television courtroom broadcasting is that television cameras or television operators will distract the various people who are required as part of the courtroom process. This includes witnesses, the jury, judges, lawyers and court staff.

This is the concern in relation to distraction effects. The empirical research effort since 1965 has been insufficient to answer and validate this concern. While there are some studies, these are too diminutive and stand alone. That is, they do not seek to verify or replicate each other. Each study, therefore, stands in splendid isolation.

Quite glaring research gaps exist in relation to our knowledge of the effects, adverse and positive, in relation to television courtroom broadcasting.

It might be suggested that because the actual size of television cameras has reduced so much, that there are no distraction effects. Some television courtroom broadcasting today does involve miniaturised television cameras. However, there is no research or statistics to show that this is universally or even predominantly the case.

There is also no research to compare the effects between situations where full sized versus miniaturised television cameras are used.

While media technology has changed, the significant point is that the research technology has also changed. Today, we have more research technology, research tools and comparative research knowledge than at any time previously.

We are better able to research distraction effects today than we were in 1965. Just because certain television courtroom broadcasting now involves miniaturised cameras, does not mean that distraction cannot occur. Indeed, even without actual distraction effects, there may still be other inhibiting effects, particularly on the non-professional persons whom may be in court.

One of the ways to conduct research in relation to where a person is looking involves new research tools called eye-trackers. An eye-tracker involves very small cameras which record where a person's eyes are looking. The result is a recorded video showing exactly where and for how long the person is looking.

If applied to the problem of distraction effects in the courtroom, we can now record and see where the individual courtroom participants are looking. We can see if they are distracted by the television cameras or the camera operator in the courtroom. We can also apply eye-tracking research to different types of television cameras in courtrooms, from small to large, from fixed to moving cameras.

We shall explore the first proof of concept demonstration of eye-tracking inside a courtroom with a view to examining television courtroom broadcasting distraction effects. Many of the eye-tracking images and topography are reproduced, as well as the implications discussed.

We can now research actual distraction effects in the television courtroom broadcasting debate.

> "Social scientists measure the intelligence of monkeys more effectively than courts have attempted to ascertain the effects of television in the courtroom."
>
> (Hirschhorn 1980: 7 and 9)

Television courtroom broadcasting arguments and the effects research are each inadequate. We have not devoted sufficiently rigorous and empirical research to the effects. The *in-court* distraction effects of television cameras, *or* television cameras plus operators, on the courtroom participants/actors in the courtroom are unknown. The US Supreme Court, in the three television courtroom broadcasting cases, has set a challenge to carry out more empirical effects-research.

New technology can now accurately track and record whether the courtroom participants/actors (real or mock courtroom participants/actors) look at the television cameras in the courtroom and for how long. We can now – for the first time – accurately research in-court distraction effects. This new technology is called "eye-tracking" technology. The author has undertaken the first demonstration of the use of eye-tracking to examine in-court distraction effects for television courtroom broadcasting.

Acknowledgement

The publication of this book is kindly assisted by a grant from the National University of Ireland.

Chapter 1

Introduction

Debate and concerns

Cameras in court or television courtroom broadcasting (TCB) is topical and controversial. This book explores one important aspect of the TCB debate.

It explores one of the central concerns in the TCB debate, namely whether there are effects of television cameras in the courtroom. Are the people in court affected or distracted by the television cameras? This is a frequent concern in the debate regarding TCB. Many people have argued that TCB will adversely affect or distract the participants in a case where cameras are permitted. This concern extends to the camera operators if they are permitted in the courtroom.

We will see that not only do these concerns remain, but that they have never been properly researched empirically. With that in mind, the author identifies how modern technology may afford a solution to this part of the wider debate regarding TCB effects.

Eye-tracking can track and record where individual persons in the courtroom are looking, for how long and ultimately whether they are distracted. Eye-tracking TCB research can provide valuable data, insights and answers, which have lingered at least since 1965 when the US Supreme Court first voiced its concerns. (The US Supreme Court shall generally be referred to as the "Supreme Court" throughout the rest of the book).

The book also points out that the debate and effects research need to be much more nuanced.

The legal starting point is the Supreme Court cases. The Supreme Court refers to the distraction-research issues and concerns. It sets the Supreme Court distraction effects research-challenge. The Supreme Court distraction effects research-challenge is significant internationally.

Any policy and legal discussion of TCB must address the effects, concerns and effects research-challenge highlighted by the Supreme Court. There are three Supreme Court cases. One could argue that they do not decide or establish any legal rule *per se*. However, the common theme in the three cases is that they all refer to and recognise that a central issue is the empirical effects research. They establish the Supreme Court empirical research-challenge in relation to the effects of TCB. This includes distraction effects.

Clearly there are concerns voiced by the Supreme Court. Many potential effects are referred to, such as distraction. Although the Supreme Court has set an empirical research-challenge, it never said how this research should occur. There are no directions, baselines or parameters established. The detail of addressing the research-challenge was left to others. This book significantly develops our knowledge of: how to support and develop our understanding, language, definitions, baseline and parameters of the distraction research necessary to deal with the distraction effects concerns that exist. It also explores and significantly develops the Supreme Court research-challenge with a demonstration of how eye-tracking can take the TCB effects research forward.

TCB has occurred frequently in the United States but in different forms. The Simpson (criminal) case and Judge Judy are very different forms. Even in the Unites States, concerns continue to be raised. The debate and concerns are topical presently for a number of reasons. There is a debate in the United States about introducing television cameras into US federal courts. A separate debate relates to whether TCB should be permitted in the Supreme Court. There has been ongoing debate over a number of decades in the United Kingdom. An official "consultation" took place in 2004 (Department for Constitutional Affairs consultation "Broadcasting Courts"). Recently a form of TCB has been permitted in the UK Supreme Court. Certain parties are now calling to expand TCB beyond the UK Supreme Court into other courts. The main proponent appears to be Sky TV (see generally Ryley 2010).

Despite the importance of the effects issues, it is perhaps surprising that the Supreme Court has only referred to television camera issues on three occasions. The two seminal cases are *Estes* and *Chandler*. The most recent case was *Hollingsworth*. It is clear from these cases that the Supreme Court was and is aware that there are substantial research gaps. The common theme in these cases is the challenge by the Supreme Court that social science and empirical research needs to be undertaken to address the research gaps.

Although the Supreme Court identifies the need for proper research of these issues, the research-challenge has not yet been fully taken up by social science researchers, the media nor the courts themselves. The gaps, concerns and effects are not addressed. This includes concerns about (adverse) distraction effects on those in the courtroom.

The debate in relation to TCB involves many arguments, both for and against cameras in court. This book focuses mainly upon one of those arguments, namely, the argument that introducing television cameras into courtrooms will distract the courtroom participants or actors. Surprisingly, this argument has not been definitively answered in a dedicated body of empirical effects research. As such, this concern remains at issue despite the existence of TCB in the United States. Eye-tracking offers a new solution to this part of the debate.

Background: Three Supreme Court cases

The Supreme Court has discussed the concerns that arise in relation to TCB on three occasions.

The cases were *Estes* (1965), *Chandler* (1981) and most recently *Hollingsworth* (2010). The Supreme Court is aware that there are substantial research gaps in relation to the effects of TCB, and has highlighted a significant research-challenge. More social science and empirical research needs to be carried out to address the research gaps. This is the Supreme Court empirical effects research-challenge. Unfortunately, the research-challenge has not been properly addressed. This is surprising given what is at stake in the courtroom. A defendant's liberty can be at stake. In certain jurisdictions even a person's life can be at stake.

There are various forms of courtroom broadcasting, for example, radio, television and more recently Internet. The present book concentrates on distraction effects of one of these forms, namely TCB. That is not to say, however, that some of the distraction issues and concerns with TCB may not also occur in other forms.

TCB has occurred most frequently in the United States – in different forms. Yet, the effects debate continues. Why is this?

One reason is that there is still so little empirical research dealing with the concerns raised, including distraction concerns. Is there definitive distraction research? How good are self-reports of distraction, or self-reports as to the lack of distraction (that is, asking participants directly if they themselves were affected)? Are the few historical third party observations of courtroom participants accurate in relation to distraction effects? Rarely does the empirical research literature seek to compare the effects of criminal cases that may be broadcast, versus the effects of broadcasting civil cases. What are the stated policies or aims of courtroom broadcasting? If it is to achieve or enhance education, confidence or information, for example, how often has empirical research sought to validate these effects? Are particular courtroom broadcasts meant to educate or enhance confidence, for example, riot sentencing (decisions), criminal sentencing, appeal decisions (criminal/civil), full or gavel to gavel (G2G) cases versus snippets of cases, in-court film only footage versus in-court film plus in-court audio footage? If we are seeking to measure effects of introducing courtroom broadcasting, be it distraction or otherwise, how frequently has the research to date undertaken baseline research, that is, gathering data *before* cameras are introduced to draw comparisons and measure effects? This applies equally to other effects issues.

Effects can occur in very different ways. Effects can be very nuanced. We may have different effects, including distraction effects, for different forms of courtroom broadcasting. Generally, the effects of different forms of courtroom broadcasting are not empirically (or otherwise) researched and compared. It is broadly assumed, for example, that TCB will achieve equal educational effects across all forms of courtroom broadcasting. Many people have also assumed that *all* forms of TCB will not distract the courtroom participants. Can this be correct?

Also ignored is the central question of what is "courtroom broadcasting"? Surprisingly, the research literature does not properly address this question. It is important to address this question because defining courtroom broadcasting and *television* courtroom broadcasting helps us to begin properly distinguishing the different effects. It also assists us in differentiating and researching the effects per individual forms of courtroom broadcasting. Consider, for example, how often the education effects of radio courtroom broadcasting have been compared to TCB. How often has TCB been compared to Internet courtroom broadcasting? Have the different forms of TCB been defined and distinguished? Have the different effects of each been researched? Consider, for example, the differences in form as between entertainment TCB, reality TCB, news TCB, documentary TCB, live TCB, Internet TCB (iTCB). The nuances of each can lead to different potential effects. Yet the research and policy debate has not yet begun to address these nuances.

The book examines one of the research gaps identified in the Supreme Court empirical research-challenge, distraction effects, and how we might address that research-challenge. The author commends the use of new eye-tracking technology to research in-court distraction effects on courtroom participants, actors or personnel. In addition, the author has undertaken a successful proof-of-concept demonstration to further advance this part of the Supreme Court research-challenge.

The debate in the United States centres in particular on legislative efforts regarding TCB in US federal courts (e.g. "Sunshine in the Courtroom" Bill(s)), the second federal courts experiment, the Supreme Court *Hollingsworth* case, and the effects and benefits generally.

A full examination of the history and prevalence of courtroom broadcasting is beyond this book (but readers might be interested in the review of US state-wide TCB, carried out by the Radio Television Digital News Association (RTDNA) annually). This book is also not about the arguments or the debate on either side *per se*.

The *Estes* case

The *Estes* case decided against permitting TCB. It effectively barred cameras from US courts for decades. It held that TCB infringed the defendant's rights to a fair trial (*Estes*: 535). Although it referred to out-of-court effects issues, the comments in relation to in-court effects are the most interesting to eye-tracking research. Responding to these comments is the challenge.

Mr Justice Clarke delivered the main opinion. It sets out many of the areas that should be addressed by a sustained body of empirical effects research. It should be noted, however, that not all potential effects issues were identified and set out in the Supreme Court judgements. The research and literature do not appear to refer to or acknowledge this point.

The *Chandler* case

The *Chandler* case was more permissive towards courtroom broadcasting. It upheld a decision in Florida to allow the televised broadcasting of a case. As such, it is sometimes viewed as overruling or distinguishing *Estes*. Kozinski and Johnson state that *Chandler* lifted the *Estes* "prohibition" (2010: 1110). They add that "the Court noted evidence that those concerns were 'less substantial factors' in 1981" (Kozinski and Johnson 2010: 110) than 1965. The ban was not actually lifted to permit unlimited courtroom broadcasting. Rather the *Chandler* Supreme Court said that the individual states were permitted to experiment with TCB. It did not expressly mandate nor judicially permit any and all forms of courtroom broadcasting. Indeed strictly speaking, it was only dealing with one form of courtroom broadcasting, namely, TCB in a criminal case. Even within TCB, there are many forms/sub-forms. Unfortunately, the discussion to date has generally not defined and examined the different forms and sub-forms of TCB. The significant nuances and different effects are effectively ignored.

The *Hollingsworth* case

The most recent Supreme Court case occurred in 2010. The Supreme Court was asked to stay the television broadcast of a federal trial. The Californian District Court had issued an order permitting live broadcasting via streaming video to a number of federal courts (*Hollingsworth*: 1). The defendants objected (*Hollingsworth*: 2). They sought a stay, which was granted by the Supreme Court (*Hollingsworth*: 2).

The case relates to the same sex-marriage law proposal (Proposition 8 or Prop 8) in California. Some parties said that they had been harassed as a result of their involvement, including receiving death threats (*Hollingsworth*: 2). They anticipated that these threats would continue or increase if TCB was permitted.

The local court had envisaged this case as an experiment of TCB in California's federal courts (*Hollingsworth*: 5). This necessitated changing a local law, which banned such broadcasting (*Hollingsworth*: 9).

The Supreme Court challenge

Despite the importance of effect issues, it is surprising that the Supreme Court has only referred to TCB issues on three occasions. The two seminal cases are *Estes* and *Chandler*. The most recent case is *Hollingsworth* in January 2010. The other two took place in 1965 (*Estes*) and 1981 (*Chandler*).

One would have expected that, in the 47 years since the first of these cases, substantial and sustained empirical research would have occurred to meet the challenge, which would have enhanced our knowledge and understanding of TCB. One would expect, for example, that there would be substantive empirical research of distraction effects in court. This is not the case. The first televised broadcast case took place even earlier than 1965.

Unfortunately, it is clear from these cases that the Supreme Court was and is aware that there are substantial research gaps. This includes the distraction effects research gap. Despite the Supreme Court identifying the need for proper research of these issues, the empirical research-challenge has not been fully taken up by social science researchers, the media, courts or policymakers. Eye-tracking offers one very clear avenue for such research. It also has substantial advantages over some of the less rigorous research previously. It can be recorded and is verifiable.

There are many research problems. We have too little research. There are many research gaps. Many studies are non-scientific and non-empirical, and rely on personal opinion, self-reports, opinion-reports and questionnaires only. Self-report research has significant flaws – in any field of research. The main problem is that they are subjective. They can also be inaccurate. The first reported TCB case occurred in 1953. This is referred to in the literature as the case of Billy Eugene Manley in Oklahoma City in 1953 (Barber 1987: 10–11). Cinema broadcasts of courtroom footage occurred prior to that. Most, if not all, of the effects literature is addressed to television as opposed to the movie theatre broadcasts. Yet, many of the same in-court distraction issues may apply to filming for the movie broadcasts. This issue is not addressed in the general literature possibly because the movie broadcasts diminished as TCB became more popular. Yet since then, there appears to be just over twenty scientific, methodical and empirical studies of TCB effects issues. These are welcome, but as yet, obviously insufficient and inconclusive.

The book suggests that with today's research methodologies, technology and eye-trackers (see Chapters 7 and 8) in particular, we can begin to empirically address some of the concerns and challenges of the Supreme Court. The author is the first researcher to identify, recommend and advance such research.

Let us see what the Supreme Court said in relation to the lack of research. The Supreme Court recognised that there was not enough proper and empirical research, and set a challenge that such research be undertaken to fill the substantial research gaps (*Estes*: 541 Clarke, J). Chief Justice Warren in *Estes*, referring to the case of *Tumey* where "the Court found the procedure so inconsistent with the conception of what a trial should be and so likely to produce prejudice that it declared the practice unconstitutional even though no specific prejudice was shown" (*Estes*: 550, 562). Keating commented in relation to a stockholders meeting that "[s]ome stockholders seemed very much aware that they were on camera" (*Estes*: n 24, at 569, 569–570 and examples of how people react when they know they are on television). *Estes* refers to Jack Gould, who states that even experienced performers can be affected, and that this "psychological and emotional burden must not be placed on a layman whose testimony may have a bearing on whether, in a murder trial, another human being is to live or die" (*Estes*: 569, 587, 588, 589, 603–604, 611–612, 615, 616).

Chandler referred to research and empirical evidence research (*Chandler*: 561, 568, 560–589, 566, 576, n 11, at 576, referring to *In re Petition of Post-Week Stations, Florida, Inc. Chandler*: 559–560, n 12 at 560, 578, 581).

Hollingsworth also referred to the lack of empirical evidence (*Hollingsworth*: 6–7).

The *Hollingsworth* Supreme Court (minority) cited the authors Cohn and Dow (1998: 62 et seq) who only found four empirical social science studies between 1953 and 1998. The four studies are as follows: Ernest H. Short and Associates (1981; California); *Federal Judicial Centre, Pilot Program Involving Electronic Coverage in Six US District Courts and Two Appeal Courts* (1994); Hoyt (1977; Wisconsin); and Borgida, DeBono and Buckman (1990; Minnesota).

The author identifies more than twenty methodical and empirical research studies (see below). Of course, although welcome, this too is hardly a sufficient body of empirical research to be determinative of effects issues in relation to TCB participants. It is also inadequate to answer distraction-effect concerns across all forms of TCB.

Research rationale of court: *Estes* and courtroom participants/actors

The *Estes* judgements variously refer to effects on courtroom participants or actors, namely the jurors, witnesses, judges and defendants.

Estes: Need to show actual prejudice?

Mr Justice Harlan in *Estes* states that the "petitioner has not asserted any isolatable prejudice resulting from the presence of television apparatus within the courtroom or from the contemporaneous or subsequent broadcasting of the trial proceedings" (*Estes*: 587). Part of the problem is that it can be very difficult to establish prejudice in a given instance. However, in a given experiment, eye-tracking can do exactly that. It can find distraction effects where they Occur, in a recorded, verifiable and demonstrated manner. This was never possible before.

In *Estes* the state of Texas argued that specific prejudice must be shown for the constitutional due process and fairness clause to apply (*Estes*: 593 Harlan, J).

> "I believe petitioner in this case has shown that he was actually prejudiced by the conduct of these proceedings, but I cannot agree with those who say that a televised trial deprives a defendant of a fair trial only if 'actual prejudice' can be shown. The prejudice of television may be so subtle that it escapes the ordinary methods of proof, but it would gradually erode our fundamental conception of trial. A defendant may be unable to prove that he was actually prejudiced by a televised trial, just as he may be unable to prove that the introduction of a coerced confession at his trial influenced the jury to convict him when there was substantial evidence to support his conviction aside from the confession."
>
> (*Estes*: 578 Warren, CJ)

To the extent that Texas was saying there are no effects shown, it beholds researchers to examine each of the separate effects issues. Unfortunately, much of the general literature has not identified and isolated an individual effect hypothesis and is hence suspect. Much of the literature cannot be said to have researched *any* actual or specific effect. To answer the Supreme Court/Texas/etc. challenge, it must be a rigorous, demonstrated, replicable, and verifiable research of a specific effect hypothesis. In meeting this challenge, the standard and scope of the research needs to be expanded, made more robust and empirical.

If the overall standard and quality is not sufficient, it does not properly address the Supreme Court research-challenge. The debate remains just that, opinion based and not evidence based.

Estes: Research

The Supreme Court recognised that there was not enough proper and empirical research. It set a challenge that research be undertaken to fill the substantial research gaps. Set out below are some of the comments of the Supreme Court with regard to the research issues and gaps.

- "[O]ur empirical knowledge of its full effect on the public, the jury or the participants in a trial, including the judge, witnesses and lawyers, is limited" (*Estes*: 541 Clarke, J);

  The Supreme Court recognised that there is a distinct lack of empirical research, and a sustained body of such research;

  By referring to the public and the courtroom participants/actors, the Supreme Court also acknowledges in-court effects-research gaps and the out-of-court effects-research gaps;
- "The State would dispose of all these observations with the simple statement that they are for psychologists because they are purely hypothetical. But we cannot afford the luxury of saying that, because these factors are difficult of ascertainment in particular cases, they must be ignored. Nor are they 'purely hypothetical.' They are no more hypothetical than were the considerations deemed controlled in *Tumey*, *Murchison*, *Rideau* and *Turner* (*Tumey*; *In re Murchison*; *Rideau* ... Referred to *Estes*: 562). They are real enough to have convinced the Judicial Conference of the United States, this Court and the Congress that television should be barred in federal trials by the Federal Rules of Criminal Procedure; in addition they have persuaded all but two of our States to prohibit television in the courtroom. They are effects that may, and in some combination almost certainly will, exist in any case in which television is injected into the trial process" (*Estes*: 550 Clarke, J). Obviously, certain equipment matters have changed over time. However, the challenge still remains and was in fact reiterated in the most recent case – in 2010;

  Although the Supreme Court is saying that it does not always need to wait for tangible psychological or other effects, it is implicit that it wants research to be undertaken in the various effects-research areas;
- The state of Texas, in defending cameras, argued that no prejudice has been shown by *Estes*, that there were no distractions and that "psychological considerations are for psychologists, not courts, because they are purely hypothetical" (referred to at *Estes*: 541 Clarke, J). It also argued that the defendant had not established any "isolatable prejudice" (*Estes*: 542 Clarke, J);

Therefore, to show effects and sufficient effects to amount to (potential) prejudice, a party needs to be aware of when and where effects or distraction can occur. However, are they properly trained and equipped to do this? Can they focus on finding effects, such as distraction, when dealing with their case at the same time? What can researchers and interested parties do in terms of general empirical research? Unfortunately, despite the challenge set by the Supreme Court, and indeed Texas itself, the various research-challenges are not yet properly addressed. Eye-trackers can help to address this particular problem;

The ABA (American Bar Association) Committee on Professional Ethics and Grievances was quoted by the Supreme Court as reporting that "courtroom photographing or broadcasting or both would impose undue police duties upon the trial judge[,] ... that the broadcasting and the photographing in the courtroom might have an adverse psychological effect upon trial participants, judges, lawyers, witnesses and juries[,] ... [and] that partial broadcasts of trials, particularly on television, might influence public opinion which in turn might influence trial results" (referred to *Estes*: 599 Harlan, J);

- The ABA House of Delegates, is reported as deciding to have a Special Committee study Canon 35 and to "conduct further studies of the problem, including the obtaining of a body of reliable factual data on the experience of judges and lawyers in those courts where either photography, televising or broadcasting, or all of them, are permitted. ... The fundamental objective of the Committee and of all others interested must be to consider and make recommendations which will preserve the right of fair trial" (*Estes*: 599, referring to 83 *ABA Rep*. 284 (1958). Harlan, J);
- "Surely possibilities of this kind carry grave potentialities for distorting the integrity of the judicial process bearing on the determination of the guilt or innocence of the accused, and, more particularly, for casting doubt on the reliability of the fact-finding process carried on under such conditions ... To be sure, such distortions may produce no telltale signs, but in a highly publicized trial the danger of their presence is substantial, and their effects may be far more pervasive and deleterious than the physical disruptions which all concede would vitiate a conviction" (*Estes*: 592 Harlan, J);
- Chief Justice Warren emphasises that "our condemnation of televised criminal trials is not based on generalities or abstract fears. The record in this case presents a vivid illustration of the inherent prejudice of televised criminal trials and supports our conclusion that this is the appropriate time to make a definitive appraisal of television in the courtroom" (*Estes*: 552 Warren, CJ);
- Warren, CJ also states that he believes that "it violates the Sixth Amendment for federal courts and the Fourteenth Amendment for state courts to allow criminal trials to be televised to the public at large. I base this conclusion on three grounds: (1) that the televising of trials diverts the trial from its proper purpose in that it has an inevitable impact on all trial participants; (2) that it gives the public the wrong impression about the purpose of trials; and (3) that it singles out certain defendants

and subjects them to trials under prejudicial conditions not experienced by others" (*Estes*: 565 Warren, CJ);

- It notes that "'television ... can ... [change] behaviour ...' (*Estes*: 569, and n 24, at 569. Warren, CJ). The present record provides ample support for scholars who have claimed that awareness that a trial is being televised to a vast, but unseen audience, is bound to increase nervousness and tension, cause an increased concern about appearances, and bring to the surface latent opportunism that the traditional dignity of the courtroom would discourage. Whether they do so consciously or subconsciously, all trial participants act differently in the presence of television cameras. And, even if all participants make a conscientious and studied effort to be unaffected by the presence of the television, this effort in itself prevents them from giving their full attention to their proper functions at trial. Thus, the evil of televised trials, as demonstrated by this case, lies not in the noise and appearance of the cameras, but in the trial participants' awareness that they are being televised. To the extent that television has such an inevitable impact it undercuts the reliability of the trial process" (*Estes*: 569–570. Warren CJ. Footnote omitted). In n 24, at 569, he refers to Tinkham, who refers to examples of how people react when they know they are on television. He also notes Gould, who refers to even experienced participants being affected, and the greater danger of effects on lay participants (*Estes*: 569 Warren, CJ);
- In the dissenting opinions it states that "[w]e deal here with matters subject to continuous and unforeseeable change – the techniques of public communication. In an area where all the variables may be modified tomorrow, I cannot at this time rest my determination on hypothetical possibilities not present in the record of this case. There is no claim here based upon any right guaranteed by the First Amendment. But it is important to remember that we move in an area touching the realm of free communication, and for that reason, if for no other, I would be wary of imposing any *per se* rule which, in the light of future technology, might serve to stifle or abridge true First Amendment rights" (*Estes*: 603–604 Stewart J. Minority opinion);

  Television and broadcasting technology may change. Yet, so too can research models, research techniques, research knowledge and research tools. One example of advanced research tools is eye-trackers (see Chapters 7 and 8). If better methods allow us to address the Supreme Court challenge in new ways, we should embrace them;
- "It is obvious that the introduction of television and news cameras into a criminal trial invites many serious constitutional hazards. The very presence of photographers and television cameramen plying their trade in a courtroom might be so completely and thoroughly disruptive and distracting as to make a fair trial impossible. Thus, if the scene at the September hearing had been repeated in the courtroom during this jury trial, it is difficult to conceive how a fair trial in the constitutional sense could have been afforded the defendant. And even if, as was true here, the television cameras are so controlled and concealed as to be hardly perceptible in the courtroom itself,

there are risks of constitutional dimensions that lurk in the very process of televising court proceedings at all" (*Estes*: 611–612 Stewart, J. Minority opinion);

- Mr Justice White, dissenting, states that "[i]n my view, the currently available materials assessing the effect of cameras in the courtroom are too sparse and fragmentary to constitute the basis for a constitutional judgment permanently barring any and all forms of television coverage. As was said in another context, 'we know too little of the actual impact ... to reach a conclusion on the bare bones of the ... evidence before us.' White Motor Co. v United States, ... It may well be, however, that as further experience and informed judgment do become available, the use of cameras in the courtroom, as in this trial, will prove to pose such a serious hazard to a defendant's rights that a violation of the Fourteenth Amendment will be found without a showing on the record of specific demonstrable prejudice to the defendant" (*Estes*: 616 White J. Minority opinion). The later point is often overlooked;
- "The opinion of the Court in effect precludes further opportunity for intelligent assessment of the probable hazards imposed by the use of cameras at criminal trials. Serious threats to constitutional rights in some instances justify a prophylactic rule dispensing with the necessity of showing specific prejudice in a particular case" (*Estes*: 616 White J. Minority opinion);
- "Here, although our experience is inadequate and our judgment correspondingly infirm, the Court discourages further meaningful study of the use of television at criminal trials. Accordingly, I dissent" (*Estes*: 616 White J. Minority opinion);
- "[W]e are concerned here only with a criminal trial of great notoriety, and not with criminal proceedings of a more or less routine nature" (*Estes*: 587 Harlan, J);
- "Permitting television in the courtroom undeniably has mischievous potentialities for intruding upon the detached atmosphere which should always surround the judicial process. Forbidding this innovation, however, would doubtless impinge upon one of the valued attributes of our federalism by preventing the States from pursuing a novel course of procedural experimentation. My conclusion is that there is no constitutional requirement that television be allowed in the courtroom, and, at least as to a notorious criminal trial such as this one, the considerations against allowing television in the courtroom so far outweigh the countervailing participants/factors advanced in its support as to require a holding that what was done in this case infringed the fundamental right to a fair trial" (*Estes*: 587 Harlan, J);
- "[A]t its worst, television is capable of distorting the trial process so as to deprive it of fundamental fairness. Cables, kleig lights, interviews with the principal participants, commentary on their performances, 'commercials' at frequent intervals, special wearing apparel and makeup for the trial participants – certainly such things would not conduce to the sound administration of justice by any acceptable standard" (*Estes*: 588 Harlan, J);
- "Within the courthouse, the only relevant constitutional consideration is that the accused be accorded a fair trial. If the presence of television substantially detracts from that goal, due process requires that its use be forbidden" (Estes: 589 Harlan, J);

- "I cannot say at this time that it is impossible to have a constitutional trial whenever any part of the proceedings is televised or recorded on television film. I cannot now hold that the Constitution absolutely bars television cameras from every criminal courtroom, even if they have no impact upon the jury, no effect upon any witness, and no influence upon the conduct of the judge" (*Estes*: 615 Steward J. Minority opinion).

So even the minority opinion raises important effects and effects-research issues.

Estes: Effects/actual effects

The Supreme Court said that in the proceedings at hand, there had been adverse effects and that there had been prejudice. For example, it stated the following,

- "The videotapes of these hearings clearly illustrate that the picture presented was not one of that judicial serenity and calm to which the petitioner was entitled" (*Estes*: 536 Clarke, J). There were 12 camera persons with television and photographic cameras (*Estes*: 536 Clarke, J);
- It was conceded that their activities "led to considerable disruption of the hearings" (*Estes*: 536 Clarke, J);
- "[T]he circumstances and extraneous influences intruding upon the solemn decorum of court procedure in the televised trial are far more serious than in cases involving only newspaper coverage" (*Estes*: 548 Clarke, J);
- The witnesses and jury "were undoubtedly made aware of the peculiar public importance of the case by the press and television coverage being provided, and the fact that they themselves were televised live and their pictures rebroadcast on the evening show" (*Estes*: 536–537 Clarke, J);
- "When he [i.e. the defendant] finally made his way into the courthouse it was reasonable for him to expect that he could have a respite from his merciless badgering and to have his case adjudicated in a calm atmosphere. Instead, the carnival atmosphere of the September hearing served only to increase the publicity surrounding petitioner and to condition further the public's mind against him" (*Estes*: 578 Warren, CJ).

Chandler: Empirical data/effect shown

The Supreme Court in *Chandler* again referred to research and empirical evidence research.

- It was held that "at present no one has presented empirical data sufficient to establish that the mere presence of the broadcast media in the courtroom inherently has an adverse effect on that process under all circumstances. Here, the appellants have offered nothing to demonstrate that their trial was subtly tainted by broadcast coverage – let alone that all broadcast trials would be tainted" (*Chandler*: 561);

- "No evidence of specific prejudice was tendered" (*Chandler*: 568);
- "Absent a showing of prejudice of constitutional dimensions to these appellants, there is no reason for this Court either to endorse or to invalidate Florida's experiment" (*Chandler*: 560–589);
- Because technology had changed since the *Estes* case, it was argued that "many of the negative factors found in *Estes* … are less substantial factors today than they were at that time" (*Chandler*: 576);
- The Supreme Court notes in a footnote that in the original experiment permitted by the Supreme Court of Florida, the court acknowledged that the research was "limited" and "non-scientific" (*Chandler*, n 11, at 576, referring to *In re Petition of Post-Week Stations, Florida, Inc.*, 1979);
- "Nonetheless, it is clear that the general issue of the psychological impact of broadcast coverage upon the participants in a trial, and particularly upon the defendant, is still a subject of sharp debate" (*Chandler*: 578);
- "Comprehensive empirical data are still not available – at least on some aspects of the problem" (*Chandler*: 578);
- It also adds that "… at present no one has been able to present empirical data sufficient to establish that the mere presence of the broadcast media inherently has an adverse effect on that process" (*Chandler*: 559–560).
  Eye-tracking was not known to the *Chandler* court;
- Even the amici briefs, supporting Florida in the Supreme Court case, admit that more experimentation is needed to evaluate the potential psychological prejudice (*Chandler*: n 12, at 560);
- "To demonstrate prejudice in a specific case a defendant must show something more than juror awareness that the trial is such as to attract the attention of broadcasters" (*Chandler*: 560);
- "The appellants have offered no evidence that any participant in this case was affected by the presence of cameras" (*Chandler*: 581).

***Hollingsworth*: No empirical data**

The dissent opinion could "find no basis [that] the applicants would suffer irreparable harm. Certainly there is no evidence that such harm could arise in this nonjury civil case from the simple fact of transmission itself … Neither the applicants nor anyone else 'has been able to present empirical data sufficient to establish that the mere presence of the broadcast media inherently has an adverse effect on [the judicial] process,' *Chandler* … 578–579 (1981) … M. Cohn & D. Dow, … 62–64 (1998) (canvassing studies, none of which found harm, and one of which found that witnesses 'who faced an obvious camera, provided answers that were more correct, lengthier and more detailed'). And, in any event, any harm to the parties, including the applicants, is reparable through appeal ... *Chandler* ... 581" (*Hollingsworth*: 6–7. Dissent).

Might eye-tracking research produce such empirical evidence? The author recommends that TCB eye-tracking studies be designed and carried out in future TCB effects research.

The four studies in Cohn and Dow (1998 and 2002: 62 et seq) is not a definitive or acceptable body of research. The research-challenge remains. In context, they found only four studies between 1953 and 2002. This is also not a complete list.

The *Hollingsworth* dissent further states that the

> applicants also claim that the transmission will irreparably harm the witnesses themselves, presumably by increasing the public's awareness of who those witnesses are. And they claim that some members of the public might harass those witnesses. But the witnesses, although capable of doing so, have not asked this Court to set aside the District Court's order ... And that is not surprising. All of the witnesses supporting the applicants are already publicly identified with their cause. They are all experts or advocates who have either already appeared on television or Internet broadcasts, already toured the State advocating a 'yes' vote on Proposition 8, or already engaged in extensive public commentary far more likely to make them well known than a closed-circuit broadcast to another federal courthouse. The likelihood of any 'irreparable' harm is further diminished by the fact that the court order before us would simply increase the trial's viewing audience from the occupants of one courtroom in one courthouse to the occupants of five other courtrooms in five other court-houses (in all of which taking pictures or retransmissions have been forbidden). By way of comparison literally hundreds of national and international newspapers are already covering this trial and reporting in detail the names and testimony of all of the witnesses. ... I see no reason why the incremental increase in exposure caused by transmitting these proceedings to five additional courtrooms would create any further risk of harm, as the Court apparently believes ... Moreover, if in respect to any particular witness this transmission threatens harm, the District Court can prevent that harm. Chief Judge Walker has already said that he would keep the broadcast 'completely under the Court's control, to permit the Court to stop it if [it] proves to be a problem, if it proves to be a distraction, [or] if it proves to create problems with witnesses.' ... The Circuit Council confirmed in a press release that the District Court 'will fully control the process' and that 'Judge Walker has reserved the right to terminate any part of the audio or video, or both, for any duration' or to terminate participation in the pilot program 'at any time' (*Hollingsworth*: 7–8, referring to News Release, Federal Courthouses to Offer Remote Viewing of Pro-position 8 Trial (8 January, 2010) ... Surely such firm control, exercised by an able district court judge with 20 years of trial-management experience, will be sufficient to address any possible harm, either to the witnesses or to the integrity of the trial (*Hollingsworth*: 7–8).

Estes: Subtle and discrete effects

The Supreme Court recognised that there may be subtle and or discrete effects.

- "Television in its present state and by its very nature, reaches into a variety of areas in which it may cause prejudice to an accused. Still one cannot put his finger on its specific mischief and prove with particularity wherein he was prejudiced" (*Estes*: 544 Clarke, J);
- Television "amounts to the injection of an irrelevant factor into court proceedings. In addition experience teaches that there are numerous situations in which it might cause actual unfairness – some so subtle as to defy detection by the accused or control by the judge" (*Estes*: 545 Clarke, J);

  Certainly in terms of eye attention and focus, we know that such effects are now no longer so subtle as to defy detection. The eye movements of simulated courtroom participants/actors, in test settings and in actual court settings, can be examined. There are many potential areas of courtroom actor eye-tracking research that can now be carried out;
- We "should not be deterred from making the constitutional judgment which this case demands by the prospect that the day may come when television will have become so commonplace an affair in the daily life of the average person as to dissipate all reasonable likelihood that its use in courtrooms may disparage the judicial process. If and when that day arrives the constitutional judgment called for now would of course be subject to re-examination in accordance with the traditional workings of the Due Process Clause. At the present juncture I can only conclude that televised trials, at least in cases like this one, possess such capabilities for interfering with the even course of the judicial process that they are constitutionally banned. On these premises I concur in the opinion of the Court" (*Estes*: 595–596 Harlan, J);
- "I do not deem the constitutional inquiry in this case ended by the finding … that no isolatable prejudice was occasioned by the manner in which television was employed in this case. Courtroom television introduces into the conduct of a criminal trial the element of professional 'showmanship,' an extraneous influence whose subtle capacities for serious mischief in a case of this sort will not be underestimated by any lawyer experienced in the elusive imponderables of the trial arena. In the context of a trial of intense public interest, there is certainly a strong possibility that the timid or reluctant witness, for whom a court appearance even at its traditional best is a harrowing affair, will become more timid or reluctant when he finds that he will also be appearing before a 'hidden audience' of unknown but large dimensions. There is certainly a strong possibility that the 'cocky' witness having a thirst for the limelight will become more 'cocky' under the influence of television. And who can say that the juror who is gratified by having been chosen for a front-line case, an ambitious prosecutor, a publicity-minded defense counsel, and even a conscientious judge

will not stray, albeit unconsciously, from doing what 'comes naturally' into pluming themselves for a satisfactory television 'performance'?" (*Estes*: 591 Harlan, J. Footnote omitted).

Conclusion

Despite the Supreme Court research-challenge, the issues and concerns relating to the in-court distraction effects of television cameras, little research has been done. We still do not have an answer to the concerns. In the cases of *Estes* and *Chandler* eye-trackers were not around. However, although eye-trackers were in existence at the time of the *Hollingsworth* decision, it appears that the Supreme Court was not aware of their existence, and of the import of eye-tracking for TCB distraction effects research.

Chapter 2

Empirical Effects Studies

Introduction

There is a variety of research, and commentary masquerading as research, in relation to TCB varying in research quality. Some of it is good, some of it is bad. The overall point remains, however, that there is far too little research.

We must also distinguish between empirical research and non-empirical or general research. The later, in some instances, does not record what was being researched and or how the research was conducted. The former is referred to below.

Prior research

Are the effects issues and questions examined extensively in empirical research? Unfortunately, a number of concerns arise. The number of empirical research studies is limited. Many gaps in the research exist. There is also a lack of replication and verification with further follow on studies of the actual research undertaken. The problem of distraction effects has not been answered. Indeed, it has not been properly addressed.

Empirical research

The prior empirical effects research in relation to TCB can be identified in the following studies, or parts of studies as the case may be,

1. Hoyt, James L., "Courtroom Coverage: The Effects of Being Televised," *Journal of Broadcasting* (1977) (21), 487–495;
2. E. H. Short and Associates, *Evaluation of California's Experiment with Extended Media Coverage of Courts, submitted to Administrative Office for the Courts; the Chief Justice's Special Committee on the Courts and the Media, and the California Judicial Council* (1981);
3. Shores, Donald Lewis Jr, *The Effects of Courtroom Cameras on Verbal Behaviour: An Analysis of Simulated Trial Witness Testimony in Courtrooms Using Television Cameras*, Ph.D. (University of Florida, 1981);
4. Pasternack, Steve Robert, *The Effects of Perceived Community Pressure on Simulated Juror Guilt Attributions: A Study*, Ph.D. (University of Tennessee, Knoxville, 1982);

5. Kassin, Saul M., "TV Cameras, Public Self-Consciousness, and Mock Juror Performance," *Journal of Experimental Psychology* (1983/4), 336;
6. Paddon, Anna R., *Television Coverage of Criminal Trials with Cameras and Microphones: A Laboratory Experiment of Audience Effects*, Ph.D. (University of Tennessee, Knoxville, 1985);
7. Borgida, E., Debono, K. and Buckman, L., "Cameras in the Courtroom: The Effects of Media Coverage on Witness Testimony and Juror Perceptions," *Law and Human Behaviour* (1990) (14);
8. Punches, Alan, *The Cognitive Effects of Camera Presence on the Recall of Testimony in a Simulated Courtroom Setting*, Ph.D. (Colarado State University, Fort Collins, 1991);
9. Johnson, M. T. and Krafka, C., *Pilot Program Involving Electronic Coverage in Six US District Courts and Two Appeal Courts* (Federal Judicial Centre, 1994) (in part only);
10. New York State Committee to Review Audio-Visual Coverage of Court Proceedings, *An Open Courtroom: Cameras in New York Courts* (New York: Fordham University Press, 1997) (in part only);
11. Netteburg, Kermit Lyol, *Cameras in the Courtroom: Is a Picture Worth a Thousand Words?*, Ph.D. (University of Minnesota, 1980);
12. Bukoff, Allen, *The Effects of Video Camera Techniques on the Pre-Deliberation Judgements and Perceptions of Role-Playing Jurors*, Ph.D. (Kent State University, 1984);
13. Alexander, S. L., *"Mischievous Potentialities": A Case Study of Courtroom Camera Guidelines, Eight Judicial Circuit, Florida*, Ph.D. (University of Florida, 1989);
14. Esposita, Steve Anthony, *OJ TV: A Narrative Analysis of Television's Pretrial Coverage of the OJ Simpson Case*, Ph.D. (Wayne State University, 1996);
15. Petkanas, William, *Cameras on Trial: An Assessment of the Educational Affect of News Cameras in Trial Courts*, Ph.D. (New York University, 1990);
16. Thaler, Paul E., *The Impact of the Television Camera on Courtroom Participants: A Case Study of the Joel Steinberg Murder Trial*, Ph.D. (New York University, 1990);
17. Keller, Theresa D., *Cameras in Courtrooms: An Analysis of Television Court Coverage in Virginia*, Ph.D. (University of Tennessee, 1992);
18. Entner, Roberta, *The Image of the Judiciary: A Semiotic Analyse of Broadcast Trials to Ascertain Its Definition of the Court System*, Ph.D. (New York University, 1993);
19. Kohm, Steven, *I'm Not a Judge But I Play One on TV: American Reality Based Courtroom Television*, Ph.D. (Simon Fraser University, 2004);
20. Stewart, Ruthie Elizabeth Reeves, *The Changing Relationship Between Camera and the Courts*, MA (Florida Atlantic University, 1998);
21. Ossinger, Jessica, *Electronic Access to Courtrooms: Television as an Educational Socializing Agent on the Judiciary*, MA (The University of Maine, 2006);
22. Allan, Kimberly, McGregor, Judy, Professor Fountaine, Susan, "The Impact of Television, Radio and still Photography Coverage of Court Proceedings, Final Report, A Report for the Department for Courts" (Massey University, April, 1998) (New Zealand);

23. Alves, Hon. Nathan Braverman, Chaor, Baron, Hon. Jean Szekeres, Groton, Hon. Thomas C. III, Leasure, Hon. Diane O., Plitt, Hon. Emory A., Jr, *Report of the Committee to Study Extended Media Coverage of Criminal Trial Proceedings in Maryland, Committee to Study Extended Media Coverage, a Subcommittee of the Legislation Committee of the Maryland Judicial Conference.*

Both the general research and the empirical research attempts have left many areas not yet addressed or validated. The challenge set by the Supreme Court still remains. Validation and replication issues are significant concerns. The first television courtroom broadcast took place in 1953 (listed by Barber, as the case of Billy Eugene Manley in Oklahoma City, see Barber 1987: 10–11). Susanna Barber (1987) indicates that from the period 1953–1987, there are only 17 (non-scientific) studies. Worse, she indicates that there are only two social science research studies between 1953 and 1987. In those particular 34 years of courtroom broadcasting, therefore, we only have two attempts to seriously or properly analyse (certain) effects of courtroom broadcasting.

The Supreme Court in both *Estes* and *Chandler*, the main cases in relation to courtroom broadcasting, "lamented the absence of hard data" (Kassin 1984: 337–349). "The overall controversy about cameras in courtrooms is unusual for the lack of specific data which have been brought to bear on the questions raised" (Hoyt 1977: 489). "In view of the practical importance of this problem for the judiciary and the Supreme Court's repeated plea for behavioural research on the matter, it is surprising that, to date, the only relevant data available are anecdotal case studies, public opinion surveys, and the verbal reports of those who had participated in television trials" (Kassin 1984: 337).

Since 1953, Ronald Goldfarb (1998) has been able to identify only eight social science studies regarding courtroom broadcasting. That is eight studies in 45 years. The first two of these are already listed in Barber (1987). So he only lists an additional six studies.

Susanna Barber lists James L. Hoyt's study of 1977 (Hoyt 1977: 487–495) as the first social science study of TCB. The Hoyt study was "attempting to experimentally test [the] speculation, to determine if, in fact, individuals are affected by the awareness that they are being televised" (Barber 1987: 10–11).

> The study simulated some of the pressures placed on witnesses in the courtroom while at the same time maintaining experimental control so that the results could be meaningfully analyzed. Subjects were shown a brief film containing rather detailed information, then were asked specific questions about the content of the film. While answering the questions they were either facing a conspicuous television camera purportedly recording their answers to be viewed by a large number of people, or an unobtrusive camera hidden behind a mirror, or no camera at all. … Based on the assumption obvious in the reasoning of Justices Clark and Warren [in *Estes*] it was predicted that when they were televised (whether by an obtrusive or unobtrusive camera) the participants would recall significantly less correct information about

> the film than when they were not being televised. Because a number of the recent proposals for courtroom coverage by television have mentioned that cameras would be camouflaged, the unobtrusive camera condition was included to determine the effects of hiding the camera.
>
> (Hoyt 1977: 490. Internal footnote reference omitted)

A review indicates that in the above studies there were,

- 9 experiments;
- 9 surveys;
- 4 reviews;
- 5 incorporated interview;
- 4 observations of court (live case);
- 1 court (not live/real case).

There is practically no meaningful research into any of the many aspects of TCB. There have been very few studies of TCB that can actually be described as research or qualitative research as we know it outside the above studies. Most of the rest amounts to reviews, observations, arguments and opinions. In terms of what might be described as qualitative research, it is limited in its scope and focus. There are many gaps. For example, it examines only self-reports for some of the courtroom participants/actors actually present. Many courtroom participants/actors are ignored in current research. This means that this research is *per se* limited in scope. The audience are not researched in terms of viewing effects or adverse effects.

In addition, almost invariably the effects literature is based upon survey type research. This utilises and relies solely upon the opinions of certain courtroom participants or actors. Sometimes these courtroom participants or actors may be interviewed but generally the courtroom participants or actors are requested to fill in a questionnaire asking them for their opinions to various predefined issues. As with any survey or questionnaire, the questions asked can vary in number and sophistication. However, the main flaws with this approach are threefold. Firstly, this is not the most reliable means of gauging effects of TCB on courtroom participants/actors. Other more scientific methods are available. Secondly, these studies are once off. Therefore, there are no internal or external checks or validations. Finally, there is no comparison or meta-analytic review of the various self-reports. Accuracy and trends cannot be considered.

Gaps in research

It is important to also point out that in addressing the Supreme Court empirical research-challenge, researchers should identify a particular effect to be researched in the context of a particular form of TCB. Too often commentators assume that an effect finding (or lack of a finding) is the same across all forms of TCB. Far too many generalisations are made from the studies to date. Significant research remains to be undertaken. The current studies are also frequently misunderstood and misrepresented.

Irony and change

According to Kowinski and Johnson, "[t]here was a time when we had no idea how these changes would add up, and it may have been reasonable to assume that the risks outweigh the potential benefits. But that was a long time ago" (2010: 1112). However, there is also considerable misrepresentation of results.

Kowinski and Johnson refer to how the audience has changed. However, that comment assumes only the audience (and arguably audience needs) can change. The Supreme Court in the camera cases also makes the claim that cameras and technology can change. It ignores the very important point that research and research methodologies can also change. It is ironic that some of the Supreme Court's comments (and Kowinski and Johnson: 1112) focus on how television technology may change in future. Neither the Supreme Court nor commentators since have recognised that research and research tools also change. Indeed the research tools have improved vastly since 1953 (the first reported television courtroom broadcast). In the case of eye focus and eye-tracking, the research and technology is significantly advanced (see below). We can track and record where courtroom participants/actors are looking and ultimately whether they are distracted. Eye-tracking is an important tool for in-court distraction effects research. It has yet to be used. The author is the first person to advance this methodology in relation to TCB.

Television technology and visibility

Kowinski and Johnson also state that today's technology is very different, "small, easily concealed and capable of operating without obtrusive lighting and microphones" (Kowinski and Johnson 2010: 1112). This is undoubtedly true. However, there is a general assumption made that this type of technology will be used in every case, or at least predominantly so. This is not uniformly the case in practice. What are the research statistics on where and how frequently miniature cameras are used? In how many instances in a pilot period are a large camera, a tripod, in-court camera operator, respectively, used? How does this compare between states, experiments, court levels, and importantly across and between different television courtroom forms? How does it change over time? Is there an obligation to use the least disruptive camera for TCB? Equally, it is not always the case that no camera operator will be located in the courtroom, even though Kowinski and Johnson correctly point out that camera technology can be operated remotely (Kowinski and Johnson 2010: 1112). There appears to be no research on these points as yet, despite their clear importance.

Kowinski and Johnson add that

> [i]f cameras in the courtroom rob criminal defendants and civil litigants of their dignity, and promote a public perception of trials as more about *sensational entertainment* than a sober search for truth, courts may be justified in parting ways with other public institutions, and public expectations, to exclude cameras in favour of forms of reporting than better advance respect for the rule of law and the guarantee of a fair trial.
>
> (Kowinski and Johnson 2010: 1112, emphasis added)

Kowinski and Johnson assume that the debate and concerns are over, and that the Supreme Court challenge no longer exists, or alternatively, is already answered. Either way, it is incorrect. Whether or not particular TCB footage is used or portrayed in a sensational or entertaining manner, really depends on the form or sub-form of TCB permitted. Also, the courtroom broadcasting effects debate does not begin and end at the courtroom door. The discussion to date is remiss in suggesting that all TCB is the same, and further that all effects are/will be the same across all forms of TCB. Why would all forms of TCB be equally distracting in court? It also assumes that civil and criminal cases are treated the same by the media. Kowinski and Johnson refer to sensationalism and entertainment. Where are the measures and statistics on the percentage of sensational versus non-sensational TCB generally, and between the different forms of TCB? Similarly, what is the percentage difference as between, for example, educational and entertainment TCB? Are certain forms of TCB cameras more distracting, and some less distracting? These are all issues that eye-tracking can help us to address.

Sample of research gaps

General: The research to date is *flawed* and in many instances *absent*. Even where there has been research, it is generally lacking in sophistication and methodology. Significantly more, and more sophisticated, TCB research is required.

Scope – definition: "Courtroom broadcasting" is not properly defined in the literature. This should be the starting point for most effects research. This research focuses on TCB as it relates to television cameras in the courtroom, filming courtroom proceedings for live and or contemporaneous television push broadcast to the general public. This definition excludes relayed or closed-circuit TCB. It also excludes radio, pull Internet, recording media, jury room, still photography and archival recording courtroom broadcasting.

Scope – researching form and effects: "Television Courtroom broadcasting/TCB" is generally not defined in the literature. Other forms of courtroom broadcasting are not defined either.

Effects research needs to define its scope in terms of the form of courtroom broadcasting, and the specific potential effect being tested. There is no proper generalised evidence of positive or negative effects because we have not properly researched for such effects. No body of replicated research has properly set out any particular effect it is seeking to investigate in relation to any particular form of courtroom broadcasting. It is difficult, therefore, to arrive at properly valid research conclusions. There is a general absence of research that has been subsequently replicated and verified.

Presumptions: The TCB arguments are also frequently presumptive. One of these, for example, is the presumption that TCB will be educational. This has not been properly researched or proven to be correct. It is also wrong to generalise that all effects are the same for every form of courtroom broadcasting. Could some forms lend themselves to being more educational than others? Is the least disruptive and most educational to be preferred?

Methodology: The general or non-empirical research is almost random and ad hoc. It is often very basic and simplistic in methodology. It does not consider in advance what effect is being examined nor how best to examine *that* effect. It is not carried out to a standard that might be replicated or validated by further studies. Many studies have not recorded details of questions asked and replies given. There is not sufficient general or empirical research of TCB to answer the arguments.

Forms: TCB arguments are fundamentally flawed. They ignore the fact that there are different types and forms of TCB. A TCB forms map would be beneficial to identify and categorise these different forms. No argument is verified without research. No argument applies (equally) across all forms of TCB. An argument should be justified in the context of a particular form (or sub-form) of TCB.

Validation and replication: Proponents/opponents fail to research, confirm or validate any of their arguments. For example, many advocate TCB because it is, or will be, educational. Yet, proponents never say why, how, in what circumstances, for what forms, etc. Nor do they show any research or validation. There is no suggestion either as to which TCB form(s) could be most educational.

Generally a proposition or argument is only accepted once repeated and verified in tests. This accepted method of study has not been recognised in the TCB debate or research to date. Future research should: distinguish between the different forms of TCB; identify in advance what exactly is being tested; involve those with knowledge and experience of conducting research; be properly conducted and recorded; be in such a manner that the research and methods may be critically examined by other researchers; be able to be replicated; and be validated by other research.

Cameras: It is important to say what camera types are involved, where the camera is located, etc. The height, location, angle, etc. of cameras are important in creating effects, as is revealed by legal-psychology research.

Participants/actors: If we are considering effects on courtroom participants/actors, we must say which participants/actors are being investigated, and how. Relevant factors/personnel have not been gauged or coded. It also means the replication of such research is not possible. Only certain people are asked relevant research questions. The study population is often statistically limited. The quality of the questions vary from study to study. There are no meta-analytic comparisons. Typically the self-report studies are not repeated and/or replicated. Generally the public in court are not asked relevant research questions. In effect, therefore, most of the courtroom participants/actors who give self-reports are legally trained or experienced. Defendants are typically not asked to undertake self-report research studies. Also, such studies generally appear not to be drafted by the persons most qualified to draft such questions and research. Nor are additional research fields and techniques generally consulted and incorporated.

Opinions and self-reports: To rely on questionnaires and self-reports as the sole indicator of whether there are effects or not, is wholly inadequate. Unfortunately, too much of the current research relies on self-reports of effects upon oneself and opinion reports of perceived effects on other courtroom participants/actors. These studies are "qualitatively inadequate" (see Slater and Hans 1982: 376). It is suggested that a wider range of research, and wider research tools be used in future in an effort to better consider the full implications of TCB. Eye-tracking tools for distraction effects have many advantages over previous research.

In-court and Out-of-court: Effects on those inside the courtroom can be referred to as in-court effects research. We also need to move outside of the courtroom – and look at the out-of-court effects issues. There has been no proper body of research into effects on the viewing (and non-viewing) audience. We should also focus on the actual courtroom broadcasting television audience, as well as the wider public audience as may discuss and consider cases covered by TCB. We need many more studies to research the impact of TCB content and forms.

Production: Just as there are many types of courtroom broadcasting, there are also many different types of television programmes and styles of presentation, filming, editing, etc. This area of research is generally ignored.

Filming: The effects-research literature does not adequately address nor differentiate the issues of whether there are differences between commercial courtroom filming and filming undertaken by the court or court service.

Education: Take the proposition that (all) TCB will educate. (Most arguments in favour of courtroom broadcasting on educational grounds refer to courtroom broadcasting generally and ignore any reference to or considerations of the different forms and sub-forms of courtroom broadcasting.) How will it educate? Why will it educate? Who will it educate? What forms will educate? What forms educate best? How do we know some, or any, of them will educate? What amount (or standard of) educative value is required for TCB to be accepted as being educational? There is no indication of what is meant by "education," "educational" and the "message" conveyed via TCB forms. For example, is the aim to educate the public on the details (or result)(or arguments) of a specific case or is it to educate generally? If the later, what general principles, issues, etc. is it aiming to impart? Is the educational effect to be one of civic information? Is the message that offenders will be pursued and prosecuted (deterrence)? Is the message that we respect the rights of victims? Is the aim to help inform citizens as to what they will face, or may see, should they ever be in court? Is it to legitimise or enhance confidence in the court system? Is it a confidence justification, that is, to increase confidence? Can sentencing TCB, for example (riot) sentencing decisions, have non-educative effects, which are not anticipated? Could there be moral panic or an increase in fear of crime or fear of crime victimisation?

The baseline requirement

In terms of baseline research, Kowinski and Johnson agree that the introduction of cameras to the courtroom does have effects and does change the "status quo" (2010: 1110). It is important to begin research *before* cameras are introduced into the courtroom to gather baseline research to compare for effects when cameras are introduced. This seldom, if ever, occurs in the existing research. Hopefully, the proposed second federal experiment in the United States will endeavour to begin gathering data in the particular courts chosen for the experiment *prior to* the introduction of TCB. This likewise applies to future pilots and experiments of TCB.

Limited research, self-reports and opinions

Kowinski and Johnson feel that the most "telling" argument is the "experience" and number of states that permit TCB (Kowinski and Johnson 2010: 1114). It is an easy and convenient argument. However, there are many forms of courtroom broadcasting permitted and the matter is still a matter of contention in many respects, even in the United States. Kowinski and Johnson also indicate that "empirical evidence from the states [is] ... positive" (Kowinski and Johnson 2010: 1114). However, what is the evidence and research in relation to effects? There are too few empirical studies. Validation research is almost entirely absent. Distraction research is distinctly lacking.

Most if not all of the general (non-empirical) studies rely on limited self-reports, opinion-reports and questionnaires. Kowinski and Johnson appear happy to rely on self-reports and survey data alone (Kowinski and Johnson 2010: 1115). But what about the empirical research-challenge? Just over 20 empirical studies is not a sufficient body of research. It also ignores the recent Maryland study (*Report of the Committee to Study Extended Media Coverage of Criminal Trial Proceedings in Maryland, Submitted by the Committee to Study Extended Media Coverage, a Subcommittee of the Legislation Committee of the Maryland Judicial Conference*, 2008). This was less than positive in its assessment of TCB effects. Opinions and self-reports (alone) are inadequate.

Kowinski and Johnson agree that the cameras in the O. J. Simpson (criminal) case "changed the proceedings in a host of ways" (Kowinski and Johnson 2010: 1117). Have we adequately researched these changes, effects and distractions? How do we know that they cannot re-occur? Eye-tracking technology (see below) can assist us in advancing proper research, and in an empirical, recorded and verifiable manner.

The case for TCB effects research to use eye-tracking technology

The Supreme Court referred to a large number of issues and concerns relating to TCB. Each of these should be the focus of specific empirical research. It is clear that not all of these issues are addressed, nor answered, in the small number of empirical studies to date. The challenge set by the Supreme Court still remains. The demonstration referred to herein and the implications from eye-tracking and Images J1.1–J1.12, Images W1.1–W1.12, Images L1.1–13 and Images ET1.1–ET1.10 are significant in beginning to address this. More work is needed. However, this is now possible.

TCB, distraction and eye-tracking

Eye-tracking (the study of eye movement and gaze) was not directly considered in the Supreme Court decisions. Neither has it been considered, as far as the author can find, in the vast general literature in relation to TCB. Eye-tracking technology can be instrumental in conducting effects research of TCB. We can examine whether cameras and camera plus operators distract.

It allows us to examine the actual in-court effects referred to by the Supreme Court. Equally, it allows us to research audience-effects, for example, education (An example of an educational eye-tracking (and content analysis) study is Barrios et al.) We are in a position to begin research of actual effects issues without having to rely solely on limited self-reports and opinion-reports. The author has already conducted the first proof of concept demonstration of eye-tracking technology in a courtroom, to demonstrate its applicability to TCB distraction effects research. Let us consider some of these avenues below in terms of eye-tracking and TCB distraction.

Eye-trackers

Eye-tracking can greatly assist in addressing the distraction-research challenge set by the Supreme Court. The device used in an eye-tracking study is known as an eye-tracker. Eye-tracking studies the eye position and direction of eye focus (Jacob and Karn, in Hyona, Radach and Deubel 2003). Such research relies on sophisticated software. Detailed experience and expertise with software, computers, computer science and statistics can also be a prerequisite to undertaking such studies. Hardware tools, as well as calibration of those tools, can be required. The data can also be recorded, played back, etc. We should apply eye-tracking to the problem of gaps in TCB research. The Supreme Court distraction-research challenge needs to be addressed. Eye-tracking can do this.

Existing eye-tracking applications

Gaze (Overview, Fixation 2010) and visual attention has been studied for a considerable time (Duchowski 2007: 3–13). Eye-tracking research and techniques (Duchowski 2007: 52–86) have been used repeatedly in advertising, marketing, psychology, eyewitness accuracy studies, Internet usage research, health research, etc. The literature on eye-tracking is constantly growing (Nielsen and Pernice 2009; Wedel and Pieters 2008: 4; Spector 2008; Henderson 2005; Hatfield 2009; Bundesen and Habekost 2008; Shah and Miyake 2005). Duchowski refers to various eye-tracking case studies (Duchowski 2007: 181 et seq; Morimoto and Mimica 2005: 4) and applications (Duchowski 2007: 181 et seq). Other examples include psychology, marketing, advertising, ergonomics (Duchowski 2007: 181 et seq; Bingemann 2007); law enforcement and policing (see, for example, Setcan.com, referring to the EyeLock training system, which comprises a forward focus camera and two eye-trackers, all of which are encompassed in a pair of glasses that a combat or police trainee wears); neuroscience and psychology (Duchowski 2007: 207); industrial engineering, aviation, driving and visual inspection (Duchowski 2007: 241); marketing and advertising (e.g. advert design and placement, label and product design and placement, television, Internet) (Duchowski 2007: 261 et seq; Lillington 2005), computer science (Duchowski 2007: 275); medical research, diagnostics, surgery, sports and performance, human machine interactions, market research, psycholinguistics, opthamology (SMI); visual systems and linguistics; gaming, medical instruments, vehicles, vehicle safety, computer interaction, medical diagnostics, security, law enforcement, video conferencing, information kiosks, interactive advertising (Tobii), and disability (Agustin 2009). Mercedes use eye-tracking technology for driver fatigue alert systems (Eye-tracking 2010; see also Ji and Yang 2002: 357). There are potential applications in security and computer security (Silver and Biggs 2008). There are also many potential mass-market applications (EyeTracking.com). Computer games development is another area where eye-tracking is utilised (see for example Sundstedt 2009). Eye-tracking applications can allow us to input instructions into technology devices with our eyes (Duchowski 2007: 205). For example, a person's gaze can be used to give instructions or point to instruction menus (Duchowski 2007: 206). Companies and researchers use eye-tracking research to track Internet use and Internet adverts. Do viewers look at the advert, for how long, or do they miss the advert entirely because of its location on screen? Where is the best location for the advert? Eye-tracking addresses these important commercial issues. There are many eye-tracker manufactures (e.g. Tobii, EyeTracking Inc, SMI, Arrington Research, Asley, SensoMotoric Instrument (SMI and Polhemus)). There are also many international eye-tracking conferences (e.g. Fixational Eye Movements and Visual Stabilisation and Eye-tracking Research and Applications (ETRA)).

Images J1.1–J1.12, Images W1.1–W1.12, Images L1.1–L1.13 and Images ET1.1–ET1.10 below now demonstrate that we can use eye-tracking for TCB distraction effects research.

Eye-tracking, law and psychology

Eye-trackers are increasingly used in legal-psychology and eyewitness identification research. Sheree and Holmes used eye-trackers recently to examine how eyewitnesses recognise suspect photograph line-ups (e.g. Josephson and Holmes 2010). Loftus in researching the weapons-focus effect (Loftus, Loftus and Messo 1987: n. 43 at 55) used a corneal reflection device (a type of eye-tracker) (Loftus and Mackworth 1978: 565) to discover where and for how long individuals would focus their attention.

Eye-tracking is used in legal-psychology to research the effects of cameras and camera perspective bias in recorded police interviews and confessions (noted by Ware 2006: 35). This is partly driven by the knowledge that there are false convictions. There are also erroneous and false confessions captured on video recordings of suspect interrogations. One result of this research is that different camera angles and focus orientations of the interview camera can alter significantly how viewers of such film footage rate the genuineness and voluntariness of the recorded "confessions." The manner in which the evidence is filmed, that is, the confession footage, can influence judgements of guilt (Schmidt 2006). Mock jurors have been found to be influenced by the camera angle from which the interrogation is filmed (Lassiter and Irvine 1986: 286). This is now known as *camera perspective bias*. This is additionally significant since the Innocence Project in the United States, which applies DNA technology and techniques to past cases. It found that a quarter of the DNA exoneration cases originally relied strongly on false confessions (InnocenceProject.org).

Most criminal investigation interviews that are recorded adopt a suspect-focused angle only. This is as opposed to focusing on the police officer or focusing on both of them at the same time. This also enhances the salience of the suspect and also the perceived voluntariness of any confession (Schmidt 2006: 25–26). Lassiter and Irvine (1986: 286–296, referred to in Schmidt 2006: 26) showed the same interview recorded on different cameras to show suspect only, police officer only, and both equally focused. The research study subjects then viewed one of the videos, depending on which group they were in. The ones who saw the suspect-only video perceived less coercion (Lassiter and Irvine 1986: 286–296, referred to in Schmidt 2006: 26). Other research also confirmed that suspect-focus videos yielded significantly higher ratings for perceived guilt and voluntariness (see for example Lassiter et al. 2002: 299). As a result of the Lassiter and Irvine study, police practice in New Zealand was changed to ensure that there are no suspect-only video recordings, and that suspect and questioner were always in frame (Schmidt 2006: 31). Pressure is increasing to change policies elsewhere also. Ware also examined camera perspective bias and used eye-trackers to monitor visual attention (Ware 2006). She also refers to studies and the literature that show that suspect-focus camera perspective creates a bias for judgements of voluntariness and guilt (Geller 1992; Kassin 1997: 221; Lassiter 2002: 204–208; each referred to in Ware 2006: 10).

What are the effects of different types of cameras and different camera locations: on different courtroom participants/actors, in different courtroom locations, in the different forms of TCB? Do we know?

Eye-tracking and in-court distraction effects

There does not appear to be any eye-tracking literature in relation to TCB. Eye-tracking and legal-psychology research can begin to address the research gaps in TCB distraction effects research. The Supreme Court has been calling for empirical research and has set such a challenge. The above three Supreme Court cases highlight some of the focus and avenues for empirical eye-tracking research.

The Supreme Court referred to various effects and potential effects (*Estes*: 545, 546, 546–547, 551, 592, 593, 609–610, 612, 613), such as effects on witnesses (*Estes*: 547), judges (*Estes*: 548, 549, 550, 565, 614) and defendants (*Estes*: 549, 551, 552–553, 555, 552–555, 566–567). Generally, defendant effects are one of the least researched areas of TCB. Eye-trackers can be used to test for distraction of each of the various courtroom participants/actors. The Supreme Court recognised that there may be subtle and/or discrete effects (*Estes*: 544, 545, 595–596). Eye-tracking can examine even discrete camera distractions. This method is more accurate than the self-reports questionnaire research to date.

Some of the potential eye-tracking research concerns are referred to below.

- We should apply eye-tracking to the various courtroom participants/actors. Do they look at the television camera?;
- If so, for how long?;
- What is the effect?;
- What difference does the location of the camera have on the different courtroom participants/actors?;

- Are there different effects for camera-only versus camera plus operator?;
- Are there different effects for different types of camera?;
- How do in-court television cameras affect different courtroom participants'/actors' self-reports while undertaking tasks?;
- The literature to date does not incorporate an analysis of the different tasks of the different courtroom participants/actors into discussion or research of the different effects issues being examined;
- We should employ eye-tracking to examine distraction, attention, etc. of courtroom participants/actors in the context of task analysis (Wickens, Vincow and Yeh refer to task analysis issues and research, see Wickens, Vincow and Yeh, in Shah and Miyake 2005: 385 et seq. See also Shah, Freedman and Vekiri regarding task demands (Shah, Freedman and Vekiri, in Shah and Miyake 2005: 450 et seq));
- A "critical variable in information space is the task that the user is expected to carry out" (Wickens, Vincow and Yeh 2005: 415);
- Almost invariably the literature (and limited research) ignores reference to and consideration of camera location and frame issues. We need to be able to describe and represent descriptively and diagrammatically the various camera issues (see Wickens, Vincow and Yeh 2005: 387 et seq). For example, how many studies furnish a map or diagram of the courtroom used, and indicate where the camera was located?
- Distraction research needs to examine the camera location issues. Self-report eye-tracking can assist in this. We also need to start recording where the camera is located in the courtroom, so that different research studies can be compared. Consider Images J1.1–J1.12, Images W1.1–W1.12, Images L1.1–L1.13 and Images ET1.1–ET1.10 later;
- It is equally important in studies to know where the different courtroom participants/ actors are located and which direction they are facing, and how this compares with the camera location. For example, are the courtroom participants/actors facing straight on, left or right when they look at the camera? We need to be able to compare this across research findings;
- "In the [*Estes*] case construction of a television booth in the courtroom made it necessary to alter the physical layout of the courtroom and to move from their accustomed position to benches reserved for spectators" (*Estes*: 572 Warren CJ); Are there effects?
- In most research, the location and height of the cameras is not considered or even documented, so we cannot look back to assess and compare different cases or research studies on these points;
- Different angles and frames can have different effects and meanings (Wickens, Vincow and Yeh 2005: 398 et seq). We need to begin examining these issues in the TCB field;
- Different frames can have different costs and benefits, advantages and disadvantages (Wickens, Vincow and Yeh 2005: 401). We need to begin examining and contrasting these for TCB;
- Many issues of confidence and ratings come up in relation to TCB research. Many opportunities arise in terms of examining these issues with eye-tracking technology.

For example, a subject wearing an eye-tracker and an observer could both look at a particular courtroom participant/actor and try to examine how many times that person focuses their attention or looks at the television camera in the courtroom;

- Will the results be the same for each?;
- Indeed, a second observer could also look at the courtroom participant/actor and try and record their perceptions during the case or after the case (e.g. the California/Short report);
- The various results would then be compared. The observers would also be tested for their confidence ratings. (Note that the Short report in California did attempt to have observers in court to ascertain if the courtroom participants/actors were affected by the cameras. However, they did not have the benefit of eye-trackers, nor do they appear to have been tested for confidence. Indeed, the test recording sheet does not appear to rate whether or how many times a particular courtroom actor is (a) distracted by and (b) focuses at the television camera. Schmidt used a press button system once the subject perceived a target effect. See Schmidt 2006: 30.) This would be interesting in terms of dealing with the problem of most TCB research, namely, of relying solely upon self-report, opinion reports and questionnaires;
- There are various types of eye-trackers. (In terms of head-mounted display applications, see discussion in Wickens, Vincow and Yeh 2005: 406 et seq). One avenue for in-court research is to use eye-trackers that are incorporated into lightweight glasses (see, for example, www.eyetracker.co.uk). This type of research allows itself to be adopted to different courtroom participants/actors and also in realistic settings and in real court settings;
- Other studies can use a variety of eye-trackers where subjects can view pictures or videos of court scenes on a PC, laptop or projection screen;
- In considering different TCB forms and, in particular, long extended footage versus short or snippet footage, we need to research what is viewed, for how long, and eye movement behaviour and visual processing speeds (note recent research by Vo and Schneider 2010: 171).

Eye-tracking and the law

Eye-tracking has not been used for in-court research before. It certainly has not been applied to the TCB research problems. Eye-tracking can be applied to TCB distraction effects research. In terms of advancing, it is a useful, if not a necessary, first step to undertake a proof of concept demonstration of eye-tracking in court (see below). Hence, the author promotes such research below.

As indicated above, eye-tracking is also used for video confessions research and camera perspective bias research (Ware 2006: 35. Note also Schmidt 2006: 3; Lassiter and Irvin 1986; InnocenceProject.org). Eye-trackers have also been used in another novel legal context, but not in court. Philip Smith (2009) refers to tobacco effects litigation in the United States, and enquires about the effect of different forms and formats of court-mandated health advertisements. Smith also uses baseline (2009) research. One of the earlier points of this author is that TCB research generally ignores the gathering of important baseline data in effects research.

The demonstration and research in this volume are the first time eye-trackers have been used in court for camera distraction effects purposes (see Images J1.1–J1.12, Images W1.1–W1.12, Images L1.1–L1.13 and Images ET1.1–ET1.10).

The Supreme Court challenge and distraction

The author recommends the use of eye-tracking technology for addressing part of the Supreme Court challenge. This is a very new and novel suggestion. As far as the author can ascertain, eye-tracking has never been considered in any courtroom on any issue (other than the out-of-court tobacco example above). Certainly it has not been addressed, nor considered, in any of the Supreme Court TCB cases nor the related TCB effects research. The literature on TCB has not considered or referred to the importance of eye-tracking technology.

The TCB effects referred to by the Supreme Court, which appear most relevant for eye-tracking research, are distraction effects caused by the television cameras (and camera operators) in the courtroom (i.e. in-court effects).

There are numerous potential effects referred to by the Supreme Court, and indeed commentators, which can be used as the primary research hypothesis for developing an eye-tracking effects study, in particular, distraction. Many issues must be addressed beforehand. A number of scoping and preparation issues also need to be considered.

The first eye-tracking demonstration

One of the issues and concerns with TCB is that the courtroom participants/actors may be distracted by the television cameras and/or the camera operators. The relevant research is TCB distraction effects research. One of the problems with the distraction hypothesis is that if there are effects, they may be different for different courtroom participants/actors. Also, the research to date is undermined to the extent that it almost solely relies on self-reports from courtroom participants/actors, as to whether they themselves were affected or not. Reports of effects on others are also opinions. Typically, the general research to date is questionnaire-based only. The empirical research in relation to in-court distraction effects is therefore minimal. It is also methodologically problematic.

Scoping

No TCB effects eye-tracking experiment has been conducted. Many complex considerations and preparations arise. One has to choose an effect to research, choose the technology and design the method of study. This is a complex task. In addition, cost factors also arise. However, that does not undermine the challenge and the necessity of research.

Eye-trackers

After one has chosen one particular potential effect to research, one must design the experiment and choose the particular eye-tracking device that is most appropriate to the experiment. Eye-tracking glasses for TCB distraction effects research would be particularly appropriate. The advantage is that they appear like normal glasses and are, therefore, much less obtrusive than other eye-trackers. Another advantage is that they are flexible and allow the (mock) courtroom actor using them to move about and operate much as they would in an authentic trial or court situation (subject of course, to which courtroom participant or actor it is).

Cost

The cost of the hardware, the software, audiovisual equipment and related material may not be insignificant. In designing, conducting and interpreting the vast amounts of data which will be generated, various specialised skills will be necessary, and which will also be a significant cost. The subjects in a given eye-tracking experiment may also have to be paid, as may any third-party researchers required.

Proof of concept demonstration

Many issues arise in relation to a TCB eye-tracking experiment, such as courtroom actor locations, camera locations, as well as how these may interact with the effect chosen to be researched. It is also important in effects research after the proposal to demonstrate the issues in a pilot study or demonstration (Mitchell and Jolley 2001). It was, therefore, necessary to undertake an initial proof of concept (see McQueen and Knussen 2006: 347). This is additionally important because of the novelty of this technology for TCB effects research.

The author, therefore, sought permission from the Courts Service in Ireland to undertake the first ever recorded demonstration of eye-tracking technology inside a courtroom as a proof of concept for TCB camera distraction-effect research. The research and results are referred to subsequently.

Conclusion

Eye-tracking has clear implications and applicability for the advancement of in-court television distraction research. This is further demonstrated by Images J1.1–J1.12, Images W1.1–W1.12, Images L1.1–L1.13 and Images ET1.1–ET1.10 in the volume. We can now independently demonstrate recordings of where individual courtroom participants/actors are looking and whether they are distracted by any of the television cameras in court. This also has potential implications in relation to types of cameras, locations and ultimate forms of TCB.

Chapter 3

Considering Distraction Effects Research

Scope and Courtroom Broadcasting (CB) forms

For all of the discussion about and interest in TCB, there is no body of properly considered and scientific TCB research in relation to the effects of TCB. Hence, the effects-research issues and the Supreme Court challenge. The Supreme Court has asked for more empirical research.

This book and the implications of this book offer valuable and important contributions to our consideration of TCB. Even in advancing distraction research, we must bear in mind that there can be different forms, types and styles of TCB.

In focusing on the effects-research issues and challenges, however, a very fundamental question arises. What exactly is courtroom broadcasting? What is *television* courtroom broadcasting? Despite the apparent obviousness and simplicity of these questions, they have never been addressed in the literature or research to date. The author defines TCB as television cameras in the courtroom, filming courtroom proceedings for live and/or contemporaneous television push broadcast to the general public. This definition of TCB has thus far been absent.

This definition is then critical in scoping what is and is not encompassed within television courtroom broadcast concerns, such as the effects-research issues and the Supreme Court research-challenge. The benefit of this definition is that it also enables the current research, and future research, to begin distinguishing between the different categories within TCB. Why is this important? This is important because once we see that there are different forms of TCB, we must consider whether there are different effects for different categories and forms of TCB. We can also ask what are the different effects for different forms of courtroom broadcasting generally. For example, will radio courtroom broadcasting differ from TCB? Is one category or form of TCB better at educating? Consider, for example, the proposition that (television) courtroom broadcasting will educate. Do we know for sure? Do we know which TCB form will educate best?

Our research, use of language and our research effort each require a new level of detail, as compared with the basic discussion heretofore.

Various legal and interdisciplinary research is recommended by the author. One of these is distraction effects research in relation to the courtroom participants or actors in court, caused by the television cameras in court. The author proposes for the first time that eye-tracking technology be used for effects research of the distraction effects on courtroom participants (referred to as participants/actors) caused by television cameras in the courtroom. This is most novel, but such interdisciplinary research is not without comparison. Eye-tracking has been used to research the effects of videotaped confessions (see, for example, Lassiter et al., in Zanna 2001: 189–253). Eye-tracking is also proposed in the United States in relation to mandated health advertisements/warnings on tobacco products and related litigation (Smith 2009). Interdisciplinary research is also published in the *Harvard Law Review* (Kahan, Hoffman and Braman 2008–2009: 837–906).

The starting point is to begin the scoping and parameter setting.

Scope exclusions

There are many types of courts, as well as many different types of television programmes. Equally, there are many different styles of presentation, filming and editing, which focus on law and the courts. Beyond the courtroom, there are many different ways to view courtroom broadcasting footage and many different types of viewing audience. The boundaries of courtroom broadcasting are wide. Arguably the boundaries are still expanding. This is the context of this book in relation to TCB effects-research issues. The term television courtroom broadcasting and the abbreviation TCB are used interchangeably throughout.

The overall topic of courtroom broadcasting is extensive and emotive. This book cannot cover all aspects of all courtroom broadcasting. It is, therefore, necessary to confine it. This book is confined to one aspect of *television* courtroom broadcasting, namely, the effects research and in particular the empirical distraction effects research.

Therefore, this book is not about the general topic of courtroom broadcasting, which implies all courtroom broadcasting. It cannot summarise the extensive and varied literature about courtroom broadcasting. There is already an extensive general literature available elsewhere (see generally Barber 1987; Freedman 1988; Stepniak 2008).

Court proceedings can be broadcast on radio, both live and recorded. Radio courtroom broadcasting, while interesting and deserving of research, is excluded from this book. (Note, however, experiments with digital recordings of cases in certain US federal courts. See "Project Expanded: More Courts Offering Digital Audio Recordings Online").

Court proceedings can be broadcast on the Internet, which has occurred in some limited instances. Again, this can be live or recorded. The task of covering Internet courtroom broadcasting is beyond the scope of this book.

It also appears that the first courtroom footage was shown in movie theatres. This is now more or less limited to historic instances only. There do not appear to be any definitions or effects research in relation to such broadcasting.

Courtrooms can also be broadcast or relayed on closed-circuit television to predefined locations, such as other rooms, courts or buildings. This book does not cover relayed or closed-circuit courtroom broadcasting.

Courtroom cases are, on occasion, recorded and made available, generally for purchase, on electronic recording media (e.g. videos, tapes, CDs and DVDs). However, the effects of these do not appear to have been researched or analysed. It does feature on occasion in the educational arguments for permitting courtroom broadcasting. However, recording media issues are beyond the scope of this book.

This book, by necessity, also excludes the recent advent of jury room courtroom broadcasting. (However, see generally, Joy and McMunigal 2004–2005: 77.) A TV station also sought access to an execution (see DeBenedictis 1991: 16).

Court activity can also be captured via still camera photography. These pictures can feature in TCB or publication in newspapers, magazines and journals. Such instances may be infrequent. There appears little, if any, dedicated literature to such photography, or its effects. Still photography is outside the scope of this book. However, it deserves to be defined and researched in future.

This book also excludes courtroom filming for purposes other than contemporaneous push television broadcast. This would exclude, for example, reconstruction or dramatised reconstruction of courtroom proceedings for contemporary television broadcast. This could occur, for example, in a celebrity trial if television cameras were not permitted into the actual courtroom. Again, this area is lacking definition and research as of yet.

Courtroom cases can also be filmed for historical, archival and record purposes. It is not intended for contemporaneous broadcast to the public. Such courtroom filming is not within the focus of this book. Such activities do not appear to be defined or researched thus far.

Some TCB uses television cameras that belong to the television station (or producer). In other instances, the cameras belong to the court or court service. The general literature, and effects research, does not adequately address nor differentiate these distinctions as of yet. This is not addressed as a stand-alone issue as it is beyond the scope of the present book. However, it is deserving of definition and research in future.

Therefore, the following are beyond the scope of this book,

- Courtroom broadcasting (CB) generally;
- History of TCB;
- General literature on TCB;
- General TCB arguments;
- Movie theatre courtroom broadcasting;
- Radio courtroom broadcasting (RCB);
- Internet courtroom broadcasting (ITCB or iTCB);
- Closed-circuit courtroom broadcasting (CTCB);
- The relay of courtroom broadcasting footage other than through a pushed television broadcast to the public (RYTCB);
- The distribution and use of courtroom broadcasting footage on CD, DVD or other electronic media recording or storage devices (recording media courtroom broadcasting (MTCB));

- Still photography of courtroom proceedings (PCB);
- Jury room (television) courtroom broadcasting (JTCB);
- Television courtroom broadcasting for archival or record-keeping purposes (record-keeping television courtroom broadcasting (ATCB)).

Some of these can be considered as distinct forms of courtroom broadcasting.

The history of TCB has been summarised elsewhere already, particularly in the United States (see, for example, Barber 1987; Stepniak 2008). We will focus on distraction effects research issues with *television* courtroom broadcasting. It also advocates that significant TCB definition and research be undertaken to address the distraction effects research gaps and challenges.

Neither is this book about the various proponents and opponents of TCB arguments whether legal, constitutional or otherwise. It does not examine or assess the various TCB arguments. To the extent that these shall be referred to, it is only to highlight the lack of TCB definition, research and validation of any of the arguments, for or against, TCB. The arguments continue to be strongly argued and ventilated. That the arguments continue suggests that no conclusions have yet been reached.

There is significant amount of commentary in relation to (television) courtroom broadcasting. This is much wider and more divergent from the focus of this book, though it is worth mentioning at least in passing. Some of the literature relates to general commentary, historical issues, description, (briefly) comparative, significantly argumentative (in terms of advocating or arguing for or against courtroom broadcasting, or some types of courtroom broadcasting), referring to specific cases or applications, particular courtroom personnel/actors, rights, media rights/right of access, defendant or party issues, rules, regulations and exceptions, facilitation or adaptation for courtroom broadcasting, or referring to peripheral but related issues. It is surprising how little definition and empirical effects research appears in the general literature. Media reporting issues are also beyond the focus of this book, as are the media arguments specific to TCB (see for example, Rotunda 1998: 295–313). Although referred to, the different forms of media and television reporting are not the core or specific focus of this book (see, for example, Tuggle and Huffman 2001: 335–344; Katz 1987: 47–75). Contempt of court issues are beyond the scope of this book. General media effects, other than in relation to TCB, are not the main focus of the book. The general issues in relation to pre-trial publicity are also outside the focus of this book. There is also general commentary in relation to the images and portrayal of law (Tuggle and Huffman 2001: 335–344; Katz 1987: 47–75). Legal documentaries and reconstructions on television are also beyond the core focus of the present book (however, see Glatt 1990: 201–230; Reith 1999: 211–221). None of the general literature reviewed refers to TCB or the definitions or forms of courtroom broadcasting. None of it refers to empirical research. However, there is some discussion and argument in relation to general effect issues. Fundamentally, this book and eye-tracking research is not about the advantages and disadvantages of courtroom broadcasting, nor about TCB *per se* (on that topic, note for example, O'Scannlain 2007: 323–330).

While effects research and eye-tracking are the main focus, the author also notes that there are also significant research-challenges in relation to each of the other forms of CB.

Scope: General

"Courtroom broadcasting" is generally not defined in the literature. Hence, TCB and other forms of courtroom broadcasting are not defined either. This is the first research identified, which defines its scope in terms of one form of courtroom broadcasting over others, and which then seeks to examine a specific aspect (namely, effects research-challenges) in relation to that specific form of courtroom broadcasting. The focus of this book is the TCB form. Specifically, this book examines the effects research-challenges of the TCB form, and how we might address (some of) them.

There is no body of empirical effects research of TCB, nor of TCB arguments, sufficient to answer the arguments. First, there is not enough research *per se*. Secondly, any research to date is either limited, flawed or unverified. None of the arguments are sufficiently defined, established or verified, whether generally or empirically.

The TCB arguments are also mostly presumptive. One example is the presumption that TCB will be educational. This has not been properly defined or researched. It has not yet been proven to be correct.

There is no proper evidence of positive or negative effects because we have not properly defined such effects nor researched for such effects. No body of replicated research has properly set out any particular effect it is seeking to investigate in relation to any particular form of courtroom broadcasting. This includes distraction effects. It is difficult, therefore, to arrive at valid, and generalisable, research conclusions. There is a general absence of research that has been subsequently replicated and verified.

It follows that there can be a critique of the naive view that any one of the arguments in favour of, or against, TCB is correct or (more) legitimate (than others). In fact, both sides in this debate are naive in assuming that they have sufficiently defined, examined, researched and verified their own arguments in any properly considered manner. No body of research currently validates any of the arguments whatsoever, including distraction.

The varied and diverse issues, which are involved in TCB, have received less than considered analysis. The different forms of courtroom broadcasting, and TCB, have not been defined. Neither has distraction. The author's definition (above) is the first properly considered definition. Effects are generally not defined. The overall body of effects research into TCB is surprisingly small.

The sophistication of research needs to develop. In addition, all research going forward needs to define and identify which TCB form, and sub-form, it is investigating, and for which issue or effect. There is a requirement for an overall map of courtroom broadcasting forms.

This book highlights some of the main challenges involved in advancing proper TCB effects research generally, and one of the avenues available for particular future TCB effects research, namely, eye-tracking and distraction. One avenue for effects research in relation to TCB is through psychology research. A cursory review of the eyewitness identification perception literature (in psychology) indicates how much we have yet to define and investigate in terms of courtroom actor effects. The author refers for the first time to definitions and form categories for TCB. This sets the scene for the research that needs to be undertaken. Eye-tracking technology can be applied to the Supreme Court research-challenge, in particular, distraction effects. Eye-tracking is already used in many fields, including, Internet, advertising, marketing, security, psychology, communications, aircraft design, vehicles, etc. The author argues that eye-tracking points the way for much future research of TCB effects. It is noted that the Supreme Court was not, and is still not, aware of eye-tracking. Eye-tracking research of TCB will also go beyond the expectations of the Supreme Court judges when they said that certain effects may be beyond properly measurable effects investigation. We can now track, record and measure actual distraction effects in relation to television cameras in courts. In addition, we are now able to properly address the distraction effects challenge with comparative research fields and comparative research tools, e.g. eye-tracking technology; legal-psychology (see below). This distraction discussion is only beginning, given modern research tools.

Forms of courtroom broadcasting

If we are considering effects on courtroom actors/personnel, we must say which courtroom participants or actor is being investigated, and how. It is important to say what camera types are involved, where the camera is located, etc. (This also ties in with eye-tracking distraction research.) Even a brief review of the literature to date indicates that some of these basic points on the map of TCB are absent. This is unfortunate. The implication is that much of the research to date is fundamentally flawed. It is incomplete. We do not know where on the map of courtroom broadcasting such research is. We realise also that particularly relevant factors have not been gauged, coded and incorporated into particular research studies. It also means the replication of such research is not possible. A map of courtroom broadcasting would clarify our understanding of the research issues. We can also gauge its quality.

Future discussion, and research, needs to address the different forms of courtroom broadcasting. Equally, no argument, whether in favour of TCB or against TCB, can be considered to have strong merit without addressing and defining the different courtroom broadcasting forms. Current TCB research is limited in focus, technique and methodology. Comparisons to other research fields indicate how basic the TCB research has been to date – if and where it exists.

Many people are already aware of most of the headline general TCB arguments, and equally some of the constitutional legal "rights" issues. No one, however, is able to say how, why or which of any of the respective arguments have been substantiated and validated.

In fact, none have been validated. Many people would have difficulty defining and differentiating different forms of TCB, as the literature has ignored this issue to date.

For example, take the proposition that (all) TCB will educate. (Most arguments in favour of courtroom broadcasting on educational grounds refer to courtroom broadcasting generally and ignore any reference to or considerations of the different forms and sub-forms of courtroom broadcasting.) How will it educate? Why will it educate? Who will it educate? What forms will educate? What forms educate best? How do we know some, or any, of them will educate? What amount (or standard) of educative value is required for TCB to be legitimised as being educational, or alternatively for any of the countervailing arguments to be outweighed? How do we define "education" and measure "educational TCB"?

Comparisons and tools

Our definitions and research methods for researching the effects of TCB need to draw on wider research disciplines and methods. Criminology and legal-psychology are just two examples of cross-disciplinary research. We cannot limit ourselves solely to narrow legal pigeon holes, such as a non-specific general legal literature, legal constitutional literature, legal contempt principles, etc, when considering TCB. We need to broaden our horizons and embrace cross-disciplinary research opportunities.

The author recognises existing legal-psychology research into crimes, witnesses and eyewitness identification to show how existing research and research tools in these areas can also aid TCB research. Research into the effects of TCB should adapt the research, and methodologies, of eyewitness identification research in relation to distraction issues. The author also advocates communications and media research, and research tools, for TCB research into distraction where relevant.

We need to rely more heavily on social science and empirical research if we are to address the Supreme Court distraction effects challenge. Let us not forget that this is not just an issue of concern for the United States. It interests and concerns us all.

Even in terms of examining the eye-tracking images and topographical issues in this demonstration, we see how we might compare distraction effects within one study and also between various distraction effects studies – and repeated. See Images J1.1–J1.12 on pages 143–144, Images W1.1–W1.12 on pages 149–154, Images L1.1–L1.13 on pages 161–162 and Images ET1.1–ET1.10 on pages 177–186.

Subjective opinions and self-reports

Most of the research to date is general (non-empirical) subjective research. It almost solely asks a few courtroom participants/actors how they subjectively feel. To rely on questionnaires and self-reports (i.e. asking a person if they have been affected by in-court cameras), as the sole indicator of whether there are effects or not, is wholly inadequate. Unfortunately, too much of the current research relies on own self-reports of effects upon oneself, and self-reports of perceived effects on other courtroom participants/actors.

Eye-tracking goes beyond the mere "self-report" personal views of certain courtroom participants/actors in relation to themselves. In these limited studies, subjects are asked questions on whether they feel that they have been affected by TCB. These opinion surveys are on their own limited and unreliable. Thus far, most TCB effects research is almost solely confined to these limited self-reports of certain individuals in the court process. It is particularly difficult to gauge one's own non-verbal communications (Valikoski 2004, and references therein).

Only certain people are asked these questions and not across all categories of persons in court. The study population is statistically limited. The quality of the questions vary from study to study. Typically the self-report studies are not repeated and/or replicated. They are, therefore, not validated by peer research. Typically the public in court are not asked any questions. In effect, therefore, it appears that many of the courtroom participants or actors who give self-reports are professionally trained or experienced.

Also, such studies generally appear not to be drafted by the persons most qualified to draft such questions and or appreciate the issues involved, nor the ample additional research fields and techniques available for TCB research. Judges and court personnel (alone) are also arguably not the best qualified to conduct this research, as appears in many instances.

A brief research history

When discussing the distraction effects of TCB, some reference to the origins of courtroom broadcasting is necessary. Television was first demonstrated in 1928 (Durant and Lambrou 2009: 244). The first reported television courtroom broadcast occurred in Oklahoma in 1953, where a camera was placed in a special booth at the back of the courtroom (referred to in Barber 1987: 10). (Indeed, one of the criticisms when trying to distinguish one courtroom broadcast form from another, or trying to compare them, is that the rules and procedures that may be applied are ad hoc and not recorded (properly)). Courtroom footage was also filmed and shown in cinemas. Cinema courtroom broadcasting would appear to be historic at this stage. It is also beyond the scope of the current work. TCB continues to be debated (see, for example, recent application for permission to broadcast in the case of *Sony, Warner, Atlantic, Arista and UMG,* 2009; Aurora Batman case 2012). It is still a "controversial and dividing issue," even in the United States (Thaler 1990: 176). The arguments in relation to effects are still "ongoing" (Stewart 1998). These debates are enhanced during the latest celebrity-related trials, such as Simpson, Kennedy Smith, Menendez, Woodward, Jackson, Conrad Murray, etc. Most televised cases in the United States are under local state rules, not national or federal rules. Indeed, a pilot scheme undertaken in federal courts was discontinued, as was a pilot scheme in New York (see, for example, Comstock et al 1978, as referred to in McQuail and Windahl 1993: 67; Stepniak 2008: 102. Note, however, that there is a recently commenced second federal pilot experiment. See "Judiciary Approves Pilot Project for Cameras in District Court") (in terms of New York see Stepniak 2008: 102).

Despite the longstanding debates, there is still no conclusion to the effects debates, be it in the United States or elsewhere. The substantial point in terms of this book is that there is no substantive and sufficiently detailed definitions and or body of research to decide the distraction effects debate.

In terms of many aspects of TCB, there is no research at all.

Large amounts of "research" of TCB must be discounted or approached with caution. This includes much of the general effects research. There are various reasons, some being that the research source appears to be no longer available; it does not record any statistics or source whatsoever; it does not define its method or methodology of investigation – or such methodology is faulty or unsound; there is no link between the investigation and the conclusions suggested; many rely solely on self-report questions. The latter ask individuals if they themselves were affected. In terms of relying on self-reports, and self-report conclusions, this cannot be strongly relied upon and is often criticised. Although self-reports of observations of others is worth undertaking (if undertaken and recorded properly), again sole or over-reliance on third party opinion-reports is suspect. Unfortunately, significant amounts of what is purported as "research" of effects cannot be overly relied upon. One of the challenges is to overcome this problem. Eye-tracking provides one of the solutions.

What research is left is diminutive in comparison to: the issues at stake, the importance of the effects debates over the decades, and the duration over which TCB, and forms of TCB, have existed. The research is surprisingly small. In terms of empirical research there are just over 20 studies since 1953. The Supreme Court challenge to carry out empirical research remains.

It is important to distinguish types of research into TCB effects. One can have general court-administered in-court surveys of effects, which are designed, recorded and reported on, to varying degrees of sophistication. Some of these are self-reports and third party opinion-reports. In addition, or alternatively, one can have scientifically or social science designed and recorded research of specifically identified effect issues. These latter studies are typically the most rigorous and more credible effects-research studies. Unfortunately, these type of effects-research studies are the ones least frequently undertaken. For example, there are few scientific or social science research studies into TCB effects. The volume of empirical research needs to be vastly increased.

That is not the whole picture in terms of research, however. The bigger picture is that vast areas of TCB and effects issues have not yet been defined and researched. A small number of previous commentators have from time to time suggested an effect research issue to be researched, or a set of research issues to be researched. Only rarely have they sought to undertake that research. This is partly understandable as such research can be complex, time consuming, expensive and cannot be undertaken individually or with only a small number of people. It is important to point out also that the research expertise may not rest with one individual or one school of research expertise. The best research will be cross-disciplinary. However, only with proper definitions and a global TCB map or matrix can we begin to contemplate all of the research effects gaps and challenges.

Education

There is frequent reference to the educational effect of TCB. Generally the concepts and definition of "education" and "educational" are not explained or researched. Also, what "message" is contained in individual TCB programmes are not routinely researched. One aim could be to educate the public on the details or result of a case. Another aim could be to educate in relation to the arguments of a specific case. Alternatively, the educative aim could be more general and non-case specific. Is it to legitimise the court system? (For example, do (new) international tribunals (see, Calvo-Goller 2006; Cherif Bassiouni 2005; Broomhall 2003) feel a (greater) need to publicise and legitimise themselves?) Equally, how does existing educational and communications research impact upon or change the argument that TCB will be/is educational? Unpicking the different strands of the educational effect(s) issues is not just useful, but a necessity if we are to properly understand TCB issues.

The research and arguments interface

Without proper and adequate definition and research into TCB, it is not possible to enter a fully informed debate of the advantages, disadvantages, policy, legal issues and the constitutional "rights" principles.

The basic headline arguments, on both sides, are naive because they have not incorporated proper and full definition and research. For example, they do not consider the different forms of TCB.

Significant amounts of research needs to be undertaken to *begin* a serious consideration of this important topic. Without such research, neither side in the debate can claim justification. Ultimately, the research may reveal implications that are far more complex than the basic research to date.

Yet, there are many opportunities available for such investigation, and which are evident in various other research fields, such as law-psychology, media, communications, social scientific research and eye-tracking.

We can only truly appreciate the overarching legal and constitutional principles once we have asked much more detailed questions. For example, what do courtroom broadcasting arguments past and present tell us about the justifications for and against TCB? What TCB arguments have been defined, validated, or indeed researched at all?

A constitution provides fundamental principles, albeit headline principles. However, these are too general to be instantly applied (or relevant) in every instance. We must ask specific and detailed questions in addition to looking at such headline guiding principles when considering (a) whether TCB can or should be permitted, (b) under what circumstances and in what situations, (c) under what conditions, rules, procedures and or regulations, (d) in relation to which TCB form(s), and (e) what research and quality of research is required.

If it is shown that there are different forms of TCB (and/or different effects for each, and/or more/less enhanced effects), we see that the headline policy, legal and constitutional principles are better informed and the legal debate changes. The rights arguments may have to be recalibrated. We are no longer looking at a provision of the constitution in isolation. For example, would a publicity rule based on publicity and volume of audience carry a different weight than a publicity rule based on the quality of the form, content or audience? It also differs in respect of whether we are talking about so-called media publicity-rule rights or public-rights. Is it the case that *any* TCB audience is good and the bigger the audience better?

Need for distraction research

The question of whether TCB should be permitted cannot yet be answered. There is no sustained empirical research. We do not know the effects. We cannot know. There is no sufficient body of empirical research or validation. Of course there are many arguments in favour, and equally against, TCB – but the central point is that too many gaps and challenges remain.

Why can we say this? We can say this because none of the protagonists, for or against, substantiate their arguments with a body of research – in particular forms and effects research. None of the arguments are demonstrably verified. Neither is there any replication research, whether by repeat studies or third party studies. Again, the author suggests that eye-tracking (and eyewitness identification studies and media and communications studies) paves the way for effects research in relation to courtroom participant or actor effects (in-court effects research).

Appreciating the form is crucial. Only by monitoring and comparing TCB systematically can we begin to fully appreciate all of the issues and arguments of TCB. It is also the only way that we can properly begin effects research into TCB and see the results of courtroom broadcasting. Only by beginning to consider distraction effects in a more nuanced manner for TCB, can be properly begin to research all of the distraction issues.

The rules relating to TCB, which already exist, suffer from the same flaws, namely that they do not identify any particular form of TCB and are thus flawed in scope. This is another separate area deserving of research.

Other than referring to the arguments vaguely, there is no systemised analysis of effects. To be effective, the research and definitions needs to be more precise and enumerated. None of the TCB arguments really address the fact that there are different ways to film courtroom proceedings, that there are different ways to present and edit footage and different ways to broadcast it to the public. The body of TCB arguments has not addressed the different TCB forms.

Conclusion

Only by embracing new knowledge and new research tools can we address the Supreme Court effects research-challenge. In terms of advancing the distraction research, the author successfully undertook the first proof of concept demonstration of eye-tracking technology for in-court distraction effects research caused by television cameras and/or camera operators in the courtroom.

Chapter 4

Effects and Courtroom Participants/Actors

The Supreme Court challenge

The most recent Supreme Court case involving TCB took place in January 2010 (*Hollingsworth*); the other two took place in 1965 (*Estes*) and 1981 (*Chandler*) respectively. One would have thought that in the 47 years since the first substantive case in the Supreme Court, substantial empirical research would have occurred to meet the challenge. Such research would have enhanced our knowledge and understanding of TCB. This has not occurred yet.

The most recent case (*Hollingsworth*) arguably avoids giving a definitive TCB research judgement, as the majority focused its decision on procedural issues. The majority opinion in *Estes* (in 1965) clearly came out against TCB and referred extensively to effects concerns. The majority opinion in *Chandler* (in 1981) has been accepted as permitting states to experiment with TCB.

The Supreme Court set a challenge in these three cases of addressing the various concerns and research gaps. Some of these it identified, some it did not. The cases implicitly called for more research and in particular more social science and empirical research. Unfortunately, despite such a challenge being set as far back as 1965, there are relatively few attempts to address the research gaps empirically. In the few instances where it does occur, it is on an individual basis. This lack of effort implicates social scientists, the media and the courts themselves.

Indeed, it is ironic that although some of the Supreme Court's comments focused on how television technology may change in future, neither the Supreme Court nor commentators since have recognised that research and research tools may also change. Indeed the research tools have improved vastly since 1953. In the case of eye focus and eye-tracking, the research and technology has significantly advanced.

It is in this context that it is suggested that today's technology and *eye-trackers* have advanced to the extent that we can begin to empirically address some of the research issues and challenges set by the Supreme Court. Self-report eye-trackers can be used for both in-court and out-of-court research; it is perhaps most relevant to in-court research of effects on courtroom personnel/actors.

First, let us see what the Supreme Court said in relation to the lack of research, some specific research gaps, and the challenges it set out.

The *Estes* research-challenge: Addressing the gaps

The Supreme Court recognised that there was not enough proper and empirical research, and set a challenge that such research be undertaken to fill the substantial research gaps. It did not set out a definitive list of specific gaps. Nor could it do so in a single case. Neither did it provide any definitions.

Although the Supreme Court said that it does not always need to wait for tangible psychological or other effects, it is implicit that it wants work to be undertaken in the various effects-research areas and has set this challenge. It is also noted that the Supreme Court felt that some effects may be difficult to ascertain. Eye-tracking now allows us to undertake empirical research, and in particular, empirical distraction effects research with eye-tracking, as demonstrated for the first time by the author's proof of concept.

Juror effects

The Supreme Court referred to various effects and potential effects. One of these was juror effects. It stated the following.

- "The potential impact of television on the jurors is perhaps of the greatest significance" (*Estes*: 545 Clarke, J);
- "The conscious or unconscious effect that this may have on the juror's judgement cannot be evaluated, but experience indicates that it is not only possible but highly probable that it will have a direct bearing on his vote as to guilt or innocence. Where pre-trial publicity of all kinds has created intense public feeling which is aggravated by the telecasting or picturing of the trial the televised jurors cannot help but feel the pressures of knowing that friends and neighbours have their eyes upon them. If the community be hostile to an accused a televised juror, realizing that he must return to neighbours who saw the trial themselves, may well be led 'not to hold the balance nice, clear and true between the State and the accused'" (*Estes*: 545 Clarke J);
- "[W]hile it is practically impossible to assess the effect of television on jury attentiveness, those of us who know juries realize the problem of jury 'distraction.' ... distractions are not caused solely by the physical presence of the camera and its telltale red lights. It is the awareness of the fact of telecasting that is felt by the juror throughout the trial. We are all self-conscious and un-easy when being televised. Human nature being what it is, not only will a juror's eyes be fixed on the camera, but also his mind will be preoccupied with the telecasting rather than with the testimony" (*Estes*: 546 Clarke, J). The author, for the first time, recommends eye-tracking technology to research these issues;
- "Furthermore, in many States the jurors serving in the trial may see the broadcasts of the trial proceedings ... jurors would return home and turn on the TV if only to see how they appeared upon it. They would also be subjected to re-enactment and emphasis

of the selected parts of the proceedings which the … broadcasters determined … and would be subconsciously influenced the more by that testimony … they would be subjected to the broadest commentary and criticism and perhaps the well-meant advice of friends, relatives and inquiring strangers who recognised them on the streets" (*Estes*: 546 Clarke, J. Footnote omitted);

- "[N]ew trials plainly would be jeopardized in that potential jurors will often have seen and heard the original trial when it was telecast. Yet viewers may later be called upon to sit in the jury box during the new trial. These very dangers are illustrated in this case where the court, due to the defendant's objections, permitted only the State's opening and closing arguments to be broadcast with sound to the public" (*Estes*: 546–547 Clarke, J).

The Supreme Court added,

- Four jurors had seen the earlier (pre-trial) broadcasts (referred to *Estes*: 551 Clarke, J);
- Pre-trial hearings can hold difficulties for defendants (*Estes*: 536 Clarke, J);
- "The presence of television would certainly emphasize to the trial participants that the case is something 'special'" (*Estes*: 592 Harlan, J);
- "To increase the possibility of influence and the danger of a 'popular verdict' by subjecting the jurors to the view of a mass audience whose approach to the case has been conditioned by pretrial publicity can only make a bad situation worse. The entire thrust of rules of evidence and the other protections attendant upon the modern trial is to keep extraneous influences out of the courtroom" (*Estes*: 592 Harlan, J);
- "The knowledge on the part of the jury and other trial participants that they are being televised to an emotionally involved audience can only aggravate the atmosphere created by pretrial publicity" (*Estes*: 593 Harlan, J).

The Supreme Court notes,

> Some of those risks are catalogued in the *amicus curiae* brief filed in this case by the American Bar Association: "[P]otential or actual jurors, in the absence of enforceable and effective safeguards, may arrive at certain misconceptions regarding the defendant and his trial by viewing televised pre-trial hearings and motions from which the jury is ordinarily excluded. Evidence otherwise inadmissible may leave an indelible mark … Once the trial begins, exposure to nightly rebroadcasts of selected portions of the day's proceedings will be difficult to guard against, as jurors spend frequent evenings before the television set. The obvious impact of witnessing repeated trial episodes and hearing accompanying commentary, episodes admittedly chosen for their news value and not for evidentiary purposes, can serve only to distort the jurors' perspective … Despite the court's injunction not to discuss the case, it seems undeniable that jurors will be subject to the pressure of television-watching family, friends and, indeed, strangers. … It is not too much to imagine a juror being confronted with his wife's television-oriented viewpoint … Additionally,

> the jurors' daily television appearances may make them recognizable celebrities, likely to be stopped by passing strangers, or perhaps harried by intruding telephone calls ..." Constitutional problems of another kind might arise if a witness or juror were subjected to being televised over his objection.
>
> (*Estes*: 612–613 Stewart, J. Minority opinion)

Witness effects

The Supreme Court also referred to witness effects, as follows,

> The quality of the testimony in criminal trials will often be impaired. The impact upon a witness of the knowledge that he is being viewed by a vast audience is simply incalculable. Some may be demoralized and frightened, some cocky and given to overstatement; memories may falter as with anyone speaking publicly, and accuracy of statement may be severely undermined. Embarrassment may impede the search for the truth, as may a natural tendency toward overdramatization. Furthermore, inquisitive strangers and "cranks" might approach witnesses on the street with jibes, advice or demands for explanations of testimony.
>
> (*Estes*: 547 Clarke, J)

> [W]itnesses would be able to go to their homes and view broadcasts of the day's trial proceedings, notwithstanding the fact that they had been admonished not to do so. They could view and hear the testimony of preceding witnesses, and so shape their own testimony as to make its impact crucial. And even in the absence of sound, the influences of such viewing on the attitude of the witness toward testifying, his frame of mind upon taking the stand or his apprehension of withstanding cross-examination defy objective assessment. Indeed, the mere fact that the trial is to be televised might render witnesses reluctant to appear and thereby impede the trial as well as the discovery of the truth.
>
> (*Estes*: 547 Clarke, J)

See Images W1.1–W1.12 on pages 149–154 and Images ET1.1–ET1.10 on pages 177–186 in terms of what a witness could see in this demonstration in court.

Judge effects

The Supreme Court also acknowledged effects on judges, namely,

- "A major aspect of the problem is the additional responsibilities the presence of television places on the trial judge. His job is to make certain that the accused receives a fair trial.

This most important task requires his undivided attention. Still when television comes into the courtroom he must also supervise it" (*Estes*: 548 Clarke, J). This is very seldom recognised, recorded or researched;

- "Judges are human beings also and are subject to the same psychological reactions as laymen" (*Estes*: 548 Clarke, J). There is apparently no empirical research of this issue. This should be addressed by research in future;
- "Telecasting is particularly bad where the judge is elected, as is the case in all save a half dozen of our States. The telecasting of a trial becomes a political weapon, which, along with other distractions inherent in broadcasting, diverts his attention from the task at hand – the fair trial of the accused" (*Estes*: 548 Clarke, J);
- "[I]t is difficult to remain oblivious to the pressures that the news media can bring to bear on them both directly and through the shaping of public opinion" (*Estes*: 548–549 Clarke, J).

> The State would dispose of all these observations with the simple statement that they are for psychologists because they are purely hypothetical. But we cannot afford the luxury of saying that, because these factors are difficult of ascertainment in particular cases, they must be ignored. Nor are they "purely hypothetical." They are no more hypothetical than were the considerations deemed controlled in *Tumey*, *Murchison*, *Rideau* and *Turner* (*Estes* referring to *Tumey*; *In re Murchison*; *Rideau*; *Turner*. Chief Justice Warren referring to *Tumey* states that "the Court found the procedure so inconsistent with the conception of what a trial should be and so likely to produce prejudice that it declared the practice unconstitutional even though no specific prejudice was shown." Referred to *Estes*: 562). They are real enough to have convinced the Judicial Conference of the United States, this Court and the Congress that television should be barred in federal trials by the Federal Rules of Criminal Procedure; in addition they have persuaded all but two of our States to prohibit television in the courtroom. They are effects that may, and in some combination almost certainly will, exist in any case in which television is injected into the trial process.
>
> (*Estes*: 550 Clarke, J)

See Images J1.1–J1.12 on pages 143–144 and Images ET1.1–ET1.10 on pages 177–186.

Defendant effects

The Supreme Court also referred to defendant effects. It should be noted that, generally, defendant effects are one of the least researched areas of TCB in both the general non-empirical studies and also the empirical studies to date. The Supreme Court states,

> [W]e cannot ignore the impact of courtroom television on the defendant. Its presence is a form of mental – if not physical – harassment, resembling a police line-up or the third degree. The inevitable close-ups of his gestures and expressions during the ordeal of his trial might well transgress his personal sensibilities, his dignity, and

> his ability to concentrate on the proceedings before him – sometimes the difference between life and death – dispassionately, freely and without distraction of wide public surveillance. A defendant on trial for a specific crime is entitled to his day in court, not in a stadium, or a city or nationwide area. The heightened public clamor resulting from radio and television coverage will inevitably result in prejudice. Trial by television is, therefore, foreign to our system. Furthermore, telecasting may also deprive the accused of an effective counsel. The distractions, intrusions into confidential attorney-client relationships and the temptation offered by television to play to the public audience might often have a direct effect not only upon lawyers, but the judge, the jury and the witnesses.
>
> (*Estes*: 549 Clarke, J)

The Supreme Court noted that the original trial judge initially imposed no restrictions whatsoever (*Estes*: 551 Clarke, J). However, as matters progressed,

> the trial judge himself was harassed ... he ... decided that a booth should be built at the broadcasters' expense to confine its operations; he then decided to limit the parts of the trial that might be televised live; then he decided to film testimony of the witnesses without sound in an attempt to protect those under the rule; and finally he ordered that defense counsel and their argument not be televised, in light of their objection. Plagued by his original error – recurring each day of the trial – his day-to-day orders made the trial more confusing to the jury, the participants and the viewers. Indeed it resulted in a public presentation of only the State's side of the case.
>
> (*Estes*: 551 Clarke, J)

Warren, CJ noted that the defendant had objected to televising, but that the motion hearing actually had at least 12 cameramen and equipment present, and photographers roaming about and taking pictures from all angles (*Estes*: 552–553 Warren, CJ). The courtroom was relatively small and the cameras were fully visible to all present (*Estes*: 555 Warren, CJ).

He added,

> That is not to say that all participants in the trial would distort it by deliberately playing to the television audience, but some undoubtedly would. The even more serious danger is that neither the judge, prosecutor, defense counsel, jurors or witnesses would be able to go through the trial without considering the effect of their conduct on the viewing public.
>
> (*Estes*: 566–567 Warren, CJ)

Also,

> Our decisions in *White* ... and *Hamilton* ... clearly hold that an accused is entitled to procedural protections at pretrial hearings as well as at actual trial and his conviction will be reversed if he is not accorded these protections. In addition, in *Pointer* ... we held that a pretrial hearing can have a profound effect on the trial itself and effectively prevent an accused from having a fair trial. Petitioner clearly did not have a fair determination of his motion to exclude cameras from the courtroom. The very presence of the cameras at the September [pre-trial] hearing tended to impress upon the trial judge the power of the communications media and the criticism to which he would have been subjected if he had ruled that the presence of the cameras was inconsistent with the petitioner's right to a fair trial. The prejudice to petitioner did not end here. Most of the trial participants were present at the September hearing – the judge, defence counsel, prosecutor, prosecution witnesses and defendant himself – and they saw for themselves the desecration of the courtroom. After undergoing this experience it is unrealistic to suppose that they would come to the October trial unaware that court procedures were being sacrificed in this case for the convenience of television. The manner in which the October proceedings were conducted only intensified this awareness. It was impossible for any of the trial participants ever to be unaware of the presence of television cameras in court for the actual trial. The snouts of the four television cameras protruded through the opening on the booth, and the cameras and their operators were not only readily visible but were impossible to ignore by all who were surveying the activities in this small courtroom. No one could forget that he was constantly in the focus of the "all-seeing eye." Although the law of Texas purportedly permits witnesses to object to being televised, it is ludicrous to place this burden on them. They would naturally accept the conditions of the courtroom as the judge establishes them, and feel that it would be as presumptuous for them to object to the court's permitting television as to object to the court reporter's recording their testimony. Yet, it is argued that no witnesses objected to being televised. This is indeed a slender reed to rely on, particularly in view of the trial judge's failure, in the course of his self-exculpating statements justifying his decision to allow television, to advise the witnesses or the jurors that they had the right to object to being televised. Defence counsel, however, stated forcefully that he could not concentrate on the case because of the *distraction* caused by the cameras. And the trial judge's attention was distracted from the trial since he was compelled to make seven extensive rulings concerning television coverage during the October proceedings alone, when he should, instead, have been concentrating on the trial itself.
>
> (*Estes*: 567–569 Warren, CJ. Italic emphasis added)

Again, the issue of the court and court personnel having to deal with applications and camera issues is seldom researched or recorded at all, neither is the issue of witness ability to object. The author recommends eye-tracking technology to research distraction effects.

TCB forms

The Supreme Court also implicitly referred to form *issues*. However, it did not explicitly set out the different forms of courtroom broadcasting. The research nor the literature to date has explicitly referred to this issue. Unfortunately, there is also no research or scoping of the implication of forms of TCB to the general discussion.

The Supreme Court said the following,

- "The probable impact of courtroom television on the fairness of a trial may vary according to the particular kind of case" (*Estes*: 590 Harlan, J);
- "When the issue of television in a non-notorious trial is presented it may appear that no workable distinction can be drawn based on the type of case involved, or that the possibilities for prejudice, though less severe, are nonetheless of constitutional proportions … The resolution of those further questions should await an appropriate case" (*Estes*: 590 Harlan, J).

It added,

> I do not deem the constitutional inquiry in this case ended by the finding … that no isolatable prejudice was occasioned by the manner in which television was employed in this case. Courtroom television introduces into the conduct of a criminal trial the element of professional "showmanship," an extraneous influence whose subtle capacities for serious mischief in a case of this sort will not be underestimated by any lawyer experienced in the elusive imponderables of the trial arena. In the context of a trial of intense public interest, there is certainly a strong possibility that the timid or reluctant witness, for whom a court appearance even at its traditional best is a harrowing affair, will become more timid or reluctant when he finds that he will also be appearing before a "hidden audience" of unknown but large dimensions. There is certainly a strong possibility that the "cocky" witness having a thirst for the limelight will become more "cocky" under the influence of television. And who can say that the juror who is gratified by having been chosen for a front-line case, an ambitious prosecutor, a publicity-minded defense counsel, and even a conscientious judge will not stray, albeit unconsciously, from doing what "comes naturally" into pluming themselves for a satisfactory television "performance"?
>
> (*Estes*: 591 Harlan, J. Footnote omitted)

What is also significant is that as no forms of courtroom broadcasting and TCB are expressly set out by the Supreme Court. This gap and challenge needs to be fully considered in future TCB discussions.

A need to show actual prejudice?

Mr Justice Harlan in *Estes* (*Estes*: 532–616) states that the "petitioner has not asserted any isolatable prejudice resulting from the presence of television apparatus within the courtroom or from the contemporaneous or subsequent broadcasting of the trial proceedings" (*Estes*: 587 Harlan, J).

The State argued that specific prejudice must be shown for the constitutional due process and fairness clause to apply (*Estes*: 593 Harlan, J). It adds,

> I believe petitioner in this case has shown that he was actually prejudiced by the conduct of these proceedings, but I cannot agree with those who say that a televised trial deprives a defendant of a fair trial only if "actual prejudice" can be shown. The prejudice of television may be so subtle that it escapes the ordinary methods of proof, but it would gradually erode our fundamental conception of trial. A defendant may be unable to prove that he was actually prejudiced by a televised trial, just as he may be unable to prove that the introduction of a coerced confession at his trial influenced the jury to convict him when there was substantial evidence to support his conviction aside from the confession.
>
> (*Estes*: 578 Warren, CJ)

Eye-tracking technology, as recommended by the author, can measure even the most subtle of eye-focus distraction effects. This supports the author's eye-tracking thesis and the point that the Supreme Court empirical research-challenge remains to be addressed.

To the extent to which Texas is saying there are no effects shown, it beholds researchers to examine each of the separate effects issues. Most of the general "research" has not identified and isolated an individual effect hypothesis. Many such studies cannot be said to have researched any actual or specific effect. To answer the Supreme Court, Texas, etc., concerns, results must be obtained through rigorous, demonstrated, replicable, verifiable research of a specific effect hypothesis. In meeting this challenge, the standard and scope of the research needs to be expanded, made more robust and empirical. If the overall standard and quality is not achieved, it fails to properly address the challenges set.

"There is no claim that the conduct of the judge, or that any deed or word of counsel, or of any witness, or of any juror, was influenced in any way by the presence of photographers or by television" (*Estes*: 613 Stewart, J. Minority opinion). Other than a very manifest example, how is a defendant meant to review and research for such effects while his case is ongoing?

The research required is difficult and complex. The defendant is normally also focused on other issues, namely, the trial hearing itself. "There is little wonder that the defendant cannot 'prove' the existence of such factors. Yet we all know from experience that they exist" (*Estes*: 547 Clarke, J).

Eye-tracking can begin to address these concerns in a verifiable manner.

Hollingsworth: Camera and effects issues avoided

The Supreme Court, however, resolved the "question without expressing any view on whether such trials should be broadcast. We instead determine that the broadcast in this case should be stayed because it appears the courts below did not follow the appropriate procedures set forth in federal law before changing their rules to allow such broadcasting" (*Hollingsworth*: 9).

The Supreme Court majority did not expressly consider courtroom broadcasting argument or effects issues. It states that its "review is confined to a narrow legal issue: whether the District Court's amendment of its local rules to broadcast this trial complied with federal law. We conclude that it likely did not and that applicants have demonstrated that irreparable harm would likely result from the District Court's actions. We therefore stay the court's ... order [which] permits the live streaming of court proceedings to other federal courthouses. We do not address other aspects of that order, such as those related to the broadcast of court proceedings on the Internet, as this may be premature" (*Hollingsworth*: 7). Neither does this research address, given the time and resources available, the wider issues of courtroom broadcasting and is rather limited to TCB, in particular the research and effect issues.

Hollingsworth: Effects and concerns

The Supreme Court again referred to effect issues, and it can be seen that the research-challenge is reiterated and remains.

Hollingsworth: Reference to witness effects issues

The Supreme Court referred to witnesses and said that the

> [a]pplicants also *have shown* [emphasis added] that irreparable harm will likely result from the denial of the stay. Without a stay, the District Court will broadcast the trial. It would be difficult – if not impossible – to reverse the harm from those broadcasts ... This Court has recognized that witness testimony may be chilled if broadcast (*Hollingsworth*: 12–13, referring to *Estes* ... 591 (Harlan, J., concurring)) ... Some of the applicants' witnesses have already said that they will not testify if the trial is broadcast, and they have substantiated their concerns by citing incidents of past harassment ... (71 news articles detailing incidents of harassment related to people who supported Proposition 8). These concerns are not diminished by the fact that some of applicants' witnesses are compensated expert witnesses. There are qualitative differences between making public appearances regarding an issue and having one's

> testimony broadcast throughout the country. Applicants may not be able to obtain adequate relief through an appeal. The trial will have already been broadcast. It is difficult to demonstrate or analyze whether a witness would have testified differently if his or her testimony had not been broadcast. And witnesses subject to harassment as a result of broadcast of their testimony might be less likely to cooperate in any future proceedings.
>
> (*Hollingsworth*: 12–13)

Hollingsworth: Evidence of harm/effects

It is interesting that the Supreme Court said that the applicants against broadcast had established effects and harm if broadcast. Perhaps more noteworthy is the comment that the respondents have not demonstrated any harm if there was no proposed broadcast. The court states that the "balance of equities favors applicants. Self-report applicants have demonstrated the threat of harm they face if the trial is broadcast, respondents have not alleged any harm if the trial is not broadcast. The issue, moreover, must be resolved at this stage, for the injury likely cannot be undone once the broadcast takes place" (*Hollingsworth*: 13).

Hollingsworth: Considered rules are required

In terms of court rules, the Supreme Court reiterated that the

> [c]ourt's interest in ensuring compliance with proper rules of judicial administration is particularly acute when those rules relate to the integrity of judicial processes. The District Court here attempted to revise its rules in haste, contrary to federal statutes and the policy of the Judicial Conference of the United States. It did so to allow broadcasting of this high-profile trial without any considered standards or guidelines in place. The arguments in favor of developing procedures and rules to allow broadcast of certain cases have considerable merit, and reasonable minds can surely differ over the general and specific terms of rules and standards adopted for that purpose. Here, however, the order in question complied neither with existing rules or policies nor the required procedures for amending them.
>
> (*Hollingsworth*: 14)

Even if the local law had been validly amended, that was not the end of the matter. The Supreme Court felt that even if it "had been validly revised, questions would still remain about the District Court's decision to allow broadcasting of this particular trial, in which several of the witnesses have stated concerns for their own security" (*Hollingsworth*: 15).

Hollingsworth: Publicity effects

The Supreme Court also noted that

> courts … have allowed the broadcast of their proceedings on the basis that those cases were not high profile [referring to *E*Trade Financial Corp.* 2008], … or did not involve witnesses [referring to *Marisol A.* 1996; *Katzman* 1996], … Indeed, one District Court did not allow the broadcasting of its proceedings because the case "involv[ed] very sensitive issues" [referring to *Schoeps* 2009] … This case, too, involves issues subject to intense debate in our society. The District Court intends not only to broadcast the attorneys' arguments but also witness testimony … *Sony BMG*, 564 F. 3d, at 11 … (distinguish[ed] broadcast of attorneys' arguments from other parts of the trial). This case is therefore not a good one for a pilot program. Even the studies that have been conducted thus far have not analyzed the effect of broadcasting in high-profile, divisive cases.
>
> (*Hollingsworth*: 16)

Hollingsworth: Education

The dissent referred to "the public's interest in observing trial proceedings to learn about this case and about how courts work (*Hollingsworth*: 7–8, referring to *Nebraska Press Assn.*) ... (Brennan, J., concurring in judgment); see also Exh. 2, at 42, Application to Petition) … [and the] statement of Chief Judge Walker … '[I]f the public could see how the judicial process works, they would take a somewhat different view of it.' 'I think the only time that you're going to draw sufficient interest in the legal process is when you have an issue such as the issues here, that people think about, talk about, debate about and consider' (*Hollingsworth*: 7–8. Referring to Walker, CJ, in *Nebraska Press Assn. …*)." It is unclear if the Supreme Court was attempting to refer to education issues and educational effects. Equally, it is unclear if there is a difference between educational TCB and informative TCB.

The Supreme Court issues and eye-tracking

We see from the three cases above that the Supreme Court referred to a large number issues and concerns relating to TCB. Each of these should be the focus of sustained empirical research.

In terms of applying eye-tracking technology, for example, to the Supreme Court challenge, one of the options is to research the effect issues identified by the Supreme Court.

The full set of effects concerns are seldom mentioned in the literature. The headline distraction effects category relates to

- Lawyers;
- Juries (in-court);
- Prospective juries (out-of-court);
- Judges;
- Defendants;
- Parties;
- Witnesses;
- Court personnel;
- Courtroom actors/personnel effects generally;
- Other in-court issues;
- Audience;
- Public;
- Other effects issues.

Conclusion

It is clear that the effect issues are not researched or answered in the small number of empirical studies to date. No effect issue has received a sustained empirical research focus. The challenge set by the Supreme Court still remains. They are not properly addressed in the small number of empirical studies nor in the general non-empirical studies thus far. For one, there is no baseline research to measure any changes. Very few studies have sought to examine in-court effects with observers and sophisticated code measurements. Eye-tracking technology probably offers the best potential for examining some of the effect concerns raised by the Supreme Court, in particular distraction and divided attention. There is also potential to examine some of the other effects raised by the Supreme Court challenge.

The author highlights the importance of television camera location and personnel/actor location in carrying out effects research. It is noted also that there is one reference to location by the Supreme Court. However, this is not a recognition by the Supreme Court of the major significance of the location issue to researching the effects of television cameras. It is pointed out elsewhere that effects will depend upon where the television cameras are located and where the courtroom personnel/actors are located. (The author also refers to location issues at Lambert, 17–18 June, 2010; Lambert, 6–8 September, 2010; Lambert, 11 August, 2010; Lambert, 26–28 November, 2010; Lambert (2010) (18); Lambert, 10 December, 2010). This is not identified as being part of the Supreme Court challenge but is equally important in terms of designing adequate and robust TCB effects research. The author suggests, therefore, that there are other research-challenges beyond the Supreme Court challenges.

It is important to point out that in addressing the TCB research-challenges and in developing TCB effects-research studies, we often need a level of sophistication that can only be obtained through cross-disciplinary research. The research questions and the research tasks demand this.

TCB eye-tracking is a new area of interdisciplinary legal research recommended by the author. This is to address the concern related to distraction-effect in relation to the courtroom personnel/actors, caused by the television cameras in court. The author proposes for the first time that eye-tracking technology be used for effects research of the distraction effects on courtroom participants (personnel/actors) caused by television cameras in the courtroom.

Although parts of the current research may well be novel, recommending interdisciplinary research is not unique. In one example, three distinguished law professors undertook detailed empirical interdisciplinary research to address an issue posed as a result of a Supreme Court case. The results were published in the legal journal *Harvard Law Review* (Kahan, Hoffman and Braman 2008–2009: 837–906). Eye-tracking has been used to research the effects of videotaped confessions (see, for example, Lassiter et al. 2001: 189–253). It is also proposed in the United States in relation to mandated health advertisements/warnings on tobacco products and related litigation (Smith 2009).

Chapter 5

Distraction and General Research Studies

Introduction

Some examples of general non-empirical studies are referred to below. Some of the flaws are also highlighted. Rarely does the research refer to distraction effects. Seldom do commentators or researchers suggest how to research for distraction effects.

Florida

One Florida study only undertook opinion surveys of certain courtroom participants/actors after the experimental period ended (*A Sample Survey of the Attitudes of Individuals Associated with Trials Involving Electronic Media and Still Photography Coverage in Selected Florida Courts between July 5, 1977 and June 30, 1978*, as referred to in Netteburg 1980: 472). The research is also understood to have other methodological flaws and is over simplic (Netteburg 1980: 472).

Various Florida studies had methodological flaws (Alexander 1990: 83). Sometimes the subject population was too low for significant conclusions (Alexander 1990: 84).

The Florida study (Courts of Florida 1978. Referred to in Alexander 1990: 491) sought to gauge responses from courtroom participants/actors, but after an extended period sometimes *up to a year after* the case. It took no account of the time differences (referred to in Borgida, DeBona and Buckman 1990: 491). Two thirds of participants refused to respond (Borgida, DeBona and Buckman 1990: 491). No account was taken of self-report issues (Borgida, DeBona and Buckman 1990: 491). It is surprising, therefore, how the study "concluded" that there were few adverse effects (Borgida, DeBona and Buckman 1990: 491). At best, the most that could have been said, despite the faulty research, was that no or few adverse effects were found. This is a significant difference. It is a fundamental flaw to misrepresent the research findings as the study referred to appears to do, and indeed as other studies have done also. Too often it is suggested that there are no effects – when the research efforts are limited and the actual research in a given study may merely indicate that a particular research hypothesis effect was not shown. There is no body of rigorous research showing actual positive effects, nor adverse effects.

Keller points out that Florida presented the first long-term opportunity to research the effects of TCB (Keller 1992: 52). The pilot programme was established in 1975 (Keller 1992: 52).

This would mean that between 1953 and 1975 various television courtroom broadcasts occurred, but without seeking to examine any long-term effect. In fact the Florida experiment only really began in 1977 (Keller 1992: 52), which extends the period further to 1953–1977.

California/Short report

Thaler notes that

> [o]ne of the most comprehensive studies was the year-long California survey-experiment in 1981, which adopted a diversified data collection method. In that experiment, researchers combined data from interviews from participants in specific trials, with general attitudinal responses gathered from questionnaires. They also confirmed interview responses with observations made by researchers attending a trial. Changes in participants' attitudes before being involved in a televised trial as well as during and after a trial were also noted.
>
> (Thaler 1990: 178)

There were even issues with the Short study (some of which are referred to in Borgida, DeBona and Buckman 1990: 492). The Short report acknowledges the issue of where the television equipment is located in the courtroom, as well as the placement of the television personnel (Short 1981: 22). Yet these are frequently ignored. They are not recorded in most studies. Even the Short study does not develop the point of making any suggestions in terms of location, nor does it recommend particular rules, restrictions or the need for further research.

The Short report concludes that the relatively positive results "thus far should not be taken as licence to grant *carte blanche* access by extended media or to ignore the guidelines in the rules" (Short 1981: 244). It continues that "California's experiment thus far with cameras in the courts has not been tainted by an *Estes* or a *Hauptman*" (Short 1981: 244). This is arguably prophetic in terms of the subsequent Simpson (criminal) case. The Short report also adds that there should be no general access for television cameras, and also that any access "should be done carefully" (Short 1981: 244–245).

The Members of the *Chief Justice's Special Committee on the Courts and the Media, The Judicial Council of California* expressly did not adopt or agree with the Short report, its finding or conclusions (See *Memorandum to Members of the Court Management Committee from Administrative Office of the Courts, Michael A. Fisher, Attorney regarding Cameras in Court Experiment (Rule 980.2)*, 11). Ephraim Margolin's Memorandum dated 16 October, 1981, attached to the above Memorandum of the Members of the Chief Justice's Special Committee, adds that "any report which fails to evaluate or even consider the use made by the media of the coverage obtained from observation of the courts leaves us with only a partial evaluation insufficient for a final determination of the wisdom of the project" (see *Memorandum to Members of the Court Management Committee from Administrative Office of the Courts, Michael A. Fisher, Attorney regarding Cameras in Court Experiment* (Rule 980.2), 11). Indeed, few empirical studies seek to review the media use of TCB footage.

The *Cameras in the Courtroom: Report on Rule 980 Reports of 2000* does not refer to any effects research carried out. It does gather statistics on types of application, which the media applied to cover, as well as response questionnaires. However, it is noted that many of the media applications contained incomplete information (Administrative Office of the Courts, Research and Planning Unit, Cameras in the Courtroom, Report on Rule 980, May, 2000: 3). The report later says that "[e]very media request form received was missing at least one piece of requested information" (Administrative Office of the Courts, Research and Planning Unit, Cameras in the Courtroom, Report on Rule 980, May, 2000: 13). The rule provided that the media were responsible for the increased court costs. This does not appear to have been developed in practice (Administrative Office of the Courts, Research and Planning Unit, Cameras in the Courtroom, Report on Rule 980, May, 2000: 9).

Baker report (Florida)

The Baker report was instrumental in Florida's move to allow cameras. It reported that there were no physical disruptions. This appears to be based on Judge Baker's views as the trial judge in a particular case (*Zamora*; Thaler 1990: 26). It also concluded that jurors were not hindered in their ability to follow the case, based on his interviews with them (Thaler 1990: 26). There appears to be no empirical research.

Virginia

The Virginia Association of Broadcasters research report on a broadcasting experiment included 35 interview data report sheets, but no analysis of these was undertaken (VAB Assessment Report to the [Virginia] Supreme Court, 1989, as referred to in Keller 1992: 12).

Bartlett

Possibly the first reference to "research" was the observations and comments of Judge Bartlett in a televised case in 1955 (Blashfield 1962: 429–434, as referred to in Shores 1981: 19). However, it appears that there were no formal definitions, research, questionnaires, interviews, coding or documented research of any type (Blashfield 1962: 429–434).

Colorado

Donald Shores refers to the introduction of television cameras to Colorado courts, and notes that there were no controlled research, experiments or surveys (Shores 1981: 19). There was equally no reference to definitions or formats.

Rhode Island

The Rhode Island research study of its pilot programme refers to various research undertaken, but none appears to be listed, nor the methodologies (Weisberger 1983: 299–311). The research apparently also included a political science academic and a psychology academic, on a limited "volunteer" basis (Weisberger 1983: 302), and was presumably limited by funding. No record is provided. In addition, it also appears that at least some of the research occurred after the pilot period expired (Weisberger 1983: 302–303).

Washington

Kermit Netteburg identifies the first effects research as being the Washington experiment of TCB. This was shown to judges but not broadcast. However, there appears to be no written report or record of the research, the questions, nor the interviews undertaken. (There are apparently recorded interviews on film. As referred to in Netteburg 1980: 470 and n 1, 470.) It appears to be opinion- and self-report-based only (Netteburg 1980: 470). Donald Shores refers to (possibly the same) Washington experiment with cameras in 1974, which only had an "informal survey" of witnesses (Shores 1981: 20).

Flaws in courtroom broadcasting research

There are numerous flaws in the courtroom broadcasting research to date. These flaws are many and varied. Any future research must deal with these flaws.

There has been far too little research carried out into this important subject of effects. The existing research is less than comprehensive. This is surprising given the important issues at stake. For this reason, the author outlines some of the research avenues, which should be pursued in future. The basis for many of these suggestions comes from extensive research in related disciplines (see Lambert (1997) (2:5): 180–187; Lambert (1995) (16:4): 139–144 as examples. On the context of open justice and court reporting, see McGonagle 1997 and 2006; Freedman 1988; Gardner 1985: 475–516; and references throughout this present work. Also, Lambert 17–18 June, 2010; Lambert 6–8 September, 2010; Lambert

11 August, 2010; Lambert 26–28 November, 2010; Lambert (2010) (18): 278–280; Lambert, 10 December, 2010: 1699–1700).

It has already been pointed out above that two of the problems with TCB research are firstly, that there are far too few research studies. Secondly, the existing research is not comprehensive. The research is also frequently unscientific and unmethodical. Therefore, little reliance can be placed upon much of the research in terms of making any definitive generalisable conclusions or determinations. Seldom do research studies extend over a long period of time. This means that it is difficult, if not impossible, to make overall conclusions or determinations regarding the extended effects of TCB. Few studies are compared with each other. None apparently attempt to replicate and/or verify the results of earlier studies. Therefore, there is a strong argument that none of the research has been conducted in any meaningful or scientific manner.

Susanna Barber (1987) has written one of the few books on this topic. In it she examines the available US studies of TCB. These studies were carried out between 1975 and 1981. Having carried out her examination, she concludes that a number of fundamental questions remained unresolved and unanswered. Some of the questions she raises are included in the following questions (Barber 1987: 92–93),

- Does television, as opposed to print (journalism), better inform the public about a particular case?;
- Can gavel to gavel (G2G) broadcasts educate the public about the administration of justice? (or better educate the public?);
- Do time constraints imposed on many broadcast news stories mean that a case is treated either unfairly or inadequately?;
- Does the public get a distorted picture of the judicial system, or a biased view of a particular trial, if stories are edited to highlight sensational testimony, cross-examination, or simply the opening and closing arguments?;
- How does the public's understanding of courts and specific cases differ when broadcast, rather than print, is the medium of communication?;
- What type or form of news coverage has consistently provided the most balanced coverage of legal issues, trial participants and court administration?

These and many other questions remain to be addressed in any meaningful, considered, logical and scientific manner as part of an examination of TCB and of TCB effects.

TCB research, and indeed legal research generally, has frequently ignored highly relevant literature and research from other (related) disciplines for too long. However, TCB issues cannot remain isolated and considered only in terms of conventional or traditional legal principles and legal texts (note an interesting chapter by Cranston, which discusses changing legal course subjects, in Zuckerman and Cranston 1995: 31–59). Of course conventional legal materials remain relevant to the topic being discussed but the legal community and the general public should be aware of the wider research opportunities available. To do otherwise would be to remain precluded from better understanding how and why the courtroom operates in the context of media attention. Research in other disciplines should be allowed to assist our understanding and assessment of TCB generally.

Decisions on TCB in the past were sometimes based upon the level of knowledge and research, if any, available at that time. Currently, there are significantly more avenues for research, many of which provide a scientific basis for assessing actual effects on courtroom participants/actors and on the general audience (i.e. the public) of TCB (see comments of Mannheim 1936). They should not continue to be ignored. The author's proof of concept demonstration of eye-tracking technology in a courtroom, to research camera distraction effects, points the way for particular future research.

Self-report research

One of the other major flaws with the effects research to date is the nature of the opinion or self-report studies themselves. (Particular) courtroom participants or actors are asked to indicate whether they themselves have been affected, or sometimes adversely affected, by TCB in a particular case they were just involved in. The nature of such questions automatically means that most courtroom personnel/actors are going to say that they themselves have or have not been affected. Sometimes they will say that it is their opinion that certain others have been affected, but certainly not them. Similarly, an eyewitness may be very confident, even certain, but still be wrong. Many eyewitness identification and recollection factors hamper a correct identification. Another inherent flaw is that even when relying on such questionnaires, there appears to be no comparisons between the answers on the effects on a person by themselves and the effects perceived by other people on the same person.

Many studies today employ various methodologies and techniques of observing and documenting actual effects and reactions on particular individuals to stimuli. Sometimes these stimuli involve a particular scene, a film, a video clip, a photograph, a written description or story, etc. In all of these instances it is possible to observe and test effects. Employing similar methodologies and techniques can bring TCB research out of the dark ages. Firstly, these methodologies and techniques can be used to test effects of TCB on courtroom personnel/actors and on the general viewing audience. However, they can also be utilised in the context of validating or contradicting opinion and self-report studies. The new methodologies and techniques can be used to see, for example, whether a particular courtroom participant/actor actually was distracted by or looked over at a TCB camera.

One of the main arguments of critics of courtroom broadcasting is that it (may) adversely affect courtroom personnel/actors. However, self-report studies and questionnaires alone cannot hope to establish or even properly research this argument. That no one had sought to expand research beyond these limited studies is striking. It may also be a matter of concern.

Opinions

The official state studies and other studies rely too "heavily" (Thaler 1990: 34) on opinion surveys and questionnaires alone. Yet,

> "[e]ven with the self-reported system and its inherent bias, these studies all revealed that a significant minority of jurors, attorneys, and witnesses reported that cameras in the courtroom had significant impact on their role in the trial. This finding alone points to the indisputable point that a trial cannot be conducted fairly if all of the participants are unable to properly perform their parts".
>
> (Stuart 1998: 57)

The 1991 Criminal Justice Section of the New York Bar Association is also criticised for having a "limited self-report" methodology and "self-reporting flaws" like other research (Stuart 1998: 58). When "examining psychological impact it may be necessary to abandon the simplistic self-reporting surveys and delve deeper into the issues" (Stuart 1998: 60). The surveys are also described as "subjective" and are "based solely on the trial participant's viewpoints as to their personal opinions and feelings ... Self-diagnosis is by its very nature problematic and distorted ..." (Stuart 1998: 56). Eye-tracking enables us to delve deeper.

In addition, the courtroom participants/actors "are set up to be impartial and truthful and when asked if affected by the influence of television, they are apt to remind the sceptical and themselves that they are indeed impartial" (Stuart 1998: 56–57) and not affected.

When "examining psychological impact it may be necessary to abandon the simplistic self-reporting surveys and delve deeper into the issues" (Stuart 1998: 60). Opinions and self-reports are often based on "intuitive judgements" (to use the words of Weisberger 1983: 305).

Opinions/self-reports

The perceptions of individuals as recorded in interviews often provide conflicting views (see Short 1981: 19). In addition to the self-report correctness problem with respondents, one is not sure if replies are being made honestly (Petkanas 1990: 113). A further problem is that replies may be made that the respondent hopes will please the questioner (Petkanas 1990: 113). Indeed, sometimes the questioner can be the judge – which potentially heaps pressure on the subject.

Saul M. Kassin also notes the self-report problems and the fact that this is widely referred to in the legal-psychology literature (Kassin 1984: 337). He also refers to a manifest example of the problem in a courtroom broadcasting survey in a Florida Supreme Court study. The jurors, witnesses and lawyers all reported their belief that the cameras had a greater effect on the other courtroom personnel/actors than on themselves (Kassin 1984: 337, with references to Davis 1980: 85–92; and also Wisenand 1978: 1860–1863).

Donald Shores also refers to the self-report bias problem with the research to date (Shores 1981: 29). He further states that "[m]any of the responses are personal estimations and speculations about contexts in which no variables were experimentally controlled" (Shores 1981: 29).

Netteburg notes,

> [a]s Warden [Warden 1965: 211] noted, "A survey of judges and lawyers on their opinion of the validity of the Pythagorean Theorem would not change its true nature." Opinion must give way to fact, and propositions must be tested against reality.
>
> (Netteburg 1980: 473)

As the author variously points out, our distraction effects research must expand.

Mixed opinions and diversions

Some of the studies when they gauge opinions of judges, include some judges with experience of courtroom broadcasting and some without. Teresa Keller raises this as an issue (Keller 1992: 24).

Also, the "concentration on fear [of effects] ... has diverted attention from other important questions pertaining to the presence of cameras in the courtroom" (Keller 1992: 26).

Little research/few studies

There is clearly not enough research. *Estes*, *Chandler* and *Hollingsworth* also note the lack of confirmed effects (Kassin 1984: 337). Steve Pasternack, for example, notes the "lack of data" and calls for not just more research but an "ongoing program [*sic*] of research" (Pasternack 1982: 3). Anna R. Padden also calls for ongoing research (Paddon 1992: 14. Also, Paddon 1985).

Steve Esposito also describes televised justice as being "relatively unexplored" (Esposito 1996: 26. See also Killian 1987: 27–43, as described in Alexander 1990: 72).

A majority of judges in the Rhode Island research felt that the pilot period "produced insufficient empirical experience upon which to base a permanent conclusion" (Weisberger 1983: 303).

Kermit Netteburg (in 1980) acknowledges that many effects questions are not answered (Netteburg 1980: 469). He continues that "[p]erhaps the most crucial question yet unanswered is whether the surveys and case studies conducted ... can be replicated with greater controls. ... [Also,] what types of trials if any should be excluded from coverage ... the frequency with which courts will be covered and the long-term effects on the court system" (Netteburg 1980: n 11, at 469). This emphasises the need for new research, such as that now made possible by eye-trackers.

Netteburg notes that self-report research is just beginning; many specific themes have not yet been researched, including some of the specific themes referred to in *Estes* (*Estes*: 469). No research addresses all issues and concerns. Research must be categorised. Specific research on specific issues can then be compared, tested and improved upon. As the author points out, there is no overall map, definitions or description of forms of TCB.

No results

The argument "about the effect … on the judicial process continues" (Thaler 1990: 16, referring also to Freedman 1988. Thaler does not refer to any page number in Freedman). The issue of different effects is still "unresolved" (Thaler 1990: 68). The research that is there is "[i]nconclusive" (Thaler 1990: 34). Evidence in relation to the various arguments "has not been systematically produced" (Hoyt 1977: 489). "Crucial questions still remain" (Thaler 1990: 70) and the debate continues (Shores 1981: 1). In terms of benefits, Kohm notes that we are still referring to only "presumed benefit[s]" (Kohm 2004: 357). Alexander argues that the (general) research to date still leaves only "speculation" and no conclusions on the effects issues (Alexander 1990: 39–40).

Confidence

There is no evaluation of confidence issues in the general research (Ossinger 2006: 21). How does TCB effect public confidence in individual courtroom participants/actors, courts and the justice process generally? There is little research, and where there is, it is non-comparative and non-longitudinal over time.

General research methods/methodology

The effects debate is still ongoing (Ossinger 2006: 9). In some respects the arguments and basis for propositions have not changed much since *Estes* in 1965 (*Estes*). Practically all of the US states' research involved unrepresentative samples and "anecdotal evidence" (Borgida, DeBona and Buckman 1990: 491).

It has been argued that US states have made "policy decisions" (Borgida, DeBona and Buckman 1990: 492) based on expedience, rather than actual research findings. This has been done without undertaking proper, controlled, replicated and validated research.

Studies are limited in only adopting one method of study. Only the Short study is referred to as adopting a multimodal method (as referred to Borgida, DeBona and Buckman 1990: 491). In one instance a law firm was engaged to assess effects on certain in-court participants/actors (Shores, referring to a one-year experiment approved by the California Supreme

Court beginning in June 1980, Shores 1981: 26). D. P. Killian also recognised the flawed methodology of the general research studies (Killian 1987, as referred to in Alexander 1990: 72). Catherine M. Boggs undertook a review of the research in 1981. Out of 72 studies at least 20 had methodological flaws undermining their reliability and validity (Boggs 1981, as referred to in Alexander 1990: 90). Edna Einsiedel did not attend the case she was researching, relying instead on interviews (Einsiedel 1978, as referred to in Alexander 1990: 87).

Netteburg criticises one of the early Florida studies. The criticism is quoted in the Short report, as having "methodological flaws, including extreme simplicity in instrumentation and the rush which the Florida's court deadline imposed on the researchers" (Netteburg 1980: 472, as referred to in the Short report 1981: 12). The studies lack proper methodology and have "no controls, disproof, or evaluation" (Gerbner 1980: 426, as referred to in Keller 1992: 70–71). Teresa Keller acknowledges that there is no clear methodology referred to in the Terry article/research (Keller 1992: 52).

Longitudinal

There is almost no TCB longitudinal research over any extended period of time. Obviously, it undermines any long-term discussion or determination of effects.

Reasons for limited effects research

Effects research has been "hampered" (Thaler 1990: 34). There is uncritical research, no definitions, nor forms, etc. The psychological effects, or some of them, may not be "easily detectable" (Thaler 1990: 68). Researching the effects issues, particularly in the courtroom environment, is also very complex (Thaler 1990: 34). Yet, more sophisticated research is required. Eye-tracking affords that opportunity.

Specific effect/specific hypothesis

Many arguments exist (Thaler 1990: 27). Yet the general studies overall are not specific in researching and testing individual effects arguments, in a manner that ensures each potential effect is isolated. Nor does it ensure that a specific "result" is not influenced by some other factor (Thaler 1990: 27).

Non-defined and non-specific studies

Many "research" studies purport to research an issue. Yet, they do not define what they are specifically researching, nor how the proposed research method will test for a particular effect. If there is an effect, can it be demonstrated that the hypothesis or proposed effect is the result of the "cause" (e.g. camera; a camera filming; a camera operator, etc.) identified, or some other cause?

Misinterpreting and generalising

Many general studies are generalised beyond their validity and data (Rimmer 1988; Alexander 1990: 90). "Reports" claim, for example, that particular research "demonstrated that audio-visual coverage does not adversely affect judicial proceedings" (Crosson, chief administrator of the courts in New York State, public report, as referred to in Thaler 1990: 30–31). However, this is wholly incorrect and mistaken. A research proposition may be that there is Y effect on person(s) A from cause X. If no positive result is demonstrated, or statistically demonstrated (or proven), then established research methods dictate that the conclusion is only that Y effect was not demonstrated. The research proposition was not established. It may also be that even if there is a minor Y effect shown in results, this may be so statistically insignificant that the research proposition may still not be proven. Many suggested "conclusions" that there are no effects are, therefore, incorrect.

Small samples

Many of the state research studies rely on "a very small sample" (Stuart 1998: 57). Virginia had 57 responses, California 56, Nevada 31 and New Jersey only "a relatively small number of respondents surveyed" (Stuart 1998: 57). James L. Hoyt's study, however, often cited, only had 12 subjects in each of the three video conditions (Hoyt 1977: 493). The courtroom participants/actors surveyed for the Short report were limited to judges, attorneys and jurors (Short report 1981: 19). There were no defendants, parties or witnesses. Only a subset of these were then interviewed (Short report 1981: 21).

Paul Thaler refers to a New York study by the Office of Court Administration after the Steinberg case. However, of the 1,095 people, only 32 were witnesses, of which only one witness was from New York City. He criticises the fact that no convicted TCB defendant was included in the survey or interviews (Thaler 1990: 178).

Low response rates

One of the other problems is that there has been a low response rate for some of the post-case survey questionnaires (Shores 1981: 22–23). Shores refers to one survey of five trials in Florida in 1977–1978, which only had responses from nine witnesses (two of whom referred to detrimental effects) (Pryor et al. 1979: 12–26, as referred to in Shores 1981: 22–23). The response rate for judges in the Florida and Wisconsin studies is indicated to be low

(Netteburg 1980: 472). The methodical witness studies to date also have relatively small subject numbers and responses (Shores 1981: 29).

Little analysis

"Early efforts included reactions from judges and surveys of participants. These methods continue, joined by more experimental methods" (Keller 1992: 51). This suggests that there is significant and frequent experimental research, however, the record shows otherwise.

Contamination

In one instance at least, participants in a given case were interviewed on their experience of courtroom broadcasting but had the self-report being videotaped (Keller 1992: 52, referring to the John Gilbert Graham trial and the research reported in Terry 1957: 354). The interviews apparently elicited "glowing testimonials to the journalistic prowess of the media" (Terry 1957: 348). There does not appear to be any consideration of whether the interview filming, or questions, may have had an effect on the responses.

Judicial process/procedure

Teresa Keller states that until the time of her study in 1992, the research has focused "primarily on whether courtroom decorum and the defendant's right to a fair trial are adversely affected. Repeatedly, surveys, experiments and legal analyses fail to find clear evidence that the judicial procedure is harmed" (Keller 1992: 71). However, there is no sustained research into court processes, TCB processes and distraction.

Camera effect/empirical/no research

Donald Shores agrees that "little factual evidence exists to support either side of the question as to what effects the camera has" on witnesses communication behaviour (Shores 1981: 37). "The effects of cameras on witnesses will never be known until systematic research efforts probe the question" (Shores 1981: 37). Burger, J in *Chandler* also agrees that "[f]urther experimentation is necessary to evaluate the potential psychological prejudice associated with broadcast coverage of trials" (Berger, J, in *Chandler*: 4146, as referred to in Shores 1981: 38). The impact is "unknown" according to another judge (Fatzer 1978: 230–243, as referred to in Shores 1981: 38). The literature acknowledges that the effects research is "sparse" (Shores 1981: 39), including distraction research.

See eye-tracking Images J1.1–J1.12 on pages 143–144, Images W1.1–W1.12 on pages 149–154, Images L1.1–L1.13 on pages 161–162 and Images ET1.1–ET1.10 on pages 177–186.

Pooling

Where pooling arrangements have been in place, it does not appear that there has been any comparative research of the footage from the different networks (note comments in Petkanas, regarding the same in one jurisdiction, Petkanas 1990: 63).

Camera shots

There is generally no comparison or research of the effects of different types of camera shots in TCB footage (Petkanas 1990: 68, regarding different types of camera angles).

Distraction, attention and other effects

One theme in many surveys is that courtroom participants/actors may see and notice the cameras, but will soon forget about them (see, for example, Einsiedel 1978, as referred to in Netteburg 1980: 470). However, if a witness for example notices the camera(s) but says they forgot about the camera(s) once they began to be questioned, could there still remain a subconscious effect? The general research does not properly investigate these concerns.

In Netteburg's research, 59 per cent incorrectly remembered that the defendant was guilty of both charges, only 5 per cent correctly recalled that the defendant was found not guilty of one charge (Netteburg 1980: 474). This was described as disturbing (Netteburg 1980: 475). He suggests further research of defendants who are acquitted in televised trials (Netteburg 1980: 475).

Kermit Netteburg finds "little evidence *to support*" some of the *Estes* decisions; "[o]ther research *fails to confirm* … detrimental effects … survey data … in Washington, Ohio, Florida and Wisconsin have *failed to demonstrate* [distraction effects]" (Netteburg 1980: 475) (emphasis added). It is clear, therefore, that such research is *not* saying that effects do not exist. It is unfortunate, therefore, that so many commentators make the wholly incorrect assumption that these and other studies have concluded that there *are* no effects or no adverse effects. Such assumptions misrepresent the research and incorrectly advance conclusions that are in fact not correct.

Consider eye-tracking Images J1.1–J1.12 on pages 143–144, Images W1.1–W1.12 on pages 149–154, Images L1.1–1.13 on pages 161–162 and Images ET1.1–ET1.10 on pages 177–186 and the import that eye-tracking brings to distraction-effect research, thus far ignored in the research and the TCB literature.

Case studies

Case studies are useful but should not be generalised (Short 1981: 11). They have a "lack of generalizability" (Netteburg 1980: 471). In terms of considering case studies and general conclusions from these, the Short report points out that a "representative sample of cases within an experimental period must be studied before general conclusions may be drawn" (Short 1981: 11). Netteburg notes,

> [Florida (*A Sample Survey of the Attitudes of Individuals Associated with Trials Involving Electronic Media and Still Photography Coverage in Selected Florida Courts between July 5, 1977 and June 30, 1978*, available from the Florida Supreme Court, as referred to in Netteburg 1980: 472) and Wisconsin (*Report of the Supreme Court Committee to Monitor and Evaluate the Use of Audio and Visual Equipment in the Courtroom* (April 1, 1979), as referred to in Netteburg 1980: 472) study] surveys are more generalizable than case studies, they still cannot be used as evidence to draw causal conclusions. For instance, we might argue that the juror who has participated in only a televised trial has no knowledge of courtroom decorum in a non-televised trial setting and little basis for deciding whether the new situation is more fair or unfair.
>
> (Netteburg 1980: 472–473)

Forms

The various different types and forms of TCB remain to be properly categorised. Effects research, including eye-tracking distraction effects research, should take account of the relevance of these differences. It is not adequate to suggest that all effects are the same for *all* potential types and forms of TCB. Steven A. Kohm expresses surprise at the lack of research of reality-based courtroom television broadcasting, despite the first show of this kind, *People's Court*, dovetailing the California Judicial Council's decision to permit TCB in the late 1970s (Kohm 2004: 90. Also Podlas 2001: 1–24). Kimberly Podlas also notes the lack of research into the impact of reality TCB, in particular *People's Court* and *Judge Judy* (Podlas 2001: 1–24). Podlas used surveys of those attending for jury service regarding their viewing habits of reality-based syndicated TCB (Podlas 2001: 1–2). She found that reality TCB viewing influenced the jurors views and expectations of how active and proactive judges would be, and in addition influenced what opinions judges would have (Podlas 2001: 2). Frequent viewers tended to look for clues as to the judge's opinion, including interpreting judicial silences (Podlas 2001: 2). Podlas also refers to TCB mis-education effect issues (Podlas 2001: 2).

In addition, "there is a marked difference between sensational trials such as O.J. Simpson's (criminal) 'trial of the century' and the more mundane kinds of disputes shown on a typical episode of *Peoples' Court* or *Judge Judy*" (Kohm 2004: 90–91).

Rebecca Stuart refers to empirical studies (supporting TCB) but does not cite them (Stuart 1998: 47–48). However, she states that results are overall positive, both civil and criminal media case coverage showed "small side effects" (Stuart 1998: 47). These are not expanded upon.

Privacy

Privacy, even in the courtroom setting, has been ignored in terms of research and evaluation, and is only addressed in comment and argument. Can TCB infringe upon privacy rights? Within privacy we have subsets of defendant privacy (see Thaler 1990: 159), party privacy, juror privacy, witness privacy, lawyer privacy, judge privacy, court personnel privacy, public attendee privacy.

Controls

All of the general (non-empirical) studies, with possibly one exception, failed to have adequate controls (Borgida, DeBona and Buckman 1990: 491).

Courtroom particpants/actors: Defendants

Very few of the general questionnaires and interviews involve the defendants (Borgida, DeBona and Buckman 1990: 92). This is a significant omission in the research. Equally, there appears to be no empirical research of defendant issues.

Audience

Susanna Barber highlights the need to focus on audience effects of TCB (Borgida, DeBona and Buckman 1990: 95 et seq). There is little audience-effects research of TCB.

Conclusion

Despite the first courtroom television broadcast occurring in 1953 (listed by Barber, as the case of Billy Eugene Manley in Oklahoma City, which occurred in 1953, see Barber 1987: 10–11), the literature reveals a scant amount of overall general research being carried out. It is particularly concerning also that there are even fewer references to quality or social science research identified in the literature on the topic. One would have expected significantly more, given the general interest in the judicial and court process and in particular in terms of the justice issues at stake.

As has already been mentioned there is actually a scant amount of even general research available on the effects of TCB. Upon examination, a number of problems and shortcomings can be identified. These include

- Not all of the research is available and/or easily accessible. Hence, it is difficult to review and is difficult for researchers in future to consider in the context of their own research;
- Not all of the research is properly cited, which hinders its availability to future researchers;
- Some of the research is not properly documented or methodical in terms of, for example, identifying who in particular undertook the research, their qualifications and expertise to do so, the exact numbers of people who were interviewed, what if any statistical recording and/or analyses was recorded;
- There is no systematisation of research such that it may be compared with other research;
- There is no accurate or scientific record of such a nature as to make any wider general conclusions in relation to TCB generally;
- Generally, we cannot tell what the courtrooms looked like and where exactly the camera(s) were located, thus making comparisons impossible;
- There is no clear theory or hypothesis presented and thus examined in the general studies, so while some of them are indeed interesting, it is unclear what, if anything, they prove.

Indeed, some of the existing courtroom broadcasting studies are not even questionnaires and contain no quantifiable data and do not even indicate how many people participated (see Barber 1987: 68).

Again Susanna Barber (1987: 80–81) notes that certain types of cases tend to predominate in TCB, in particular "notorious or sordid" cases. Studies further reveal that few trials are broadcast "in any substantial detail" and fewer still gavel to gavel over the whole length of the case (Barber 1987: 81).

Overall, we need definitions, consideration of forms and significantly more empirical research, and more eye-tracking research addressed to TCB distraction research.

Chapter 6

Legal-psychology and Eye-tracking

Introduction

Our TCB distraction research needs to expand significantly. It needs to become interdisciplinary. Incorporating legal-psychology to TCB research is necessary in order to address the Supreme Court research-challenge. Existing legal-psychology research uses eye-tracking technology. Legal-psychology is, therefore, very relevant for courtroom broadcasting research.

TCB research often seeks to answer questions and issues by relying upon self-reports and opinion-reports. It also relies upon the expressed confidence of (some) courtroom participants/actors. The issues of opinion-reports, self-reports (even Mason's research in Europe appears limited to self-report type research (Mason)) and confidence appear extensively in the existing psychology literature. Courtroom broadcasting research can and should refer to this extensive literature and research.

One area of psychology investigation is eyewitness identification research. The models and tools of such research are very relevant to courtroom broadcasting. For example, psychologists research the factors involved in witness "identification." On occasion they recommend improved procedures, and on some occasions they also testify in court on these issues. Re refers to a case where the warning to jurors was not sufficient (see Re 1984: 519). While many factors may be already within the knowledge of jurors and other courtroom participants/actors, the extent to which all of these factors are known to the public, that is, jurors, is less certain. Holtenson strongly argues that judicial warnings are insufficient (Holtenson 1988: 521–547). Judges are not (always) experts in the mental processes that occur during the identification process and are not in the best placed position to advise on identification evidence and Holtenson therefore advocates expert psychological testimony. Many psychologists have testified in courts as to eyewitness identification factors (see Heaton-Armstrong et al. 2006). Cases include *US v Amaral* and *Estate v Galloway.* Oliver P. Holtenson also refers to cases (Holtenson 1988: 542 et seq. Note also Roberts 2010: 57–62).

A recent eyewitness research study indicates that 75 per cent of people exonerated through the use of DNA evidence were originally convicted due largely to mistaken eyewitness identifications (Wells and Bradfield 1998: 360, as referred to in TerBeek 2007: 21–22). Calvin J. TerBeek strongly recommends using empirical and scientific based research in relation to eyewitness identification issues (Wells and Bradfield 1998: 21–51). He also notes that the courts have not been shy to refer to and use statistical evidence in other instances (Wells and Bradfield 1998: 51, referring to the case of *Roper v Simmons*, but no citation given). Research also suggests that not all courtroom participants/actors are familiar with psychology research findings. For example, research in Sweden involving police officers, prosecutors and judges found that a number of wrongful beliefs and understandings existed (Granhad, Stromwall and Hartwig 2005: 709–727). It also found that there were some differences between the subject groups (Granhad, Stromwall and Hartwig 2005: 709–727).

Eye-tracking research can also be utilised, and is referred to in the next chapter. It is increasingly used for applications in many different fields. However, eye-tracking tools have been used in psychology research too. It should now be applied to TCB.

No body of research has sought to investigate effects and distraction effects on courtroom participants/actors, other than by opinion-reports and self-reports. This is, in terms of the research capabilities available today, a glaring failure of courtroom broadcasting research. Can we seriously continue to rely wholly upon propositional, limited and flawed research and research methodologies, such as have been used in the past?

Out-of-court research

One of the flaws to date is that predominantly all identified courtroom broadcasting research focuses on potential effects inside the courtroom (*in-court*). It ignores any substantial or sustained reference and consideration to audience effects and effects on persons outside of the courtroom (*out-of-court*). There was, however, one study found where viewer reaction to a particular case was gauged via a questionnaire in Arizona. One thousand questionnaires were used with a 25 per cent response rate. Of the respondents, 95 per cent watched the trial more than once and 84 per cent agreed with the guilty verdict. (See *New Law Journal* 30 November, 1987: 13 et seq). This means we have only begun research into one half of the TCB spectrum. Can we, therefore, stand over the research effort to date? Legal-psychology, media and communications studies should also be applied to TCB issues.

In-court research

The in-court research is limited. It focuses on some but not all of the courtroom participants/actors. In addition, it is flawed because it relies on limited models of research. Primarily it uses questionnaires to ask (some) courtroom participants/actors if they themselves have been affected (self-reports). Sometimes, but not always, researchers will ask a courtroom participant/actor if they feel other courtroom participants/actors have been affected (opinion-reports). Such opinion-reports and self-report studies are limited, flawed and ignore an abundance of other opportunities for research, such as legal-psychology and eye-tracking.

In-court self-reports and opinion-reports

The majority of studies into TCB are limited to self-report and opinion report studies. People in actual cases (or in mock cases) are asked for their opinions on whether they feel that they have been affected by the television cameras filming in the courtroom. While gathering such opinions is in itself a worthwhile exercise, self-reports are not the most accurate indicator of an individual being affected by television cameras in the courtroom. Self-report studies should not be relied upon as the sole indication of the in-court effects of TCB. Wider ranging, more reliable and cross-disciplinary research is needed, such as employment.

Legal-psychology eyewitness research

Eyewitness research and eyewitness identification research tools in psychology are potentially very useful for effects research into TCB (see generally Heaton-Armstrong et al. 2006). Courts and the public have long recognised that there can be flaws with identifications and eyewitness identification evidence. In court, certain eyewitness identification requires additional corroboration evidence. Sometimes judges also give a warning to the jury in relation to such evidence. (There are increasingly strong arguments in psychology to suggest that these may be insufficient. For example, not every judge or every juror is familiar with the research identifying the process through which witnesses make identification, recall what they witnessed, and the various factors that effect witness perception and recall. Note also TerBeek 2007: 21–51). Many psychologists, who are familiar with such evidence and research, have assisted the courts in understanding these issues more fully. Loftus is just one such example (see also Holtenson 1988: 521–547).

Wells and Murray state in their review of 31 psychology studies that "the eyewitness accuracy-confidence relationship is weak under good laboratory conditions and functionally useless in forensically representative settings" (referred to in Hollin 1989: 161. Also Wells et al. 1979: 440–448). Eyewitness recall (or, perhaps recall by a participant in a televised trial, or a television viewer of a televised trial) is not the most reliable indicator.

Eyewitness evidence is highly malleable and subject to influence by many factors (Hollin 1989: 161. Also Wells et al. 1979: 440–448. See also Martin and Macrae 2010: 163). Post-event factors are one category of influence, such as questions, briefings, personal anticipation, cross examination and feedback or alleged feedback, from other witnesses or participants/actors (Cutler and Penrod 1985: 195. Also Bell and Loftus 1989: 669–679). Psychology research examines the context of questions to witnesses, information given to witnesses, the replies and the effects of the context, questions and information. Generally, no similar examination occurs with TCB research. Indeed, the context of the research, and sometimes the questions themselves, are not recorded. This makes it impossible for later researchers to examine these studies or to attempt to make comparisons across studies. It is important to record the questions asked, the context, all of the results and to describe how the research was carried out.

Identification, corroboration and warnings

There have been many notorious examples of eyewitness unreliability (see, e.g., in Re 1984: 509). Trained observers can give wrong identifications. Even "the most positive identification made by a confident witness may be wrong" (Re 1984: 510).

Lord Justice Scarman in *R v Dunne* states that "there is no branch of human perception more fallible than identifying a person." Heffernan also comments that "[e]yewitness testimony, however sincere and persuasive, is notoriously unreliable and the courts have long recognised that the frailties of human observation and memory may lead to mistaken identity and ultimately wrongful conviction" (Heffernan 2005: 284, and also Chapters 4 and 7).

Courts, aware of the potential unreliability of visual identification evidence, frequently warn juries about such evidence and also advise juries of the importance of having supporting collaborative evidence (Heffernan 2005: 284; TerBeek 2007: 47).

The courts afford certain safeguards and warnings against eyewitness identification, particularly when uncorroborated by additional evidence (See Re 1984: 517; Tapper 2007: 578 et seq; Keane 2008: 549 et seq). The warnings attempt to restrict instances of bias, mistake, etc. Legal appeals are also possible (*People (AG) v Stafford*; *R v Turnbull*). Cutler and Penrod note that jurors do not/cannot assess the detrimental impact that reading or seeing media reports may be having upon them, and thereby cannot guard against it. It has also been found, they note, that the judge's warning to a jury does not do away with jury prejudice. "The only certain safeguard against the effects of pre-trial publicity is to impanel a jury which has not been exposed to pre-trial publicity" (Cutler and Penrod 1985. Note also references to warnings, corroboration, etc. in Chapter 10. Also note references to Twining under the heading Witness. Twining also points out that warning the jury about the perils of convicting on identification evidence alone is not a sufficient safeguard. Twining 1990: 152–175).

No such general warnings are given in relation to television media presence in court. A warning may be of little use if it is given after the information has been given to the subjects and is thus processed by the brain. However, warnings before the information is received seems to ensure that they read the information slower and increase their resistance to suggestion.

TCB factors

Many different reasons and factors contribute to mistaken identification. One flaw with TCB is that it frequently assumes that limited and basic courtroom actor questionnaires are not undermined by bias, drafting, self-reports, confidence, etc. issues. Frequently these issues are left unanswered and even unconsidered.

A review of existing legal-psychology research confirms that we must start to address the research flaws in courtroom broadcasting. We cannot continue to assume that courtroom actors/personnel and their replies are better than eyewitnesses accounts, or better in all instances. They should at least be similarly tested and researched.

Similarly legal-psychology, media and communications can assist out-of-court effect issues, for example, research of effects while multi-tasking in the courtroom.

Legal-psychology: The mistaken eyewitness

Legal-psychology research identifies many of the factors that contribute to incorrect identifications. Courts have long held the view that eyewitness identification must be considered very carefully. This research is already applicable to the many gaps in the courtroom broadcasting research. For example, how do we as courtroom participants/actors see cameras in the courtroom? How do we identify them? What do we see? What do we see, and not see, in the courtroom? How does the process of viewing, recall and identification work in the courtroom setting?

> In the High Court of Australia, Evatt and McTiernan JJ. ... analysed the elements which underlie an assertion by a witness that he recognises a certain person. In a joint judgement they stated "An honest witness who says 'the prisoner is the man who drove the car'" whilst appearing to affirm a simple clear and impressive proposition, is really asserting: (1) that he observed a driver; (2) that the observation became impressed upon his mind; (3) that he still retains the original impression; (4) that such impression has not been affected, altered or replaced ... and (5) that the resemblance between the original impression, and the prisoner is sufficient to base a judgement, not of resemblance, but of identify.
>
> In recent years psychologists have undertaken research which reveals that each of the stages listed by Evatt and McTiernan JJ. is subject to factors/personnel which may weaken the value of the final identification and lead to a wrongful conviction.
>
> (Re 1984: 510, referring to Evatt and McTiernan, JJ., in *Craig v The King. Craig v R*)

Many of the various factors identified as being applicable to eyewitness identification and eyewitness evidence can apply to research of the courtroom broadcasting issue. L. Re (1984: 510), for example, identifies many acquisition stage factors, event stage factors/personnel, witness factors, recollection factors, post-event information factors, displacement factors, context importance factors/personnel, etc. Elizabeth F. Loftus and James M. Doyle (1987: Chapter 2. Note also second edition/supplement published in 1994 by Lex Law Publishing) also identify many factors. The research processes through which legal-psychology investigates and identifies various factors are important to courtroom broadcasting, given that courtroom broadcasting has not yet been so rigorous in its research.

Another point is that some studies have asked opinion-report questions on, for example, whether the particular courtroom act ›r saw the witness or judge acting up or in some way being affected by the courtroom cameras. Self-reports may be useful. However, it should not be the sole definitive evidence and form of study. For one thing, courtroom participants/ actors may be able to give their opinions and experience to a certain extent. However, they are arguably not qualified in all aspects and areas where a change may be effected and/or visible. The TCB research and research tools need to be expanded.

In addition, asking courtroom actor A about his or her opinion on whether courtroom actor B was affected or changed in some way (e.g. distraction) due to the cameras, ignores the fact that courtroom actor A was actually busy doing something in court as their primary task. Therefore, their task was not to observe meticulously everything that courtroom actor B may, or may not, have been doing. Equally, this applies to observing what the cameras, equipment and cameraman were doing. Such questions are also focused on main perceivable effects, and not more internal or non-observable effects. As previously pointed out, self-reports and opinion reports are limited in that they may not on their own demonstrate in-court effects. In addition, they are not corroborated by any further or additional set of research techniques and studies. Again, we need to cast a wider net and involve more than one type of research technique to properly evaluate courtroom broadcasting effects.

Consider the advantages of having recorded images available, which can be checked, re-examined and made available to other researchers, as compared to subjective self-reports. See eye-tracking Images J1.1–J1.12 on pages 143–144, Images W1.1–W1.12 on pages 149–154, Images L1.1–L1.13 on pages 161–162 and Images ET1.1–ET1.10 on pages 177–186.

Valentine, Pickering and Darling (2003: 989) point out that in the United Kingdom, the Turnball guidelines (*R v Turnball*. Note also Roberts 2010: 57–62) enshrine "some" of the factors needed to be considered in assessing eyewitness identifications, but that other factors need to be taken into account also. Graham Davies and Laurence Griffiths (2008: 435–449) suggest that despite our history of knowing that mistaken identifications occur, procedural changes following the 1976 Devlin report, and more recently CCTV and DNA evidence, mistakes still arise. They call into question the continued use of a single confident witness as being sufficient to convict an accused person (Davies and Griffiths 2008: 435–449).

TCB safeguards

In terms of TCB research, there are generally no comparable safeguards. The courtroom broadcasting research does not identify or research the flaws of relying solely upon self-reports and opinion-reports. It appears some researchers may not be even aware of these issues. There are no suggestions made as to how to address the self-report and opinion-report concerns. Eye-tracking, however, offers a concrete direction for effects research.

In addition, not all courts that permit TCB have procedures and restrictions, whether in place or documented. Judges are not generally aware of or advised on all of the issues involved in media, communication, production, editing, selection, etc., and have no direct input or control over what happens to the footage once it is filmed and leaves the court.

One could refer to contempt of court rules as a court mechanism to protect and regulate proceedings in relation to cameras. However, is relying on contempt of court rules alone a sufficient safeguard? Do contempt rules cover every issue that may arise in court and out of court in relation to TCB? Contempt rules were developed prior to the advent of TCB. Does contempt law reflect modern communications technologies such as courtroom broadcasting?

Surprisingly, no research has been carried out into in-court safeguards, or out-of-court safeguards, for TCB. While there are "use" rule restrictions in relation to parliamentary broadcasting, there is no research of use-issues and use-safeguards in relation to TCB.

Legal-psychology research on effects

Elizabeth Loftus and Katherine Ketcham point out that human memory is extremely fragile and malleable (Loftus and Ketcham, in Lloyd-Bostock and Clifford 1985: 159–170; Twining, in Lloyd-Bostock and Clifford 1985: 255–280, and other sections therein. Also Loftus 1979, 1996, 2005: 361–366). Memory can be "supplemented, altered or even reconstructed by as simple an instrument as a strong verb, embedded unnoticed in a question" (Loftus and Ketcham, in Lloyd-Bostock and Clifford 1985: 159–170). Individuals in studies have said that certain objects existed at a crime scene (Loftus and Ketcham, in Lloyd-Bostock and Clifford 1985: 159–170). However, none of those objects in fact existed (Loftus and Ketcham, in Lloyd-Bostock and Clifford 1985: 159–170). In one study 175 of those who received false information, identified a non-existent barn. In experiments to test later recall, 805 people gave incorrect information as the period was prolonged (Loftus and Ketcham, in Lloyd-Bostock and Clifford 1985: 159–170). Other examples of false recall include the fact that an assailant had curly hair, when in actuality he had straight hair; that broken glass was present when there was none at the accident; and giving incorrect colours of objects (see Loftus and Ketcham; Twining, in "Legal Processes: Redefining the Problem," in Lloyd-Bostock and Clifford 1985: 255–280, and other sections therein. Also Loftus 1979, 1996).

Confidence reports

The "relations between identification accuracy, confidence, and event factors are complex" (Hulse and Memon 2006: 322). However, in the context of the TCB research confidence and self-reports concerns are not investigated.

The (professionally trained) police officers in the Hulse and Mermon study tended to downplay their emotional responses (Hulse and Memon 2006: 323). The study found that there were significant differences in self-report arousal and recorded arousal (Hulse and Memon 2006: 323). The police officers' recall may be susceptible to the same arousal biases as other people (Hulse and Memon 2006: 323).

According to psychology research, juries are impressed by confident eyewitness identifications (see Re 1984: 515). TCB research predominantly relies on confidence reports. This occurs in the self-reports, opinion-reports and limited interviews of courtroom personnel/actors. These are useful but cannot be overly relied upon. Nor should they be solely relied upon.

Psychology research suggests that third parties largely accept eyewitness testimony based upon the *confidence* of the eyewitness and the degree of detail given in the eyewitness testimony (Culter and Penrod 1985: 195; Hollin 1989: 165. See also TerBeek 2007: 24 et seq, and 40 et seq). Unfortunately, a person's individual confidence cannot be overly relied upon.

In the context of TCB, for somebody involved in a trial to admit that they were affected by cameras could be tantamount to an admission that, but for the cameras, they may have acted differently, or perhaps rendered a different decision. It is not altogether surprising for them to express the effect upon themselves in the negative. Even if they were aware of cameras during a case, any decision reached by a courtroom actor should be clearly reached without influence from the cameras present. One might also add that it should also be without the appearance of such influence. Yet, official research almost invariably ignores these issues and leaves research questions unaddressed.

We should not be uncritical in our assessment of confidence in self-report studies. Additional research and research tools need to be applied to this important topic, but also as a verification and additional test of opinion reports and self-report studies.

That a witness, or courtroom actor, indicates confidence that they were not affected is not conclusive. Psychology research has found jurors equally willing to believe an incorrect witness as a correct witness (TerBeek 2007: 19, referring to Wells et al. 1978; Wells 1978: 1546–1557, also Loftus 1979, 1996: 177). Interestingly, many of the questionnaire and self-report studies of courtroom broadcasting do not appear to code or rate courtroom participant/actor confidence. Confidence is rated in psychology research as one of the two least important factors in testing accuracy of eyewitness identifications (see Cutler and Penrod 1985: 112).

Do we know if it is any different for TCB surveys? How can eye-tracking assist and enhance the research? The demonstration described in this book will assist.

It would be possible to introduce some confidence type tests to TCB research, for example, testing if courtroom participants/actors felt they were affected by cameras; testing if others thoughts so; and testing the confidence of each.

Can one's confidence, and indeed certainty, in subjective self-report opinions be verified by eye-tracking and recorded images, similar to those in Images J1.1–J1.12 on pages 143–144, Images W1.1–W1.12 on pages 149–154, Images L1.1–1.13 on pages 161–162 and Images ET1.1–ET1.10 on pages 177–186?

Consent bias

Some of those involved in courtroom self-report studies were initially asked if they consent to the use of TCB. If they initially agreed and gave some tacit support to the presence of courtroom cameras, it may be inconsistent for them later to say that they were adversely affected by the use of cameras. (Also when people are questioned or surveyed, they may pay greater attention and may be less likely to be confused, for example, in trade mark litigation surveys for instance. This point is made in Jacoby (in Kassin and Wrightsman 1985: 194). Some commentators also make a similar point with regard to courtroom broadcasting. They feel courtroom participants/actors will be more responsible when being filmed. Whether this is true or not, something which has not been shown either way, it remains a fact that only a small percentage of cases will be covered. This is so even with a whole channel devoted to courtroom broadcasting.) This has not been researched. Clearly this is relevant. Again, legal-psychology research can be applied to investigating of this problem.

Other courtroom participants/actors may not have consented. Given this acceptance, they could be less likely to disagree with courtroom broadcasting or identify any negative effects, if subsequently asked. This issue has not been researched to date. Legal-psychology research can assist the consideration and investigation of this issue.

Courtroom broadcasting studies do not appear to gauge views of those actual and potential courtroom participants/actors who objected to courtroom broadcasting. This would be very useful and would also assist comparison. Legal-psychology research and eye-tracking can also assist in designing such research.

Inconsistent bias

An individual courtroom actor may feel that others may be affected by cameras in the courtroom, but that they *themselves* are not so affected. Many of the opinion-report studies concentrate on asking whether individuals feel that they themselves or other participants/actors were or were not affected. Legal-psychology research and eye-tracking should be used to assess how correct or credible this is.

Psychology also shows us that people often reject information inconsistent with views they have of themselves (McQuail and Windahl 1993: 47. Generally also Loftus 1979, 1996; Heaton-Armstrong et al. 2006). If a courtroom actor feels everyone else is positive about TCB, if and when asked, this potentially affects their own replies. Another issue is the extent to which we can, or should, rely on opinion reports of effects on others as a sole validation for testing effects.

It is feared that incorrect information is most likely to be accepted when it comes from a position of authority or so-called impartiality (see Loftus and Ketcham 1985; Twining 1985. Also Loftus 1979, 1996). Again, this raises issues for TCB research to date. Is research biased or prejudicial against recording negative effects because of who asks the questions?

If TCB is described as having no adverse effects or as being educational, beneficial or impartial, it may be more difficult for courtroom participants/actors to disagree – even when they do feel effects (see Goodman and Hahn, in Weiner and Hess 1987: 258–283). The legal-psychology research emphasises the point that TCB studies need to become more sophisticated in focus.

Arousal in court

Arousal research suggests that once aroused, our focus narrows (Hulse and Memon 2006: 314). Therefore, potentially arousal, stress or excitement at TCB cameras could lead to more focus on the camera and less on the overall events. It does not appear that we have properly considered or investigated issues such as stress and arousal on the different categories of courtroom participants/actors, and how the introduction of cameras and TCB may impact this (Hulse and Memon 2006: 313–325). Eye-tracking is a relevant research avenue. There are also other parallels with courtroom broadcasting and the instant study. Defendants in the courtroom broadcasting context have been seldom researched. Also, there is no apparent TCB arousal research (note comments in Hulse and Memon 2006: 313). Even professionally trained police officers' recall performances can be affected both qualitatively and quantitatively when they witness an arousing type event, for example, a shooting. Can it be assumed that television cameras in courts will not have some effect on professional police officer witnesses? What about other courtroom actors/personnel, both professional and otherwise?

Weapon focus and camera focus

Legal-psychology research into the weapons-focus effect is relevant. Weapons focus is the phenomena whereby victims or witnesses of crimes involving a weapon are sometimes less able to identify the attacker because they were focusing on the weapon. The focus on the weapon "impairs" (see references and definition in Pickel et al. 2008: 72; Hope and Wright 2007: 957–958) the ability to see and remember other accurate information. Studies show that with a weapon present, recall for and identification of the face of the person holding the weapon is "impaired" (Hulse and Memon 2006: 314, 321). Studies also show correct identifications are reduced and incorrect identifications increase with a weapon present (Hulse and Memon 2006: 321). This has also been shown to be the case for adults and children (see, for example, Davies, Smith and Blincoe 2008: 19–28). Nancy Steblay provides a general review of the weapon-focus research (Steblay 1992: 413–424) (note also Loftus, Loftus and Messo 1987: 55–62; Maass and Kohnken 1989: 379–408; McCraty, Atkinson and Sundram 1999; Pickel 1998: 277–295; Safer et al. 1998: 99–117; Sporer et al. 1995: 315–327; Woolnough and MacLoud 2001: 395–411; Yuille and Cutshall 1986: 291–301; Yuille et al.

1994: 931–936; Pickel, French and Betts 2003: 277–292; Pickel, Ross and Truelove 2006: 871–893; Oue, Hakoda and Onuma 2006: 443–451).

Opponents and proponents of TCB should use eye-tracking and weapons-focus research methodologies to conduct research into whether courtroom participants/actors may be distracted by, or may look at, television courtroom broadcasting cameras. Similarly, effects could occur because of other equipment and/or cameras operators. This can also be researched.

Why is it implicitly assumed that everyone in the courtroom will react in the same way? Research should examine whether some courtroom participants/actors may be more affected than others.

Will eye-tracking reveal that professionally trained participants/actors are less amenable to being distracted by TCB than non-trained and non-regular participants/actors in the courtroom? Will witness (coded as "W") images reveal different eye directions than those of a solicitors/barrister/lawyer (coded as "S" and "L")? Would significant difference mean significant changes to the TCB forms preferred or permitted? Is additional safety required?

Consider the argument that even if there are distraction effects, these will diminish over time. That may or may not be so in a long legal case. However, not every case is a long legal case. Not every court appearance, applications, etc. encompasses all of a case. Importantly also, not every courtroom actor will be present in court for a long period as their case may not involve an extended period in court. Is research required to consider diminished distraction effects incorporating differences between how long the case takes and also differences between professional and non-professional courtroom participants/actors? It would appear so.

Indeed, is someone more likely to be affected if the television camera is close to them or pointing at them than another courtroom participant/actor who is a much greater distance from the television camera?

In one of the psychology studies, Elizabeth Loftus, Geoffrey Loftus and Jane Messo showed individuals a series of slides showing a crime being committed (Loftus, Loftus and Messo 1987. Generally see also Lindsay et al. 2007). The researchers then monitored subjects' eye movements with the use of a video camera. The study found that the subjects focused more often, and for longer periods of time, on the weapon as opposed to other objects that appeared in the scene. This does not mean that facial, clothing or other details are completely ignored, rather that the weapon is given a disproportionate amount of focus. The point is that because subjects pay less attention to the details of the criminal or other details in the scene, they may then be less likely to be correct in a subsequent identification. In another study, 26 per cent of individuals who saw a video where a weapon was present gave a correct identification at a later test. Of subjects who saw the weapon-hidden video, 46 per cent gave correct decisions, which is significant (Cutler and Penrod 1985: 102, referring to Cutler et al. 1987: 223–258).

Weapons focus raises concerns for distraction effects in courtrooms. Video technology can be used to carry out experiments for effects of courtroom broadcasting. Consider eye-tracking Images J1.1–J1.12 on pages 143–144, Images W1.1–W1.12 on pages 149–154, Images L1.1–1.13 on pages 161–162 and Images ET1.1–ET1.10 on pages 177–186.

Some of the weapons-focus research also refers to arousal levels (Husle and Memon 2006: 313). This highlights that potentially courtroom cameras, or TCB, may have different effects and/or arousal levels on different courtroom participants/actors. This needs to be considered. For example, could the defendant or the parties be more prone to be affected than other courtroom participants/actors? If so, what does that mean for TCB issues and rights arguments? In addition, the areas of arousal and weapons focus may be areas of legal-psychology interest to TCB effects research. Hulse and Memon note that "[p]erceptual and attentional narrowing during encoding is unlikely to be the only explanation for the effects of arousal and weapon presence on memory" (Husle and Memon 2006: 314). Many complex research issues arise for TCB that have been considered or examined before.

Kerri L. Pickel et al. found that the witness in their study reported fewer correct, and more incorrect details when the subject carried a weapon versus carrying a book (Pickel, Ross and Truelove 2006: 871). However, they found some differences with "educated" witness subjects (Pickel, Ross and Truelove 2006: 871). They also refer to discussions and research that looks at why someone focuses on the weapon, for example, that it is threatening (Pickel, Ross and Truelove 2006: 871). So, for example, could different courtroom participants/actors be threatened in different ways by cameras and TCB? Could some be threatened, but not others? Consider that certain forms of TCB can be permitted in some local jurisdictions in the United States – even if one of the courtroom participants/actors has objected. Consider further, that some courtroom participants/actors may on occasion object not to the cameras, but to being shown in the footage. What effect does this have? Are there different effects for a courtroom actor who knows that the camera(s) cannot focus or point at them and a courtroom participant/actor who is filmed but will have their face digitally blocked? Is this out-of-court "safeguard" different from an in-court "safeguard"? One study also found that weapon-focus effect can occur even in states of low anxiety level (Kramer, Buckhout and Eugenio 1990: 167–184, as referred to in Pickel, Ross and Truelove 2006: 872). There is much for TCB research to consider.

L. Hope and D. Wright found that subject reaction in dealing with a second task was impaired in the weapon-present group and unusual-object-present groups, as compared to the control group (Hope and Wright 2007: 951–961).

Jo Saunders refers to the issues of introducing post-event questioning (PEQ) and post-event narratives (PENs) after the witnessed event and the influence these can have on recall and retrieval by individuals (Saunders 2009: 326, and references therein). This also ties in with TCB effects research, which rely upon and do not properly record the manner of how views, opinions and self-reports of courtroom participants/actors are obtained. Without proper recording, examination and scrutiny, yet another flaw arises for the current body of TCB research.

Courtroom proceedings involve many complex visual and aural elements. Introducing television cameras and TCB brings more complexity. Courtroom participants/actors have roles and tasks to undertake, both visually and aurally. Pickel, French and Betts undertook research to see if a weapon's presence impairs memory for auditory information, similar to the way it does for visual information (Pickel, French and Betts 2003: 277–292). They found diminishing memory accuracy when the task involves more demanding auditory content (Pickel, French and Betts 2003: 277–292).

Certainly weapons-focus raises many questions, but also opportunities, for TCB effects research, and also distraction research.

Legal-psychology eyewitness tools

Modern high-speed video and film techniques and other tools are currently being used in a variety of research forms. Legal-psychology uses videos and high-speed cameras for research of, amongst other things, attention, weapons-focus and eyewitness-focus issues. These technologies and techniques are an obvious avenue of research into TCB distraction and attention. These tools can permit accurate research into where courtroom participants/actors are actually looking and also for how long. So far, they have been ignored. High-speed cameras and eye-tracking are very beneficial tools for carrying out television courtroom actor effects research.

While self-report questionnaires are useful, it is possible with cameras and high-speed cameras to see where a person is actually looking, for how long, and how frequently. These can be cross-referenced with the questionnaire answers. They can also be used in laboratory settings and mock court settings. It is not necessary to get access to actual live-courtrooms to undertake such research. The use of high-speed cameras has application in relation to in-court effects. High-speed cameras can also be used for certain out-of-court research studies of the audience.

Many experiments involve test participants in a mock trial jury, as part of research into various factors involving eyewitness identification and testimony issues (See Cutler and Penrod 1995: 9, 101–102). These can be repeated both with more demanding effects research. This needs to expand to eye-tracking.

Elizabeth F. Loftus (1996: vii) indicates that many studies have examined how malleable eyewitness memory can be, and also how affected by post-event factors or post-event information. She indicates that the procedures of some research can be quite straightforward (Loftus 1996: vii). The participants of the study are shown an event. Half of the participants are then given new misleading information regarding the event. The other half of the participants do not receive any new information (Loftus 1996: vii). Both groups are then tested in relation to the original event they witnessed. It would not be difficult to expand such models of research by introducing cameras to the event situations, and to test different effects.

A large variety of studies have researched and tested eyewitness identification issues (see Heaton-Armstrong et al. 2006). Some of these could be followed in a non-live courtroom setting. As well as testing courtroom participants/actors in relation to identification of recall of participants such as a policeman or other witness, research could also test the identification and recall of a camera operator. Similar research could test recall and identification of various pieces of evidence. Research could also examine the camera type and model. Someone saying that they were not affected could be asked to identify pieces of evidence and other details in court. What are the implications if they can correctly identify the camera, but not one or more pieces of important evidence?

Other experiments into courtroom broadcasting can also involve filmed events, which are then shown to subject participants in the study. Subjects are divided into two or more study groups. Then each group is tested and examined in relation to the particular matter or effects hypothesis being researched (see for example, reference to such experimentation in Loftus 1979, 1996: 25).

Lynn M. Hulse and Amina Memon in their study used a novel system of live action real-time events shown on screen, and required officers to interact with and respond to the scenes (Hulse and Memon 2006: 316). They also tested anxiety and arousal levels before the experiments (Hulse and Memon 2006: 317). Then, during the experiments they monitored participants with wireless heart monitors (Hulse and Memon 2006: 317). This raises very important research possibilities for TCB. This could also involve eye-tracking.

Distraction focus

The various tools and methods utilised in weapons-focus research can be used to actually see whether or not courtroom participants/actors are distracted by or look at television cameras. Some tools have a research subject look at a particular pre-recorded scene and examine eye movements to see which objects and parts of the film the subject watches most. Therefore, it is possible to construct a similar study where subjects watch a particular court case with a camera present and to see if, how frequently, and for how long they focus on the courtroom camera. One of the results of some of the weapons-focus research is that subjects focus on the weapon for longer than other objects in a scene. Is this true of some of the courtroom participants/actors? Is there a camera-focus issue? This is something we can test. Other studies can have two subject groups, one with a camera present and the other with none. The focus of such a study would be to examine the effects of courtroom cameras, specifically on how courtroom cameras influence what information is taken on-board by a courtroom participant/actor, and how their recall for pertinent details of a case are affected. It is also possible to have follow-up studies at medium and long-term intervals.

The viability of eye-tracking research is demonstrated in the eye-tracking videos and in the still images. See, for example, Images J1.1–J1.12 on pages 143–144, Images W1.1–W1.12 on pages 149–154, Images L1.1–1.13 on pages 161–162 and the topography Images ET1.1–ET1.10 on pages 177–186.

Legal-psychology, importance and salience

In some psychology studies regarding eyewitnesses, there is examination of salience (see references in, for example, Hulse and Memon 2006: 26. Note also references in Vo and Schneider 2010: 173) or importance. Applying such studies to courtroom broadcasting, we can stage a trial, film a trial, etc. and list all of the items that each courtroom participant/ actor category would have seen. Then, we get them to list, or rate, these in order of importance. For example, among the most important items that they saw, one would have included a courtroom television camera. These have been overlooked in terms of TCB research so far.

Camera effect issues

Further testing can be undertaken into courtroom broadcasting forms, by varying the type, size, colour, movement, location, noise, etc. of the television camera or cameras. Research regarding recall and identification of central versus peripheral details can also be undertaken and would also be relevant here (see Loftus 1979, 1996: 63; Cutler and Penrod 1987: 183). Additional research should also investigate the effects of television cameras appearing only for certain witness testimony. Does the camera presence enhance the importance and/or credibility of that witness in the eyes of the jury?

Research can focus on how long each courtroom actor may focus on the courtroom camera, and compare this to their opinion as to whether they saw or looked at the camera. Also, if they did, for how long did they do so?

The research can also involve pictures and drawings (see, for example, the many examples of drawings in Loftus 1979, 1996), some of which, for example, may have a courtroom camera present and a courtroom camera absent. This would also be somewhat easier to arrange than live or pre-recorded filming of a mock courtroom scene.

Research studies can be both laboratory-based and more realistic field studies (see references in Cutler and Penrod 1985: 10). They can also be court-based. Typical of such studies should be research examination of one isolated factor in TCB filming. As with all research, one needs to define and describe the effect or test being carried out. This is not always evident in TCB research. It is a significant flaw of many TCB research studies that no hypothesis is generally proposed and identified, and then tested. Arguably, no effect can be shown for TCB with this type of research.

Ewing, Rhodes and Pellicano have found that gaze direction affects judgements of facial attractiveness (Ewing, Rhodes and Pellicano 2010: 321–330. See also Martin and Macrae 2010: 161–170). Clearly research is needed into the effects of different in-court camera positions, heights, angles and directions, and how this affects the audience when they see the footage. Douglas Martin and C Neil Macrae also refer to how different processing strategies can be "primed," which also suggests that research is required into cameras and camera footage for TCB (Martin and Macrae 2010: 163). They also refer to research demonstrating that specific processing orientations impact performance for face-recognition (Martin and Macrae 2010: 167).

Landstrom, Hjelmsater and Granhag found evidence in their study to show that different effects were obtained from using three differently located cameras to film the same interview (Landstrom, Hjelmsater and Granhag 2007: 199–208). They found camera perspective bias. They also refer to concurring previous research. (They give the example of Lassiter et al., in Zanna 2001: 189–253, referred to in Landstrom, Hjelmsater and Granhag 2007: 205). They also state that "the camera should not be considered a passive bystander, objectively recording what is said and done. Instead, factors such as camera shot (i.e. the distance between the camera and the suspect; ... and the camera focus (e.g. if the camera is focused on the suspect alone or on both the suspect and the interrogator; ... can contribute to biased assessments" (Landstrom, Hjelmsater and Granhag 2007: 200). "Research has shown that ... particular camera focus can bias judgements on the suspect's guilt, voluntariness, and credibility" (Landstrom, Hjelmsater and Granhag 2007: 200).

Martin Safer et al. found that when shown four pictures, taken from different standpoints in the same witnessed event scene, participants chose the close-up picture (Safer et al. 1998: 99–117, as referred to in Hulse and Memon 2006: 314–315). This emphasised critical details matching their memory if the event was emotionally arousing versus neutral (Safer et al. 1998: 99–117, as referred to in Hulse and Memon 2006: 314–315). Eye-tracking can enhance research and can be cross-referenced.

Witness stress

Stress is meant to have a significant influence on witnesses (see Loftus 1979, 1996: 33). However, TCB research has never looked at this issue. TCB research should add stress as a factor to be researched in any new studies. Again, there is legal-psychology research that can be helpful in designing and contextualising such research. They also report that participant viewers relied heavily on verbal cues (Loftus 1979, 1996: 199).

Context and effects

Legal-psychology research has recognised the stages of recall and identification (namely, acquisition, retention and retrieval (see, for example, Loftus 1979, 1996: 50, 113, 114)). Can these be related to (as appropriate in) TCB research? To date, there is no effort to examine how and when different courtroom participants/actors can be affected. Nor does research examine (that is, when research is carried out) the time and context of any possible effect.

It is important to also refer to when questions are asked of courtroom participants/actors. Legal-psychology research indicates that the longer the time between the event and the questions and recall, the more inaccurate and incomplete the witness will be (see Loftus 1979, 1996: 53). This point is not always recognised in the research.

Equally, post-event information, discussions and questions (see Loftus 1979, 1996: 54, 94) can alter, change or influence a witness as much as a courtroom participant/actor. These issues are beyond the current study.

Oue, Hakoda and Onuma found that the visual features of the weapons affected the witnesses' memory, suggesting the shape of the weapon is a factor attracting witness attention (Oue, Hakoda and Onuma 2006: 443–451). The types, models, size, locations, etc. of cameras need to be considered in TCB effects research. This opportunity has been missed so far. Eye-tracking allows these avenues to be expanded.

Similarly, it is most important to be careful that the questions or queries do not taint or influence the answer. Many TCB studies, however, are conducted by people who would not otherwise draft questionnaires or experiments and who may not be aware that their queries, although well intentioned, may be influencing the reply.

Timing of post-event information can be very relevant in a number of studies (see Loftus 1979, 1996: 64). So, for example, if a camera is already present, or indeed permanently in the courtroom, this is potentially less relevant, obvious, affecting, etc. It is potentially less disrupting than a television camera moving about in the courtroom. It is also potentially less disruptive than a television camera plus a camera operator coming into the courtroom (a) after the case starts or (b) after many or all of the courtroom participants/actors have come into and prepared themselves in the courtroom. Again, these issues are ripe for research.

There are also interesting differences in the form of retrieval. For example, differences have been found between asking subjects what they saw and asking them to reply to a predetermined list of questions (see Loftus 1979, 1996: 90). Also, the interrogator is not always neutral (see Loftus 1979, 1996: 97).

Consider a judge after a televised courtroom trial asking jury members if they were affected by the camera broadcasting. Many potential bias issues arise. The judge is not always a neutral party. He may have considered an application to allow cameras and decided in favour – possibly in sight of the jury. They may also be otherwise aware of the decision. The judge may have made some positive comments. The jury before being asked are aware of the views of the judge in terms of reinforcing acceptance of the cameras and a judicial view of no adverse effects. Yet, this is what has occurred in some TCB research. Gary Wells and Amy Bradfield, amongst others, have been researching confirmations and feedback given to witness and found that it can influence the witness (Wells and Bradfield 1998: 360, as referred to in TerBeek 2007: 25–26).

Melissa L.-H. Vo and W. X. Schneider also make the point that in looking at a given scene or carrying out a given task, we also rely on our existing knowledge and experience, which they refer to as "implicit knowledge" (Vo and Schneider 2010: 172). Again, this appears not to have been considered or researched in the TCB literature to date.

TCB recall research

Another avenue for examination is to carry out studies with cameras present in the courtroom and with cameras absent. Then, each group would be tested for the recall accuracy for details in the courtroom scene. Is there better and more detailed recall in the camera-absent scenario? Does camera presence affect recall of central and peripheral details? Equally, these tests could be replicated in different courtroom broadcasting forms.

One tool is to test jurors or mock jurors for their recall and retention. The jurors are shown a particular case or take part in a case. One group has cameras present and the other does not. Thus, it is possible to compare results and see what the possible effects of the cameras were. Research can be conducted to see if the camera-present group recalls fewer pertinent details of the case. One of the advantages of conducting studies is that it can be possible for the juries not to know what is actually being tested for, thus avoiding bias. In terms of medium- and long-term retention, it is also possible to conduct follow-up studies on both sets of jurors.

The videotaping of courtroom scenes or interviews of subjects after seeing or recalling events can be used in research studies (see references in Vo and Schneider 2010: 183). Another study method is to stage a mock crime, then conduct interviews of the subject witnesses, and later arrange a mock trial where the witnesses are cross-examined. Various factors can be tested (see example referred to in Vo and Schneider 2010: 185).

Blocking effect

It is possible to study the effects of digital image blocking. Do witnesses (or indeed other courtroom participants/actors) who have been able to have their image digitally blocked react any differently than those who know that their image will be shown? Is there any difference between those whose image is automatically blocked by a pre-existing court broadcasting rule or those who are asked for their preference or have to apply to have their image blocked? Similar studies can be used to test effects on those who may have objected to the TCB but were overruled. Cameras can also be used, whether in a real TCB context or a mock trial situation, to test for accuracy of self-reports and third party reports of effects. A study could use (miniature) cameras to examine effects of broadcast cameras on courtroom participants/actors and compare these to self-reports *and* third party reports.

Conclusion

Legal-psychology provides an abundance of relevant research opportunities, some of which is relevant in relation to distraction concerns and television eye-tracking research. Sole reliance upon limited self-report studies does not answer any of the arguments in the TCB debate. The extensive literature of legal-psychology research shows that we should not rely on self-reports and opinion studies alone. More robust and scientifically based research is required following the lead of other fields of research, such as legal-psychology.

Chapter 7

The Eye-tracking Distraction Solution

Eye-tracking and TCB

Eye-tracking (the study of eye movement and gaze) was not directly considered in the Supreme Court TCB decisions. Neither has it been considered in the general literature in relation to TCB. However, eye-tracking technology offers a significant research opportunity. It can research distraction effects of TCB.

S. L. Alexander, for one, notes the lack of empirical research (Alexander 1990: 39).

It is now clear that the Supreme Court is not aware of eye-trackers and did not refer to eye-tracking previously. Eye-tracking can be used for conducting in-court effects research, in particular research of distraction effects.

The basis of the arguments in the television courtroom debate are largely unchanged since 1965 (Stewart 1998: 9). Legal-psychological, media and communications research has also advanced. Eye-tracking technology, in particular, provides definite avenues for examining the actual in-court (and audience) effects gaps referred to by the Supreme Court. We are now in a position to begin research of actual effects issues without having to rely solely on limited self-reports and opinion-reports. Let us consider some of these venues below.

Eye-tracking technologies are important (see Overview, Fixation 2010). Eye-tracking research and techniques (see Duchowski, regarding eye-tracking techniques generally, Duchowski 2007: 52–86) have been used successfully in advertising, marketing, psychology, eyewitness accuracy studies, Internet usage research, health research, etc. The literature on eye-tracking is constantly growing (Nielsen and Pernice 2009; Wedel and Pieters 2008; Spector 2008. See also Henderson 2005; Hatfield 2009; Bundesen and Habekost 2008; Shah and Miyake 2005) and recognised (Davis 2003: 367, 378).

While William Petkanas suggests that recordings of TCB may be shown to audience subjects, and that they may then be interviewed afterwards, for example, in terms of what they found informative and interesting (Petkanas 1990: 118), no reference is made to eye-tracking. He further suggests that another study might have one group viewing film footage, while the other reads reports of the same case (Petkanas 1990: 118).

Eye-tracking also helps with other research issues. For example, Tuula-Riitta Valikoski (2004: 178) notes that many responses to in-court research questions of attentional focus issues (in this instance prosecutors) do not provide evidence of cognitive processes. It only identifies reported indications of attentional effects. Eye-tracking provides direct and accurate recorded measurement of eye movement and eye focus. The era of Eye-tracking TCB research should be upon us.

Advantages of eye-tracking

Eye-tracking "provides a more direct and continuous measure of attention" than manual measurements (Armstrong and Olatunji 2009). It also overcomes the limitations of opinion-reports and self-reports. Furthermore, it can be used to test and validate opinion-reports and self-reports. "[E]ye movements are a direct indicator of overt attention" and provide "a highly direct measure of visual attention, eye systems also allow continuous measurement of eye movements" (Armstrong and Olatunji 2009). We should be researching this in the context of TCB. Eye-tracking permits testing and direct observation of eye fixation, focus and attention of television cameras (see Ware 2006: 11). Eye-tracking research also has the advantage that it tracks and documents exactly what people see (see www.prsresearch.com/prs-tools/). Eye-tracking gives accurate, verified and observable data.

Eye-tracking and legal-psychology

Eye-trackers are increasingly used in psychology and eyewitness identification research. Sheree Josephson and Michael E. Holmes used eye-trackers recently to examine whether eyewitnesses use scanpaths to recognise suspects in photograph line-ups (an example is Josephson and Holmes 2010). Elizabeth Loftus used eye-tracking to research the weapons-focus effect (Loftus, Loftus and Messo 1987: n 43, at 55. Note also Loftus and Mackworth 1978: 565–572; Kwak 2009). However, while there has been legal-psychology and eye focus research on particular legal issues, primarily eyewitness identification issues, the issue of in-court TCB distraction effects is largely, if not entirely, ignored.

More recently there has been noted an increasing use of eye-tracking in relation to legal-psychology research into the effects of cameras and camera perspective in recorded police interviews and confessions (this is also noted by Ware 2006: 35). This is partly driven by the knowledge that there can be false convictions, and erroneous and false confessions captured on video recordings of suspect interrogations. One result of this research is that it has been found that different camera angles and focus orientations of the interview camera can alter significantly how viewers of such film footage rate the genuineness and voluntariness of the recorded suspect "confessions." The manner in which the evidence is filmed, that is, the confession footage, can influence judgements of guilt (Schmidt 2006: 3). Mock jurors have been found to be influenced by the camera angle from which the interrogation is filmed (Lassiter and Irvine 1986: 268–276, referred to in Schmidt 2006: 9–10). This is now known as *camera perspective bias* (see Lambert 2010: 128–130). It is additionally significant since the Innocence Project began. It applies DNA technology and techniques to past cases. It found that a quarter of the DNA exoneration cases originally relied strongly on false confessions (see InnocenceProject.org; Schmidt 2006: 11).

Most criminal investigation interviews that are recorded, adopt a suspect-focused angle only. This is as opposed to focusing on the police officer or focusing on both of them at the same time (see Schmidt 2006: 25–26). G. Daniel Lassiter and Audrey A. Irvine showed the same interview recorded on different cameras to show suspect-only, police officer only, and both equally focused (Lassiter and Irvine 1986: 268–276; Schmidt 2006: 26). The research study subjects then viewed one of the videos, depending on which group they were in. The ones who saw the suspect-only video perceived less coercion (Lassiter and Irvine 1986: 268-276; Schmidt 2006: 26). Other research also confirmed that suspect-only videos yielded significantly higher ratings for perceived guilt and voluntariness (see for example Lassiter et al. 2002: 299–305; Schmidt 2006: 28). As a result of the Lassiter and Irvine study, the police in New Zealand changed their practices to ensure that there was no suspect-only video recordings, and that suspect and questioner were always in frame (see Schmidt 2006: 31). Pressure is increasing to change policies elsewhere also.

Lezlee J. Ware also examined camera perspective bias and used eye-trackers to monitor visual attention (Ware 2006). She refers to studies and the literature that shows that suspect-only camera perspective creates a bias for judgements of voluntariness and guilt (Geller 1992; Kassin 1997: 221–233; Lassiter 2002: 204–208; Ware 2006: 10).

Eye-tracking research

The device used in an eye-tracking study is known as an eye-tracker. One of the initial stages in designing eye-tracking experiments is formulating a hypothesis to research (Overview, Fixation 2010: 157. There are also different types of research design, see Overview, Fixation 2010: 159 et seq).

The aim of eye-tracking research is to study the eye position and eye movement of the subject (Jacob and Karn, in Hyona, Radach and Deubel 2003: 573–605). Such research relies on sophisticated software (see reference in Hyona, Radach and Deubel 2003: 88–91). Detailed experience and expertise with software, computers, computer science and statistics can also be a prerequisite to undertaking such studies (note also, Hyona, Radach and Deubel 2003: 171). Hardware tools as well as calibration of those tool is often (but not always) needed (see comments in relation to calibration issues, Hyona, Radach and Deubel 2003: 87–99, and 301). Eye-tracking involves research of

- Fixation;
- Fixation (gaze) duration;
- Fixation rate (overall);
- Fixation duration mean (overall);
- Number of fixations (overall);

- Scanpath (fixation sequence);
- Area of interest (AOI);
- Gaze percentage (proportion of time) per AOI;
- Number of fixations per AOI;
- Gaze duration mean per AOI.

Eye-tracking allows researchers to examine,

- Fixation count/duration/order;
- Areas of interest (per region);
- Transitions between regions;
- Time to fixation (first);
- Counting of visits and re-visits;
- Task completion duration.

However, such studies can be expensive, complex and require collaboration and expertise across research fields (Sundstedt 2009). The eye-tracking hardware and software can be expensive too. Notwithstanding that, we need to apply eye-tracking to the problems of gaps in TCB research. The Supreme Court distraction challenge needs to be addressed.

Eye-tracking forms: Interactive and diagnostic

Andrew Duchowski refers to various eye-tracking case studies (see Duchowski 2007: 181 et seq. See also Morimoto and Mimica 2005: 4–24) and applications (Duchowski 2007: 203 et seq). At a headline level, the two headline application categories are interactive (input) applications and diagnostic applications (Duchowski 2007: 205. Also Sundstedt 2009).

Diagnostic eye-tracking can be used in the fields of psychology, marketing, advertising, human factors and ergonomics (Duchowski 2007: 205; Bingemann 2007). It is also used in law enforcement and policing security (see, for example, Setcan.com, referring to the EyeLock training system, which comprises a forward focus camera and two eye-trackers, all of which are encompassed in a pair of glasses that a combat or police trainee wears).

Interactive eye-tracking applications include using eye-tracking to input instructions to or interact with a (technology) device of some sort using eye focus (see Duchowski 2007: 205). For example, a person's gaze can be used to give instructions or input instructions. Quadriplegics, for example, can use their eyes to move a pointer or cursor (Duchowski 2007: 206. One enterprising father also wrote his own iPhone application, called the iComm, to allow his disabled daughter to point instructions of the iPhone screen using her eyes). Additional applications include the fields of human computer interaction, visual displays and computer graphics (Duchowski 2007: 206).

Other eye-tracking applications

Companies and researchers use eye-tracking research to track displays. For example, companies using or advertising on the Internet can use eye-tracking to test an advert or the location of an advert. Do viewers look at the advert, for how long, or do they miss the advert entirely because of its location? Where is the best location for the advert? Eye-tracking addresses these important commercial issues.

Andrew Duchowski refers to various eye-tracking examples in neuroscience and psychology (Duchowski 2007: 207 et seq), industrial engineering and human factors (e.g. aviation, driving and visual inspection; Duchowski 2007: 241 et seq), marketing and advertising (e.g. advert design and placement, label and product design and placement, television, Internet; Duchowski 2007: 261 et seq) and computer science (Duchowski 2007: 275). Lillington refers to IBMs Webgaze Analyser for researching how people read Internet pages (Lillington 2005).

SMI (SensoMotoric Instruments) refer to eye-tracking applications in medical research, diagnostics, surgery, psychology, sports and performance, human machine interactions, market research, neuroscience research, psycholinguistics, opthatmology, ergonomics, etc. (see Smi.com).

Further eye-tracking applications exist in visual systems and linguistics, and also in relation to gaming machines, medical instruments, vehicles, vehicle safety, computer interaction, medical diagnostics, security, law enforcement, video conferencing, information kiosks, interactive advertising, etc. (referred to by Tobii.com). "Eye movements are the only means of communication for some severely disabled people" (Agustin, as referred to in the eye-tracking blog of Martin Tall 2010). Mercedes use eye-tracking technology for driver fatigue-alert systems (see Eyetracking.com. Note also Ji and Yang 2002: 357–377). There are also potential applications in general security and computer security (Silver and Biggs 2008). There are also many market research applications (see Eyetracking.com).

Computer games development is another area where eye-tracking is increasingly utilised (see for example, Sundstedt 2009).

Eye-tracking might also be used to develop more general mass-market applications, such as gaze controls for heating, lighting (see "An Affordable Future for Eye-tracking in Sight" 2010) or perhaps television. Overall, there are many current applications (see also Richardson and Spivey, in Bowlin and Wnek 2004) and more promised.

There are various eye-tracker manufacturers. Examples include Tobii (Tobii.com), Eye Tracking Inc (Eyetracking.com), SMI (Smivision.com), Arrington Research (Arringtonresearch.com), Asley (Asleyetracking.com), SensoMotoric Instrument (Smi.com), and Polhemus (Polhemus.com). There are increasing numbers of international conferences relating to eye-tracking. One is the Fixational Eye Movements and Visual Stabilisation conference. (Note also the Communication by Gaze Interaction (COGAIN) eye-tracking project, which aims, inter alia, to advance the technologies, and attempt to reduce the substantial cost of eye trackers. See "An Affordable Future for Eye-tracking in Sight" 2010.) Another is Eye-tracking Research and Applications (ETRA) (see Etra.cs.uta.fi/ 2010). Lund University Humanities Lab is one university to offer courses in eye-tracking technology (see Lund Eye-tracking Academy (LETA)). Various other universities and university departments use eye-tracking as a valuable tool of research. The University of Bournemouth, UK; Ball State University, US; Trinity College, Dublin; and University College Dublin are just a few examples.

TCB and eye-tracking

There does not appear to be any reference in the literature or conference papers to the eye-tracking legal applications in relations to TCB, for example, distraction. This is the first research to explore these possibilities. Indeed, the in-court proof of concept demonstration undertaken by the author is the first such research in relation to TCB and eye-tracking anywhere. Eye-tracking and psychology research can begin to address the legal research gaps in TCB effects research. The Supreme Court has been calling for empirical research and has set a challenge. The three Supreme Court cases highlight some of the avenues for empirical research.

Eye-tracking comes to court

Some of the research gaps referred to in the cases, and where eye-tracking may be applied to TCB, are referred to below,

- We should apply eye-tracking to the various courtroom participants/actors;
- Do they look at the television camera?;
- If so, for how long?;
- What is the effect?;
- What difference does the location of the camera have on the different courtroom participants/actors?;
- Are there different effects for camera-only versus camera and camera operator?;
- Are there different effects for different types of camera?;
- How do in-court television cameras affect different courtroom actors'/personnels' self-report undertaking tasks?

The TCB literature to date does not incorporate an analysis of the different tasks of the different courtroom participants/actors into discussion or research of the different effects issues being examined.

We should employ eye-tracking to examine distraction, attention, etc. of courtroom participants/actors in the context of task analysis. Wickens, Vincow and Yeh refer to task analysis issues and research (Wickens, Vincow and Yeh, in Shah and Miyake 2005: 385 et seq. See also Shah, Freedman and Vekiri, in Shah and Miyake 2005: 450 et seq regarding task demands). A "critical variable in information space is the task that the user is expected to carry out" (Wickens, Vincow and Yeh, in Shah and Miyake 2005: 415).

Almost invariably the literature and limited research ignores reference to and consideration of camera location and frame issues. We need to be able to describe and represent descriptively and diagrammatically the various camera issues (see generally discussion of frame representation issues in Wickens, Vincow and Yeh 2005: 387 et seq).

Distraction and distraction research need to examine the camera-location issues. Now eye-tracking can assist in this. We also need to start recording where the camera is located in the courtroom. The different research studies need to be able to be compared, including comparison of camera locations.

It is equally important in studies to know where the different courtroom participants/actors are located and which direction they are facing, and how this compares with the camera location. For example, are the courtroom participants/actors facing straight on, left or right when they look at the camera? We need to be able to compare this across research findings.

Are alterations required? In the *Estes* case "construction of a television booth in the courtroom made it necessary to alter the physical layout of the courtroom and to move from their accustomed position to benches reserved for spectators" (*Estes*: 1965: 572. Warren, CJ). What are the effects of alterations?

In most research, the location and height of the cameras is not considered or even documented, so we cannot look back to assess and compare different cases or research studies on these points.

Different angles and frames can have different effects and meanings (see Wickens, Vincow and Yeh 2005: 398 et seq). We need to begin examining the various issues in the TCB field. Different frames can have different advantages and disadvantages (Wickens, Vincow and Yeh 2005: 401). We need to begin examining and contrasting these for TCB.

Many issues of confidence and ratings come up in relation to TCB research. Many opportunities arise in terms of examining these issues with eye-tracking technology. For example, an eye-tracker and an observer could both look at a particular courtroom participant/actor and try to examine how many times they focus their attention or look at the television camera in the courtroom. The observer could press a button to record each time they perceive the courtroom participant/actor looking at the camera.

Indeed, a second observer could also look at the courtroom participant/actor and try and record their perceptions during the case or after the case (e.g. the Short report).

The various results would then be compared. The observers would also be tested for their confidence ratings. Note that the Short report in California did attempt to have observers in court to ascertain if the courtroom participants or actors were effected by the cameras. However, they did not have the benefit of eye-trackers, nor do they appear to have been tested for confidence. Indeed, the test recording sheet does not appear to rate whether or how many times a particular courtroom actor is (a) distracted by and (b) focuses at the television camera. Schmidt used a press button system once the subject perceived a target effect (see Schmidt 2006: 30). This would assist in dealing with the problem of most TCB research, namely, of relying solely upon self-report, opinion-reports and questionnaires.

There are various types of eye-trackers. One avenue for in-court research is to use eye-trackers that are incorporated into lightweight glasses (see example reference to same at Eyetracker.co.uk). This type of research allows itself to be adopted to different courtroom participants/actors and also in realistic settings and in real court settings. There are also various types of head-mounted eye-tracking tools (in terms of head-mounted display applications, see discussion in Wickens, Vincow and Yeh 2005: 406 et seq).

Other studies can use a variety of eye-trackers where subjects can view pictures or videos of court scenes on a PC, laptop or projection screen. This model would assist in increasing subject numbers in respective TCB studies.

In considering different TCB forms and in particular long, extended footage versus short or snippet footage, we need to research what is viewed, for how long, eye movement behaviour and visual processing speeds (note recent research by Vo and Schneider 2010: 171–200).

Eye-tracking out of court

Distraction is an in-court issue. However, various studies can be undertaken with eye-trackers in relation to out-of-court effects. Some of the potential studies can involve the following.

The actual footage and segments broadcast potentially have effects. We need to begin researching the use and integration of different footage segments: presenter discussion, analysis, etc. Is there continuity, discontinuity, visual momentum (see Wickens, Vincow and Yeh 2005: 402) and what effects occur for the viewer? We should ask "what do you think you see?" (see SMI article of the same heading available at Smi.com) in the context of the audience of TCB.

Eye-trackers can help us to see what the audience focuses upon in a given picture or broadcast.

Is TCB designed best to educate? Or are certain forms of TCB best configured to educate? Some researchers refer to preparation and deliberate design of multimedia presentations in order to enhance learning and education (see Mayer, in Shah and Miyake 2005: 479).

How and what do the audience learn from TCB? In the first instance, we can now at least track what they are looking at and what they see, and for how long, in television courtroom broadcasts and pictures of television cameras in courts. Eye-tracking now permits this research. Of course we also have other issues to consider in dealing with measuring audience education and information gain, such as understanding, coding, differences between pictures, videos, text and audio, different channels and different speeds (see general comments in Mayer, in Shah and Miyake 2005: 479–481).

We should also begin to research camera-focus issues in terms of witness test. Just as research has found that there are problems and biases created by police interviews, which only record the suspect being interviewed, issues arise in court also. If a television camera focuses on a witness or suspect being examined or cross-examined, does this create different impressions and effects than the television camera focusing on the questioner and the person being questioned? Legal-psychology studies and eye-tracking can assist in initiating this research (see Schmidt 2006; generally and 39, and also references therein).

Some TCB seeks to focus on the defendant for a "reaction shot" when a witness is being interviewed. The witness testimony could be carried as audio is played over a close-up of the defendant. What issues does this raise? For one, there may be effects. It would appear that the research referred to above in relation to videotaped confessions and eye-tracking may assist in investigating these issues for the first time.

The video confession research is also concerned that "as the salience of the suspect in the video is increased," perceived voluntariness may also increase (see Ware 2006: 18–19, and references therein). Does this hold relevance for television camera zooming in the courtroom? Research of these issues could involve eye-tracking, confidence and test of various subject judgements, awards, verdicts, etc.

How useful are news snippets of TCB? Are they educational? Eye-tracking research can begin to assist us in addressing these questions. Consider, for example, the eye-tracking research undertaken by Melissa L.-H. Vo and W. X. Schneider (2010: 179) into the information we obtain from mere glimpses. They found "strong evidence for the influence of flashed scene previews on the guidance of eye movements which indicated that participants were able to generate, store, and make use of initial scene representation for subsequent target search … the results … add to the growing evidence that initially generated scene representations can be stored across saccades continuously exhibiting their influence on eye movement control" (Vo and Schneider 2010: 187). However, one group was found to process information faster than the other group (Vo and Schneider 2010: 191. The information shown to the groups was different (see Vo and Schneider 2010: 192). Does this have implications for TCB?

Complex issues such as emotions and emotional content in the footage also need to be examined. Reiko Graham et al. found that during longer presentations "validity and emotion interacted such that cuing by emotional faces, fearful faces in particular, was enhanced relative to neutral faces" (Graham et al. 2010: 331–368). These results converge with a growing body of evidence that suggests that gaze and expression are initially processed independently and that they interact at later stages to direct attentional-orienting. In Graham et al.'s study the participant subjects were asked to perform a task and then tap a spacebar on a computer (Graham et al. 2010: 339). This assisted in recording time spent reacting to the stimulus. Different subject groups can be compared.

Helena Rutherford and Jane Raymond also refer to research that found that "presenting negative versus neutral targets in short alternating blocks and examining [inhibition of return (IOR)] on the first trial of each new block, we show that the emotional modulation of IOR stems from the affective context in place before visual orienting is initiated, not by perceptual processing of the targets after cue effect" (Rutherford and Raymond 2010: 389, 389–412).

Newspaper reports consist of different layouts, articles, texts, headlines, photographs, captions, "tickers, drop quotes, fact boxes, maps, diagrams, tables, etc." (Holsanova, Holmberg and Holmqvist 2008: 1). Television programming contains some of these plus many additional elements. How does the audience interact with, use and (possibly) learn from TCB and different forms of such broadcasting? What viewing, learning and cognitive processes are involved? Significant research has yet to be undertaken in relation to audience-effects issues in TCB. Eye-tracking tools can clearly assist in examining these issues.

Holsanova, Holmberg and Holmqvist used eye-tracking to research the effects of reading information graphics in a newspaper study (Holsanova, Holmberg and Holmqvist 2008: 1–12. The main measures of online reading compared were reading order; reading time; and text-graphic integration (Holsanova, Holmberg and Holmqvist 2008: 8)). They found that different spatial layouts had a significant effect on readers' eye movement behaviour (Holsanova, Holmberg and Holmqvist 2008: 1, 10). They indicate that the results are important in contributing to the study of "attentional guidance in printed media" (Holsanova, Holmberg and Holmqvist 2008: 1). Research identifies different reading and scanning speeds with different tasks and purposes (see references in Khosla et al. 2008: 237–251 and 238). Khosla et al. researched different instructional tasks, namely, word search, question – answer tasks and finding subjectively most interesting answer, and tracking time for the various tasks (Khosla et al. 2008: 238–240). They also refer to different subject states, namely, scanning, reading and decision state (Khosla et al. 2008: 245–246, and 249). The decision state suggested a more careful analysis (Holsanova, Holmberg and Holmqvest 2008: 248). We need to start undertaking research into attention, education, information, etc., in relation to the TCB audience.

Holsanova, Holmberg and Holmqvist also refer to research regarding cognitive load (see for example Chandler and Sweller 1991: 293–332, as referred to in Holsanova, Holmberg and Holmqvist 2008) and the cognitive theory of multimedia learning (Holsanova, Holmberg and Holmqvist 2008: 2–3. See also the following, Henderson and Ferreira 2004: 1–58; Holmqvist et al., in Hyona, Radach and Duebel 2003: 657–670; Holsanova, Rahm and Holmqvist 2005: 65–93; Jeung, Chandler and Sweller 1997: 329–343; Mayer 2001; Mayer 2005: 183–200; and Scheiter, Wiebe and Holsanova, in Zheng 2009). In term of suggesting effects for TCB, for example, education; educational benefits equally across all forms of television broadcasting, etc.; we need to incorporate additional factors such as competing programmes, forms, tasks, dual-tasks being undertaken, environment, etc. Arguably, research of TCB is more complex because it is multimedia and multimodal based (see for example Folker, Sichelschmidt and Ritter, in Bara and Bucciarelli 690–695, 2005). Considerations such as distraction, priming, negative priming, attentional capture, attentional orientation, visual search, divided attention also arise (Bundesen and Habekost 2008: 16–102).

Eye-tracking can be used to carry out similar type research of TCB effects.

Courtroom design

In terms of designing TCB, and forms, we should consider how to get the best broadcast footage for educational purposes and the optimum scenario for filming without adverse effects upon courtroom participants/actors. Considerations that have not been considered before are how best to tailor initial design features (consider generally Wickens, Vincow and Yeh, in Shah and Miyake 2005: 383–425) to try and accomplish these aims. Additional design features, both in terms of in-court and out-of-court effects, are camera type, height and location. These design features have not been addressed in the general TCB literature nor in the limited effects literature. Wickens, Vincow and Yeh, for example, refer to and examine issues involved with framing, with design applications and visual spacing (Wickens, Vincow and Yeh, in Shah and Miyake, 2005: 384) and refer to different effects (Wickens, Vincow and Yeh, in Shah and Miyake 2005: 418–419).

Eye-tracking and dual tasking

The issue of dual tasking and multi-tasking in the courtroom has not been researched or addressed yet. What are the effects on a courtroom actor of doing various tasks at once? These complex issues have yet to be considered in the courtroom broadcasting context. There is some eye-tracking research referring to this issue in other fields; this is a complex issue, which needs consideration in the courtroom broadcasting context. The issue of carrying out dual tasks simultaneously also appears in eye-tracking research (Duchowski 2007: 239). This applies to distraction research also.

Viewer strategies and tactics may also be involved. For example, in terms of reading and eye-tracking research, Khosla et al. (depending on whether the subjects perceive a forthcoming task as difficult or not) note that subjects adopt different strategies, which can influence their fixation times (Khosla et al. 2008: 249; O'Regan, in Kowler 1990: 395–453; O'Regan, in Rayner 1992: 333–354, each as referred to in Duchowski 2007: 239).

In terms of TCB, numerous research possibilities arise. Various types of research experiments can be conducted with eye-tracking monitoring of different cameras and courtroom "photographic stimuli" (to use the words of Sato and Yoshikawa 2010: 369–388).

One could have separate subject groups who also have to perform tasks and tap a spacebar. Reaction times and eye movement can be tracked and coded. The groups might in one scene have to tap the spacebar as soon as the judge arrived into the courtroom. In one group, the scene may have a camera and camera operator moving; in another a camera and camera operator with no movement; another with camera only; and a final control group with no camera at all. In each, the judge arrives in (after introducing the camera focus element). The research can then be compared.

Khosla et al. state that

> "[t]he finding that eye movement patterns differ when different processing demands are encountered can be used for developing an interactive information search application that learns and adapts to users' goals and intentions (Khosla, Simola, Salojarvi and Kojo 2008: 249–250). For example, by examining which parts of a search engine results are read in different states, such as *reading* or *decision* states, it is possible to infer about the intentions and interests of the user."
>
> (original emphasis).

Should we not research audience viewing of TCB? Take a gavel to gavel (G2G) criminal trial for example. How does the intention, tasks and cognitive load on the viewer affect what they see, how their eyes fixate and for how long? Does this change occur during different segments of the trial (e.g. opening, testimony, arguments and motions, closing), and/or between different courtroom participants/actors (e.g. judge, witness, expert witness)? Eye-tracking can assist us in the task of beginning to unlock the answers to these queries.

Eye-tracking and distraction

One of the concerns with TCB is that the cameras in court "might be so completely and thoroughly disruptive and distracting as to make a fair trial impossible" (*Estes*: 611–612. Stewart, J. Minority opinion). Mr Justice White states that

> the currently available [research] materials assessing the effect of cameras in the courtroom are too sparse and fragmentary …, 'we know too little of the actual impact … to reach a conclusion … evidence before us.' It may well be, however, that as further experience and informed judgment do become available, the use of cameras in the courtroom, as in this trial, will prove to pose such a serious hazard to a defendant's rights that a violation of the Fourteenth Amendment will be found without a showing on the record of specific demonstrable prejudice to the defendant.
>
> (*Estes*: 616. White, J. Minority opinion)

Again, one of the concerns with TCB has been the distracting effect on the courtroom participants/actors. Up until now, however, the Supreme Court has not realised that research tools actually exist to examine these issues. Eye-tracking provides tangible methods for examining actual distraction of courtroom participants/actors caused by television cameras in court. We should apply eye-tracking to the various courtroom participants/actors who are involved in televised cases. Do they look at the television camera? If so, for how long? What is the effect? Eye-trackers allow us to begin this research.

Are there different effects for camera only versus camera plus camera operator? Can there be different effects for different types of camera? Again, eye-trackers allow us to begin the research. Consider Images W1.4 on page 148 and W1.9 on page 151 and also Images ET1.1–ET1.10 on pages 177–186.

Many issues of confidence and ratings arise in relation to TCB research. Many opportunities also arise in terms of examining these issues with eye-tracking technology. For example, an eye-tracker and an observer could both look at a particular courtroom participant/actor and examine how many times they focus their attention or look at the television camera in the courtroom. The observer could press a button to record each time they perceive the courtroom participant/actor to look at the camera. The observer in court can be tested against what is recorded by the eye-tracker. Thus far the use of observers in court to record the effects of TCB has not been independently assessed. This is important in the context of eye-tracking verifying observer-reports and also in terms of a modern critical assessment of the general research carried out historically.

The various results would then be compared. The observers would also be tested for their confidence ratings. Note that the Short report in California did attempt to have observers in court to ascertain if the courtroom participants/actors were affected by the cameras. However, they did not have the benefit of eye-trackers, nor do they appear to have been tested for confidence. Indeed the test recording sheet does not rate whether or how many times a particular courtroom actor is (a) distracted by and (b) focuses at the television camera. Schmidt used a button system, pressed once subject perceived a target effect (see Schmidt 2006: 30, 38). This would assist in dealing with the problem of most TCB research, namely, that of relying solely upon self-report, opinion-reports and questionnaires.

First in-court demonstration

Some of the one off in-court television broadcasts in the United Kingdom took literally years of negotiation before approval and agreement was reached. As noted above, the Supreme Court (and possibly courts elsewhere) is not aware of the existence of eye-trackers when discussing TCB issues, particularly distraction effect issues. No commentator has discussed or identified the utility of eye-tracking of TCB effects research. It is, therefore, very timely to suggest and recommend, as the author does, eye-tracking in order to address the Supreme Court research distraction effects challenge.

There also appears to be no explicit consideration of effects-research issues, including distraction and eye-tracking in the recent proposals for TCB of UK appeal decisions and/or sentencing decisions, as proposed by David Cameron and Kenneth Clarke.

Self-report eye-tracking experiments can be costly, complex and can produce very large volumes of data. It would be useful, and would assist in scoping eye-tracking experiment of

TCB in-court effects, to bring an eye-tracker into an actual courtroom and to examine how it will operate. This will assist in scoping actual eye-tracking experimentation, deciding upon which eye-trackers to use, developing hypothesis and models of examination for effects, etc. (see below for more details of the eye-tracking in-court proof of concept demonstration).

With this in mind, the author entered into dialogue with the court authorities in Ireland to discuss the possibility of obtaining permission to undertake a recorded demonstration of eye-tracking technology in a real courtroom. After a period of discussion, the Courts Service in Ireland granted permission in principle to such a demonstration. Certain criteria were required to be formalised and documented.

The ultimate demonstration involved a head-mounted eye-tracker. The subject wearing the eye-tracker sat in the respective positions of the main courtroom participants/actors, namely, barrister, solicitor, witness, court clerk and judge. It was initially hoped to undertake the demonstration in two courts, one normal commercial/civil court, and one with a criminal jury box courtroom. In the later court, it was proposed that the subject wearing the head-mounted eye-tracker will also sit in the jury box. Ultimately this did not occur.

One of the advantages of an eye-tracker is that whatever the subject looks at, can be monitored accurately, and also recorded. Therefore, the demonstration of where the subject is looking, and can look (their cone-of-vision) can be recorded in relation to their position in the courtroom. Location issues should be incorporated into future research.

In addition, while not a full eye-tracking experiment (given that, a different type of eye-tracker would be more appropriate; significantly more detail and planning would be required; as well as dealing with issues of official and university approvals), it was proposed to introduce an actual tripod television camera into the courtroom. This would act as an example of distraction focus.

The proposal was to record the subject's eye movements and focus in their cone-of-vision in their respective locus; and then, to introduce the tripod television camera to a fixed position within the cone-of-vision, to record and demonstrate how an eye-tracker can accurately monitor, track and record when a subject actually looks at the television camera.

Conclusion

Researchers use eye-tracking and content analysis to examine education. An example of one study using both eye-tracking and content analysis can be seen in Barrios et al. (see Barrios et al. 2004). Why should we not use eye-tracking in addressing the many effects gaps posed by TCB and the Supreme Court?

Kari-Jouko Raiha, Professor of Computer Science at the Finnish University of Tampere and project coordinator of the Communication by Gaze Interaction (COGAIN) project, states that we should "think of all of the other potential applications for this technology that we just haven't thought about, or imagined yet" (referred to at "An Affordable Future for Eye-tracking in Sight"). Eye-tracking to examine distraction effects of TCB is recommended by the author as one such application.

We do not know how frequently the potentially least instructive television technology is utilised. Eye-tracking can begin this research.

H. C. Schmidt also states that the current research in psychology into videotaped confessions is motivated by the Supreme Court's treatment of confession evidence cases (Schmidt 2006: 74). It is surprising that more research has not been undertaken into the effects of TCB, given that the Supreme Court first called for empirical research studies as far back as the *Estes* case in 1965.

The time has come to address the research-challenge set by the Supreme Court and also to ensure that the research effort into the effects of TCB advances beyond the criticism that "[s]ocial scientists measure the intelligence of monkeys more effectively than courts have attempted to ascertain the effects of television in the courtroom" (Hirschhorn 1980: 7 and 9). It is time to move beyond limited self-reports and opinion-reports and embrace eye-tracking research.

Eye-tracking can be particularly beneficial in addressing distraction-effect research. We should embrace the opportunity. This involves expanding upon the initial proof of concept demonstration described in the following chapters.

Chapter 8

The First TCB Eye-tracking Demonstration

Introduction

The linking of eye-tracking and TCB effects research is timely and internationally significant. It is the first proof of concept demonstration of eye-tracking technology for TCB effects research, in an actual criminal courtroom.

The Supreme Court has discussed some of the issues and concerns that arise in relation to TCB on three occasions. The cases were *Estes* (1965), *Chandler* (1981) and most recently in *Hollingsworth* (2010). The Supreme Court is aware that there are substantial research gaps, and has set a challenge that more social science and empirical research be carried out to address the research gaps. Unfortunately, the distraction-research challenge has not been properly or fully tackled.

One of the issues and concerns with TCB is that the courtroom participants/actors may be distracted by the television cameras and/or the camera operators. The relevant research is TCB distraction effects research. Unfortunately, there is a dearth of such research.

One of the problems with the distraction hypothesis is that if there are effects, they may be different for the different courtroom participants/actors. Also, the research to date is undermined to the extent that it almost solely relies on self-reports from courtroom participants/actors, as to whether they themselves were affected or not. Other reports on the effects on other parties are also opinions. Typically, the general research to date is questionnaire-based only. The empirical research in relation to in-court distraction effects is very minimal.

Eye-tracking and the law

Eye-tracking has not been used for in-court research before. It certainly has not been applied to the TCB research problems. The author links TCB and eye-tracking. Eye-tracking can apply to TCB distraction effects research. It is a useful, if not a necessary, first step to undertake a proof of concept demonstration of eye-tracking in court.

By way of background and context, it is useful to refer to eye-tracking generally. Regardless of TCB research, eye-tracking is used widely across many fields. Some of the fields where eye-tracking is used include medicine, psychology, advertising, marketing and design. There are even some legal security research applications. Various legal-psychology research into eyewitness identification and witness memory also used eye-tracking (for one recent example, see Kwak 2009).

Eye-trackers examine how eyewitnesses recognise suspects in photograph line-ups (an example is Josephson and Holmes 2010). They are used for examining the weapons-focus effect (Loftus, Loftus and Messo 1987: n 43, at 55; Kwak 2009; Loftus and Mackworth 1978: 565–572; Ware 2006: 34–35).

Eye-tracking is also used to research effects of cameras and camera perspective in recorded police confessions (this is noted by Ware 2006: 35). The way in which the confession evidence is filmed, can influence later judgements of guilt based on viewing the confession footage (Schmidt 2006: 3). Mock jurors can be influenced by the camera angle from which the confession interrogation is filmed (Lassiter and Irvine 1986: 268–276. Referred to in Schmidt 2006: 9–10). This is called *camera perspective bias*.

In the G. Daniel Lassiter and Audrey A. Irvine (Lassiter and Irvine 1986: 268–276; Schmidt 2006: 26) research study people who saw the suspect-only video perceived less coercion (Lassiter and Irvine 1986: 286–276. Referred to in Schmidt 2006: 26). Other research also confirms that suspect-only videos yield significantly higher ratings for perceived guilt and voluntariness (see for example Lassiter et al. 2002: 299–305; Schmidt 2006: 28; Schmidt 2006: 31; Geller 1992; Kassin 1997: 221–233; and Lassiter 2002: 204–208; each as referred to in Ware 2006: 10).

Eye-trackers have also been considered in relation to tobacco health advertisements (Smith 2009). Smith also used baseline (Smith 2009) research.

The Supreme Court challenge and distraction

The author has recommended the use of eye-tracking technology for addressing part of the Supreme Court challenge. This is very new and novel technology. As far as the author can ascertain, eye-tracking has never been considered in any courtroom on any issue. Certainly it has not been addressed, nor considered, in any of the Supreme Court TCB cases nor the related TCB effects research. The literature on (television) courtroom broadcasting has not considered or referred to the utility of eye-tracking technology.

The TCB effects referred to by the Supreme Court, which appear most relevant for eye-tracking research are distraction effects caused by the television cameras (and operators) in the courtroom (i.e. in-court effects).

There are numerous potential effects referred to by the Supreme Court, and indeed commentators, which can be used as the primary research hypothesis for developing an eye-tracking effects study, in particular distraction. There are many issues which must be addressed beforehand. A number of scoping and preparation issues also need to be considered.

Scoping

There has never been a TCB effects eye-tracking experiment conducted. Many complex considerations and preparations arise. One has to choose an effect to research, choose the technology and design the method of study. This is a complex task. In addition, cost factors arise.

Choice of eye-trackers

Once one has chosen one particular potential effect to research, one must design the experiment and choose the particular eye-tracking device that is most appropriate to the experiment. Currently the author favours Tobeii eye-tracking glasses for TCB distraction effects research. The advantages are that they appear like normal glasses and are, therefore, much less obtrusive than other eye-trackers. Another advantage is that they are flexible and allow the (mock) courtroom actor using them to move about and operate much as they would in an authentic trial or court situation (subject of course, to which courtroom actor it is).

Cost

The cost of the hardware, the software, audiovisual equipment and related material will not be insignificant. In designing, conducting and interpreting the vast amounts of data that will be generated, various specialised skills will be necessary, and will also be a significant cost. The subjects in a given eye-tracking experiment may also have to be paid, as may any third party researchers required.

Proof of concept demonstration

Many issues arise in relation to a TCB eye-tracking experiment, such as courtroom actor locations, camera locations, as well as how these may interact with the effect chosen to be researched. It is also important in effects research after the proposal to demonstrate the issues in a pilot study or demonstration (see Mitchell and Jolley 2001: C-13). It was, therefore, felt necessary to undertake an initial proof of concept (see McQueen and Knussen 2006: 134–135, and 347). This is additionally important because of the novelty of this technology for TCB effects research.

The Courts Service in Ireland granted permission for the first ever recorded demonstration of eye-tracking technology inside a courtroom as a proof of concept for TCB effect research.

There was no guarantee that permission would be granted. Indeed, the author was very conscious of the fact that the makers of *The Trial* programme in the United Kingdom had to prepare and negotiate for many years with the relevant courts, judges and officials before obtaining permission to film their programme.

The author initially obtained permission "in principle" from the Irish Courts Service (and expresses his kind appreciation). However, there were a number of prior specific criteria to be met and satisfied. There was still no guarantee that the eye-tracking demonstration would be finally permitted or fully feasible.

The necessity of an actual courtroom for demonstration

By way of explanation again, an eye-tracker is a double miniature camera, which is affixed to a person's head, one focused in the direction that the person is looking, and the other focused on the person's eye, or incorporated into glasses.

Eye-trackers allow us to track and record where an individual is actually looking and for how long. This is relevant for research of "distraction" effects of courtroom participants caused by television cameras/operators in mock and non-live court settings. There has been no courtroom broadcasting research as of yet that incorporates eye-tracking technology.

It is necessary to undertake the same in an actual court environment as it is difficult to replicate an actual courtroom layout without great expense; the demonstration is less valid and less real if undertaken in a room or environment, which does not in any way look like a courtroom; no environment sufficiently similar to a courtroom is actually available; the results of the demonstration are more valid and more useful to researchers and other interested parties for having been undertaken in a real court environment. The demonstration should allow greater insights in relation to the actual detailed practicalities and methodologies required for undertaking a full empirical in-court eye-tracking mock trial experiment.

The author also undertook certain research and review work at the new criminal court complex in Dublin, which included some of the new layouts and technology incorporated into these courts (undertaken on 20 December, 2010. The author also acknowledges the kind assistance and information furnished by a certain senior barrister). Baseline research needs to begin *prior to* the introduction of TCB.

The demonstration

A full eye-tracking experiment is complex and costly. For the moment the author wished to demonstrate the technology in an actual (non-live) court environment. It would hopefully demonstrate as a proof of concept that it can be used to address in-court effects research as referred to in the Supreme Court distraction challenge.

This is a necessary first step before carrying out a full eye-tracking experiment. It is the first such demonstration of eye-tracking in a courtroom environment for courtroom broadcasting effects research anywhere.

The author requested access to an empty courtroom for two hours with an eye-tracker, laptops, audio visual equipment, still camera, related equipment and technical experts. It was also suggested by the author that it would be useful to get access to more than one courtroom, as the layout of courtrooms can vary. In the end, one courtroom was used. It was a criminal trial/remand courtroom.

It was also useful to take still photographs, which would be of necessary assistance in designing an actual eye-tracking effects experiment, and also in choosing which particular effect to study, and how to do so.

The research, as well as requiring the author's legal knowledge and experience, also required technical assistance to operate the eye-tracker and to compile the data.

Research aim

The research aim was to undertake and record the use of an eye-tracker in an actual non-live real court environment and to demonstrate and record what someone might see from different courtroom actor positions in the court – both with and without the television camera.

Research method

The demonstration was conducted to undertake and record the use of an eye-tracker in an actual non-live real court environment, including the use of a static non-working camera as an example distracter.

One of the researchers had the eye-tracker placed upon them. The eye-tracker was then calibrated to the individual. This is an exercise necessary with most eye-trackers. The subject then positioned themselves in a number of directed positions within the courtroom, which would be used as the normal locus of different courtroom participants/actors within a courtroom.

The subject wearing the eye-tracker then looked about in various directions simulating what a person in that position might see. The purpose was to demonstrate what is available in the immediate cone-of-vision for the person to see. The eye-tracker recorded (a) what they could see and (b) what they looked at.

This exercise was undertaken with and without the television audiovisual equipment (camera distracter) being present and visible. The eye-tracker and laptop equipment tracked and recorded what the person saw and where they looked.

This is not, for the avoidance of doubt, an actual eye-tracking effects experiment. It is only a demonstration of an eye-tracker in a non-live court environment.

The first proof of concept demonstration

The author undertook the world's first proof of concept demonstration of eye-tracking in court for research of in-court distraction effects caused by television broadcast cameras and operators. This demonstration research exercise was carried out in a real court in Dublin, Ireland on 29 October, 2010. (The author acknowledges the kind assistance and permission afforded by the Courts Service. In addition, extensive gratitude is expressed to Anarta Ghosh and Mirko Arnold, Trinity College, Dublin, each of whom provided invaluable technical expertise in relation to the use, operation and recording of proof of concept demonstration results with the eye-tracker).

Incidentally, this is also understood to be the first use and demonstration of eye-tracking technology for any purpose in a real courtroom.

The courtroom used was a District (lower-level) criminal arraignment and criminal trial court. The courtroom was empty of lawyers and the public.

Equipment

An Ergoneer (see www.ergoneers.com) Dikabilis Cable (wired) head-mounted eye-tracker system was used for conducting the demonstration (the system comprises the ergonomic head unit with EyeCam, nasal fitting, elastic band and infrared diode for illumination of the eye (see *Dikabil Manual*, Section 2.1: 5)).

In addition, a Sony DVCAM Model DSR 1P television camera and Sachler tripod was used as a distraction foil. It was not plugged in or operating.

A number of still photographs were also taken on a Sony Cyber-shot 14.1 mega pixel camera.

Procedure

One of the technical assistants wore the eye-tracker (the "subject"). The subject took up the following directed courtroom participant/actor positions using the eye-tracker,

- Judge (J);
- Court Clerk (C):
- Witness (W);

- Sitting solicitor (in certain courtrooms, including the instant courtroom, this position could have also been a senior prosecuting Garda (police officer))(S);
- Standing solicitor/barrister (L) (L1, L2, L3).

The tripod-mounted television camera was located in four different positions within the courtroom. These are marked as C1, C2, C3, C4 on Image ET1.4: TV camera locations (circle pointer).

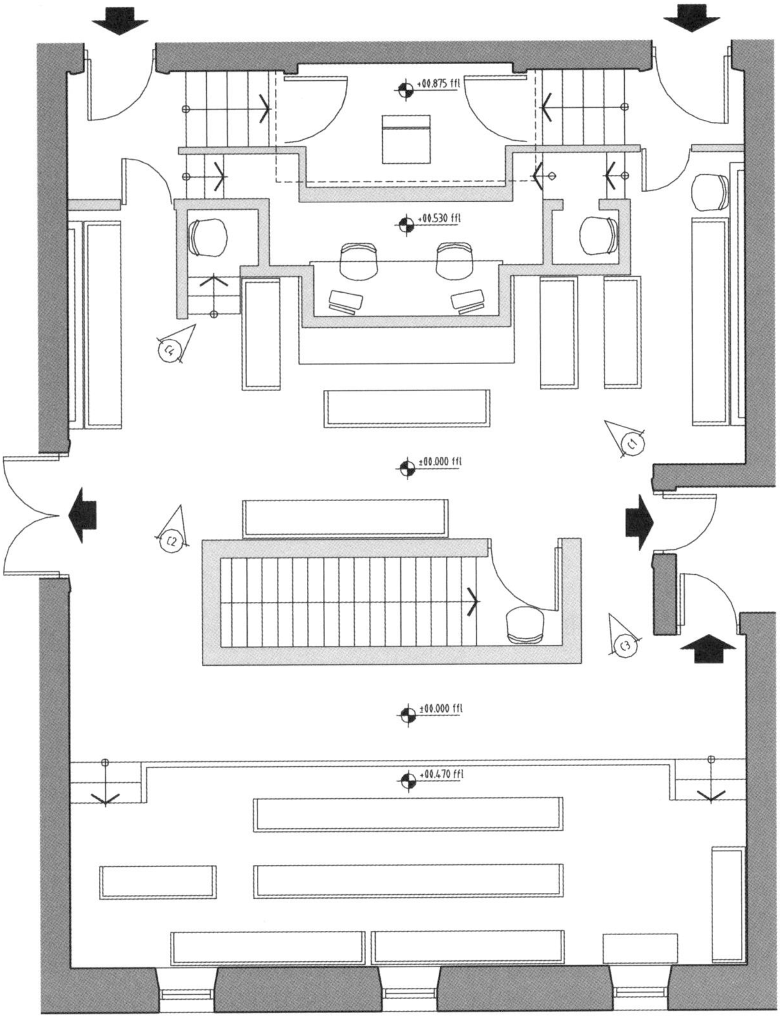

Lambert ET1.4: TV Camera Locations

The proposed predetermined research conditions were as follows,

Judge conditions
No camera
Camera position 1 (C1)
Camera position 2 (C2)
Camera position 3 (C3)
Camera position 3 (C4)

Clerk conditions
No camera
Camera position 1 (C1)
Camera position 2 (C2)
Camera position 3 (C3)
Camera position 3 (C4)

Witness conditions
No camera
Camera position 1 (C1)
Camera position 2 (C2)
Camera position 3 (C3)
Camera position 3 (C4)

Sitting solicitor conditions
No camera
Camera position 1 (C1)
Camera position 2 (C2) (There was no Camera Position 3 in this instance, as the television camera was located close to the back of the courtroom. It was, therefore, not directly visible. It was not in the direct visible forward cone-of-vision.)
Camera position 3 (C4)

Standing solicitor/barrister conditions
No camera
Camera position 1 (C1)
Camera position 2 (C2)
Camera position 3 (C3) (if visible)
Camera position 3 (C4)

It was also intended to record the eye-tracker subject from a public seated position but this was not technically or logistically possible in this instance. However, it should be possible in future demonstrations and/or experiments.

Results

The eye-tracker used for the demonstration was successful for the demonstration and proof of concept. The demonstration was a success. However, the eye-tracker used, like many eye-trackers, is very conspicuous and would be very obvious to the courtroom actor wearing it, as well as to other courtroom participants/actors. This would, therefore, not be the best type of eye-tracker to use for any in-court experiment.

In addition, these types of eye-trackers offer less flexibility to the wearer, again hindering the authenticity of an actual eye-tracking experiment for in-court TCB effects.

Video recorded files were created and close to 20,000 still images with the eye-tracker were produced. In addition there were a number of still camera photographs taken. The latter were mainly to record some background and environment photographs of the subject courtroom. In addition, they also recorded the markers for the four different television tripod positions in the courtroom.

Samples of the eye-tracker still images are set out below. The eye-tracker + marker on the still images (and respective video) marks where the subject courtroom participants/actor is actually looking.

We should next look at some of the respective eye-tracking images and directional + markers for the courtroom participants/actors.

Chapter 9

The Judge

Introduction

These images come from the real-time video footage recorded by the eye-tracker. The eye-tracker tracks the direction of the eye gaze and marks where the individual is looking. The eye-tracker records a video, and the images below are still images taken from that video. On the pictures the eye gaze of the individual is tracked and marked with the eye-tracker + marker, marked in white.

In the images below, the individual subject wearing the eye-tracker is sitting in the judge's position in the courtroom. The images therefore demonstrate where the judge would be able to look and what they would see. In each instance the eye tracker + marker records and demonstrates where they are looking in a demonstrable and recordable manner. This is unlike any of the TCB distraction effects research to date. Distraction can be verified.

Judge: No camera

Image J1.1 shows no camera present and the judge (J) looking at the witness box (W), as shown with the eye-tracker + marker.

Image J1.2 shows two solicitors or lawyers sitting (S), with the judge (J) looking at the one on the right, as shown with the eye-tracker + marker. No camera is present.

In the similar image, Image J1.3, the judge (J) looks at the solicitor or lawyer on the left (S). Again no camera is present.

It is interesting, to say the least, how wide the judge's cone-of-vision is and how much they can see in court, be it television cameras and/or camera operators. This is clear in Image J1.3, Image J1.4 and Image J1.5, for example.

Image J1.4 shows a standing solicitor or lawyer (S), and an adjacent seated solicitor or lawyer (S). The judge (J) is looking at the lawyer standing (L), as shown with the eye-tracker + marker. No camera is present.

Image J1.5 shows a standing lawyer (L3), standing behind the bench with a seated solicitor or lawyer (S). The judge (J) is looking at the standing lawyer (L3), as shown with the eye-tracker + marker. No camera is present.

Camera position 3

Image J1.6 shows the eye-tracker + marker showing that the judge (J) is looking at the television distractor in camera position 3 (C3), at the back left of the courtroom. The camera operator is also present. There is also a seated solicitor or lawyer (S). The cone-of-vision for the camera includes the seated solicitor (S).

Image J1.7 shows the camera in camera position 3 (C3) but with no camera operator present. Again, the judge (J) is looking at the camera, as shown with the eye-tracker + marker. The cone-of-vision is again wide.

Camera position 1

Image J1.8 shows the judge (J) looking at the camera and camera operator in camera position 1 (C1). There is also a seated solicitor or lawyer (S). The cone-of-vision includes the seated solicitor(s).

Image J1.9 also shows camera position 1 (C1). However, there is no camera operator present. The judge (J) is shown looking at the camera, as shown with the eye-tracker + marker. Again, there is a wide cone-of-vision.

Camera position 2

Image J1.10 shows the judge (J) looking at the camera operator. There is a camera and camera operator at camera position 2 (C2). There is also a seated solicitor or lawyer (S). The camera is directed at the judge (J). The cone-of-vision is again wide, including the camera, camera operator and lawyers (S; L).

Image J1.11 shows the camera in camera position 2 (C2) again. However, there is no camera operator. The judge (J) is shown looking at the camera, as shown with the eye-tracker + marker. There is also a seated solicitor or lawyer (S). Again, a wide cone-of-vision is evident.

Image J1.12 is also of camera position 2 (C2). There is a camera, standing lawyer (L1) and seated solicitor or lawyer (S). The camera is directed at the standing lawyer (L1). The judge (J) is looking at the seated solicitor or lawyer (S), as shown with the eye-tracker + marker. The cone-of-vision, when directed at the standing barrister (L) includes the camera distraction.

Further images

Further images show solicitor sitting (S) and barrister standing (L). The eye-tracker + marker shows that the judge is looking at the barrister (J to L). The television distractor is evident to the right, in camera position 2 (C2).

Images J1.1–J1.12

Images show the eye-tracker + marker showing that the judge (J) is looking at the television distractor in camera position 2 (C2). The image also shows the solicitor sitting (S) and barrister standing (L).

Images show the barrister is facing towards the witness box (L to W). The eye- tracker + marker again shows that the judge (J) is looking at the television distractor in camera position 2 (C2). It is noted that the television distractor appearing to be "unobtrusive" at the side of the courtroom is in the centre of the judge's cone-of-vision as s/he looks between the barrister and the witness.

Images show the judge (J) looking at the television distractor in camera position 2 – with camera operator present. The television camera is pointing and focusing upon the barrister (and or solicitor) position(s).

Images show the judge (J) looking at the television operator distractor in camera position 2 (C2) – with camera operator present. The television camera is pointing and focusing upon the judge.

Images show the judge (J) looking at the television camera distractor in camera position 2 (C2) – with camera operator present. The television camera is pointing and focusing upon the witness position.

Images show the judge (J) looking forward and focusing on the standing barrister (L). The television camera is not visible.

Chapter 10

The Witness

Introduction

As indicated in the last chapter, the following images are still images selected from the eye-tracking video footage. In this instance the images are taken from the position of an individual subject in the witness box. The direction and focus of the subject witnesses eye gaze is tracked and indicated with the eye-tracking + marker.

Witness: No camera

Image W1.1 indicates the eye-tracker + marker showing that the witness (W) is looking at the judge's position (J). No camera is visible/present.

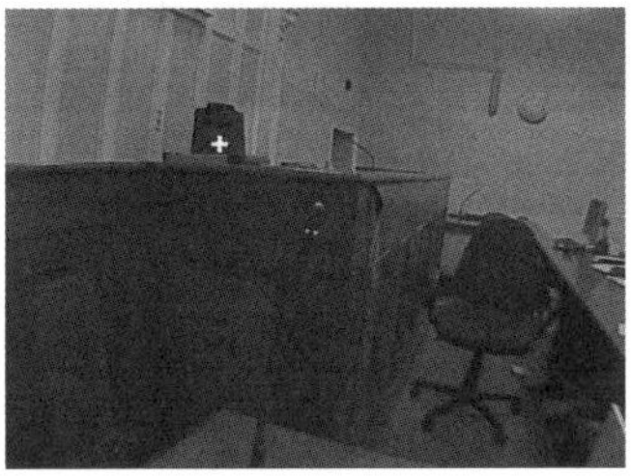

Image W1.2 shows a seated solicitor or lawyer (S) and a standing barrister or lawyer (L2). The standing lawyer (L2) appears to be examining/cross-examining the subject witness (W). No camera is visible/present. The eye-tracker + marker shows that the subject witness (W) is looking at the standing lawyer (L).

Witness: Camera position 1

Image W1.3 shows a solicitor or lawyer sitting (S). The distractor television camera is in camera position 1 (C1). No camera operator is present. The television camera is focused on the witness (W). The eye-tracker + marker shows that the witness (W) is looking at the seated solicitor or lawyer (S).

It is noted that in camera position 1 (C1), the distractor television camera and the seated solicitor/lawyer (S) are very close. They are each central in the subject witness' (W) cone-of-vision. It is not possible to say that the subject witness (W) does not/cannot see the distractor television camera when they are focused on the seated solicitor or lawyer (S). The camera position is directly in the witness' (W) cone-of-vision, and also directly behind the solicitor position (S). It is highly visible even when the witness (W) is looking at the solicitor (S).

What implication does this have in relation to distraction effects? What are the implications of television camera location for effects on different courtroom actors/personnel, and in this instance the witness (W)?

Image W1.4 shows the solicitor or lawyer sitting (S). The eye-tracker + marker shows that the witness (W) is looking at the distractor television camera. The distractor television camera is focused on the subject witness (W). The distractor television camera is in camera position 1 (C1).

Image W1.5 shows a seated solicitor or lawyer (S) and a standing lawyer (L2). The distractor television camera is present in camera position 1 (C1). The eye-tracker + marker shows that the witness (W) is looking at the seated solicitor or lawyer (S). We see that the distractor television camera, seated solicitor or lawyer (S) and standing lawyer (L) are all in close proximity in the central field of the cone-of-vision of the subject witness (W). We can see that even when focused on the seated solicitor or lawyer (S), and arguably also the standing lawyer (L), the subject witness (W) is still able to see the distractor television camera.

Image W1.6 is similar to Image W1.5 above, with the seated and standing solicitor/lawyer and distractor television camera in camera position 1 (C1). In this image the eye-tracker + marker shows that the subject witness (W) is looking at the standing lawyer (L2).

If the subject witness does not have to move their head when looking variously at the lawyers and the distractor television camera, how are opinion reporters or observers in court able to discern and opine on whether the subject witness (W) was distracted? The TCB research to date has not even tried to investigate this point. We can say that the present demonstration shows that eye-tracking technology allows us to begin this research. The future of TCB in-court distraction effects research is tied to eye-tracking. Eye-tracking needs to be fully embraced.

Image W1.7 is also similar to Image W1.5 above. In this image the eye-tracker + marker shows that the witness (W) is looking at the distractor television camera in camera position 1 (C1). As pointed out above, the subject witness (W) would probably not have to tilt their head to vary the focus of their visual attention as between the two lawyers and the distractor television camera. If one is an observer close to the subject witness, would one be able to discern where the witness (W) is looking? Most of the research into TCB in-court effect does not use independent third party observers. In the few studies that have used observers, it is not clear where the observers were located and sitting in the courtroom. There are clearly issues in relation to the veracity of the observer reports to date *per se*. There are also issues in relation to the location of the camera, the location of the courtroom actor/participant and the location of the observer in the observer reports. We need to reassess the observer reports to date. In addition, we should also rely upon a new body of eye-tracking research to move beyond the limits of observer reports.

Image W1.8 shows a seated solicitor or lawyer (S) and distractor television camera in camera position 1 (C1). In addition, there is a camera operator present. In this image the eye-tracker + marker shows that the subject witness (W) is looking at the seated solicitor or lawyer (S).

We again note that the distractor television camera, operator and seated solicitor or lawyer (S) are all central in the cone-of-vision of the subject witness (W). One can also speculate on the implication of whether the combination of the distractor television camera and operator are more visually attention grabbing than a single seated solicitor or lawyer (S). This discussion would also cross over with future research in relation to the implications of the location of the television camera and the location of an instant courtroom actor/participant.

Image W1.9 is similar to Image W1.8. There is a seated solicitor or lawyer (S), distractor television camera and camera operator in camera position 1 (C1). In this image the eye-tracker + marker shows that the subject witness (W) is looking at the distractor television camera.

One of the implications is that both distractor camera and operator are in central focus. A further implication is that it may not be possible without eye-tracking technology to discern that the subject witness (W) is looking at the distractor television camera – at least in part because of the location of the distractor television camera.

Witness: Camera position 2

Image W1.10 shows the solicitor or lawyer sitting (S). The distractor television camera is located to the right of the witness subject and close to the side of the courtroom. The distractor television camera is in camera position 2 (C2). The eye-tracker + marker shows that the subject witness (W) is looking at the distractor television camera located to the right.

On this still image it is clear that the subject witness (W) can easily pan from the seated solicitor or lawyer (S) to the camera and vice versa. It is also clear that even where the witness subject (W) is looking at the seated solicitor or lawyer, the distractor television is within the witness' (W) cone-of-vision. Distraction is still possible.

Image W1.11 shows the solicitor or lawyer sitting (S) as well as a lawyer standing (L2). Again the distractor television camera is located to the right of the witness subject (W) and close to the side of the courtroom. The distractor television camera is still in camera position 2 (C2). The eye-tracker + marker shows that the subject witness (W) is looking at the distractor television camera located to the right.

It is evident that both lawyers and the distractor television camera are all within the cone-of-vision of the subject witness (W). Indeed, the standing lawyer (L) and the distractor television camera are within closer proximity than the seated lawyer in Image W1.5. The eye-tracker + marker shows that the subject witness (S) is looking at the distractor television camera operator located behind the distractor television camera. It is evident that both lawyer, the distractor television camera and the distractor television camera operator are all within the cone-of-vision of the subject witness (W).

Image W1.12 shows the solicitor or lawyer sitting (S). The distractor television camera is located to the right of the witness subject and close to the side of the courtroom. The distractor television camera is still in camera position 2 (C2). In addition to the distractor television camera, there is also a distractor television camera operator. The witness (W) is looking at the camera operator, as indicated by the eye-tracker + marker.

There does not appear to have been any previous research directed to researching the effect, or additional effect, of TCB camera operators.

Comment

It would also seem to be clear that in this demonstration, the subject witness (W) can look at the various courtroom lawyers and the distractor television camera in camera position 2 (C2), without having to tilt their head left or right. What is the implication of this? If the limited self-reports, opinion-reports and in some limited instances observer-reports in previous research rely upon an expressive visual cue such as courtroom actor head tilting or turning, this may be flawed.

The current demonstration would appear to indicate that the subject witness (W) can look at or be distracted by the television camera without turning, or visibly turning, their head. There is, therefore, a real possibility that there are effects that no previous research has gauged. Indeed, it can also be said that no previous TCB research has sought to research for such subtle or non-head-tilt effects. This is a significant research gap.

Further images

Further images show the eye-tracker + marker showing that the witness (W) is looking at the judge's position (J).

Images show the eye-tracker + marker showing that the witness (W) is looking at the court clerk's position.

Images show solicitor sitting (S). The eye-tracker + marker shows that the witness (W) is looking at the solicitor (S).

Images show solicitor sitting (S) and barrister standing (L). The eye-tracker + marker shows that the witness (W) is looking at the barrister (L).

Images show solicitor sitting (S). The eye-tracker + marker shows that the witness (W) is looking at the distractor television camera located to the right. The distractor television camera is in camera position 2 (C2).

Images show solicitor sitting (S). The eye-tracker + marker shows that the witness (W) is looking at the distractor television camera operator located to the right. The distractor television camera is in camera position 2 (C2).

Images show solicitor sitting (S). The eye-tracker + marker shows that the witness (W) is looking at the distractor television camera located to the right. The distractor television camera is in camera position 2 (C2). There is no camera operator present.

Chapter 11

The Solicitor/Barrister/Lawyer

Introduction

The still images below are taken from the eye-tracker video recordings from the gaze direction measured in relation to the standing solicitors/barrister/lawyer wearing the eye-tracker. Again the gaze direction is indicated with the eye-tracker + marker in white.

Standing solicitor/barrister: No camera

In Image L1.1 the eye-tracker + marker shows that the standing lawyer is looking at the judge position (J). No camera is present/visible.

Camera position 1

In Image L1.2 the television distractor is in camera position 1 (C1). The standing lawyer (L3) is looking at the television camera, as indicated by the eye-tracker + marker. No camera operator is present.

Image L1.3 shows the standing lawyer is looking at the witness position (W) as indicated by the eye-tracker + marker.

Image L1.4 again shows the camera in camera position 1 (C1). This time the camera operator distractor is present. The standing lawyer (L3) is looking at the camera operator, as indicated by the eye-tracker + marker.

Image L1.5 shows the standing lawyer (L) looking at the solicitor bench.

Camera position 2

Image L1.6 shows the camera in camera position 2 (C2). The eye-tracker + marker shows that the standing lawyer (L) is looking at the distractor television camera located to the left. There is a camera operator present.

Image L1.7 show the standing lawyer (L) looking at the witness box (W), as indicated by the eye-tracker + marker.

Image L1.8 shows the distractor camera and camera operators present in camera position 2 (C2). The witness (W) is looking in the direction of the camera. Both are present and visible in the witness cone of vision.

Image L1.9 again shows the standing lawyer (L) looking at the witness area (W) but able to see the camera, still located in camera position 2 (C2). (Image not included).

Image L1.10 shows the camera in camera position 2 (C2) with the camera operator. In this example, however, the camera is focused not on the witness (W) or judge (J), but rather on the standing lawyer (L).

It is worth noting that there is no great distinction in the research to date between distraction effects where one can see cameras in one's cone-of-vision but not focusing upon one's self, and where the camera is directly focusing upon one's self.

Image L1.11 is similar but this time focusing on the judge (J).

Camera position 4

Image L1.12 shows the standing lawyer (L) focusing on the witness (W). This time the camera is in camera position 4 (C4), as indicated with the eye-tracker + marker.

It is noted that it is difficult for the standing lawyer (L) not to see the camera given its proximity to the witness (W) in the cone-of-vision.

Image L1.13 also shows the camera in camera position 4. The standing lawyer (L) is starting to look at the camera. There is no camera operator present.

Further images show the eye-tracker + marker shows that the lawyer is looking at the distractor television camera located to the left of the witness box. The distractor television camera is in camera position 4 (C4). There is no camera operator present.

In addition, in further images the eye-tracker + marker shows that the lawyer is looking directly at the witness box. However, the distractor television camera, located behind and to the left of the witness box is still visible at the periphery of the cone-of-vision. The cone-of-vision includes the witness position, the clerk position and the judge position. The distractor television camera is in camera position 4 (C4). There is no camera operator present.

Other images show the eye-tracker + marker showing that the lawyer is looking at the witness box. The distractor television camera is in Camera Position 4 (C4). It is focused on the judge's position (J). There is no camera operator present. In further images, which are similar, the cone-of-vision is altered to have the witness (W) more centred. Within the cone-of-vision is the distractor television camera, witness box, judge's position and clerk's position.

Images show the eye-tracker + marker showing that the lawyer is looking at the witness position (W). The distractor television camera located behind and to the left of the witness

Images L1.1–13

box, plus camera operator, is visible. The distractor television camera is in camera position 4 (C4). It is focused on the judge.

Images show the eye-tracker + marker showing that the lawyer is looking at the distractor television camera located behind and to the left of the witness box. The distractor television camera is in camera position 4. There is a camera operator present.

Chapter 12

Location Issues

Introduction

It has already been indicated by the author that location is an important issue for TCB. In particular, the location of the courtroom participants/actors and of the in-court television camera. Equally, the location of the in-court camera operator – when present – is important and must be gauged. Location issues have never been properly addressed in the body of general and empirical research to date. It is important to point out also that the research to date is flawed and unreliable to the extent that location issues and location factors/personnel are ignored.

This is important because the location of the television camera and the camera operator, respective to the location of the courtroom participants/actors, could influence the courtroom actors/personnel in the courtroom. These issues also potentially influence the viewing audience outside of the courtroom.

The locus of the camera, and operator, can influence the courtroom participants/actor and what goes on in the courtroom (in-court effects). Indeed, we need to assess courts and trial procedures (see generally, Smith 2003) in this research also. In addition, there can be effects outside of the courtroom too.

In making assessments about the effects of TCB we need to be aware of where the camera is located. Therefore, research studies need to record and indicate where the camera was located. By way of background and context, we will now look at how the literature occasionally and implicitly refers to location. However, the body of the general and empirical research both avoid the location issue. It is not addressed.

Location and the research literature

The general non-social science studies not unexpectedly refer very little to the location issue. They do not record the actual location of cameras in particular experiments. This is unfortunate, as it means we cannot properly consider and evaluate the efficacy of those experiments as influenced by location factors.

However, what is more disturbing is how seldom the television camera location is recorded even in the empirical studies. The instances where there is some record of location available in the literature are referred to below.

It must be pointed out, also, that it does not appear that any of the non-empirical or empirical research studies refer to the camera operator issue. While it can be said that, for example, of course the camera operator will always be beside the television camera, this is a simplistic appraisal. If we are properly researching for in-court distraction effects, we need to record if there is a camera operator present, how many, where, are they moving, what are they doing, are there assistants, etc.

In terms of the empirical research the following references to location and/or operators have been identified by the author.

Nevada is referred to as requiring camera operators to dress appropriately for court (as referred to in Netteburg 1980: 43). The camera locations are not recorded.

In James L. Hoyt's study it was indicated that in the camera obtrusively present control condition, the camera was "in front" of and pointing "directly at" the subjects (Hoyt 1977: 491). No recorded diagram or photograph is produced.

The Short report does not address the camera location effect issue, but does attach diagrams of some of the courts, which mark the location of the television camera (Short 1981: 57–63) (see Appendix 1).

Donald Shores refers to one of his control groups where the camera operator noticeably adjusts the camera and also turns it on and off (Shores 1981: 59). The location issue is not mentioned.

Saul M. Kassin indicates that in his study the camera was "directed at the jury box from the witness stand" (Kassin 1984: 339–340). No diagram was attached. The location issue is not mentioned.

Eugene Borgida, Kenneth G. DeBono and Lee A. Buckman used a camera behind a one-way mirror, approximately 17 feet from the witnesses (Borgida, DeBona and Buckman 1990: 495–496). They do not refer to the location issue.

Alan D. Punches does record and include a diagram of where the two cameras were, both facing the subject head on from left and right (Punches 1991: 40–41). He does not, however, refer to the location issue.

Allen Bukoff in his research on video recording refers to the issue as follows, television "[c]amera *position* and angle, closeness of focus, lighting, and other video production techniques may be able to influence a juror's perception of the physical attractiveness of the witness and attorneys by recording them in a more or less visually appealing view" (Bukoff 1984: 22. Emphasis added). In his study, he indicated that the cameras and equipment were set up "approximately ten feet from the witness" (Bukoff 1984: 58). No diagrams, layouts or photographs of the experiment environment marking the cameras are included.

S. L. Alexander refers to Paul Goldman and Richard Larson, who produced a diagram of camera location in one actual experimental case study (Alexander 1990: 65, referring to Goldman and Larson 1978: 2001–2061). Also referred to is the feedback from one media representative, who felt that the judge(s) had too much discretion in relation to where equipment (and presumably cameras too) would be located (Alexander 1990: 129). One case is referred to where the pooled camera was located at the rear of the courtroom (Alexander 1990: 138). The location issue is not referred to or documented.

Paul Thaler, in his case study of the Steinberg case, indicated that in the pre-trial stages, cameras were permitted in the "well" of the courtroom, but during the trial they were located at the end of the jury box behind the lawyers, thus shooting over the lawyers' shoulders (Thaler 1990: 62). In fact the lawyers were asked to move on a number of occasions to permit line of sight access to witnesses (Thaler 1990: 62). The location issue is not referred to.

The first Federal pilot study refers to media representatives, who indicate that single camera footage of a case can cause a problem for gavel to gavel (G2G) recording, as occasionally courtroom participants/actors move and/or block the camera line of sight (Johnson and Krafka 1994: 37). No camera locations are recorded.

The following did not refer to nor record television camera location, nor do they refer to the separate location issue itself, namely, the first Federal pilot study (Johnson and Krafka 1994); Kermit Netteburg (1980), Donald Shores (1981), Steve Pasternack (1982), Anna R. Paddon (1985), Steve Esposito (1996), William Petkanas (1990), Stephen Kohm (2004), Ruthie Elizabeth Reeves Stewart (1998: 1–2, and 32), Jessica Ossinger (2006), the New York study (*New York State Committee to Review Audio-Visual Coverage of Court Proceedings, An Open Courtroom: Cameras in New York Courts* 1997), Teresa Keller (1992: 125) and Roberta Entner (1993). Susanna Barber (1987), Warren Freedman (1988), Ronald Goldfarb (1998, in particular 116 et seq), nor Marjorie Cohn and David Dow (2002) refer to it either. Even Daniel Stepniak in one of the more recent texts (2008) does not address this issue (Stepniak 2008). It appears that the author is again the first to raise location issues as a significant consideration to be addressed in effects research in future.

The Supreme Court in the three camera cases, *Estes*, *Chandler* and *Hollingsworth*, does not refer at all to the camera and location issues. Neither does the Supreme Court research-challenge refer to the location problem, nor does it recommend this as an empirical research issue. The author has previously made the point that though the Supreme Court challenge refers to many issues to be empirically researched, we should not assume that the Supreme Court has definitively referred to all such potential issues and effects.

The *Cameras in the Court: A State-By-State Guide* (available at www.rtdna.org), produced by Radio Television Digital News Association in the United States, refers to local state laws in the United States relating to TCB. The issue of location and effects is not referred to at all. However, in many instances, particularly the Tier 1 category identified therein, judges are given wide discretion (www.rtdna.org) and, therefore, at least in these instances should be able to specify where the television camera(s) will be put. Most states also provide a limit on the number of cameras and/or camera operators (www.rtdna.org). In one instance (North Carolina) the camera and camera personnel must be behind a partition or booth, albeit this may be waived (www.rtdna.org). This is the only location reference. The impact of the location issue is not addressed in the law reviewed.

The Guidelines for Media Access to Judicial Proceedings in the Rhode Island experiment (1981–1982) specified that the location of the television camera would be as directed or designated by the judge (referred to and appended in Weisberger 1983: 300 and 308). The importance of the location issues is not identified, however.

TruTV (Formerly *CourtTV*)

TruTV generally uses a single camera, without an operator in court (Harris 1993: 804). It is unclear if camera location, camera operator location, etc. are ever recorded and documented. Given that *TruTV* undertakes so much of the TCB that occurs, it would be useful for researchers, both now and in the future, to have these details documented and made available. A further issue is that in future experimental periods, including the second proposed Federal pilot period, there should be a requirement to properly record location issue data.

Distraction

The research needs to properly address in-court distraction effects. This has long been voiced as one of the reasons militating against camera access.

Unfortunately camera location and actor location, and their interplay, have never been addressed. Take lawyers for example. Sometimes cameras are placed somewhere in front of where they are seated or standing. Therefore, the camera is within their cone-of-vision. It is logical, therefore, that the camera may be a distraction. If there is a camera operator present, this possibility of distraction may be enhanced.

However, if the television camera is located somewhere in the courtroom that is behind the lawyers, then the possibility of distraction in the lawyers' visual cone-of-vision is less. It is important, therefore, that in considering effect and research of effects, we know which actor we are considering, what effect, what cause, and where the cause (camera in this instance) was located.

A camera in front of the lawyers would seem to enhance the possibility of distraction. But one should not assume that a camera located behind the lawyers precludes distraction effects. Psychological concerns still arise. There have already been recorded instances where television cameras and operators have recorded (and attempted to record) discussions between lawyer and client, and also recorded documents and notes on the lawyers table. It appears that this is the reason why these concerns are explicitly addressed and prohibited in some of the US state laws regulating TCB (see survey and summary of state laws at www.rtdna.org). When a lawyer is in discussion with his or her client, or witness, or other lawyers or assistants, he or she is frequently altering their cone-of-vision sideways or backwards. The television camera is, therefore, potentially within focus, even if behind them.

The cases and the literature recognise that lawyers may not be the only persons in court who might be distracted. Take the jury for example. Depending on the layout of a courtroom, they may be seated along one side of the courtroom. Let us assume the jury box is on the right-hand side of the courtroom. They might then have to turn to their right to see the lawyers, the judge and the witness box. If the television camera is located in the upper end of the courtroom, then the camera will be in the right-facing cone-of-vision of the jury. It is a potential distraction. If the camera moves, tilts, pans, zooms, etc. then the possibility of jury distraction may be higher. If there are lights on the camera, or there is a camera operator, then potential distraction effects may be heightened.

Yet, the location issue and the recording and linking of the actual location of the camera and the location of the courtroom participants/actors are not addressed in the research literature. Therefore, because of this gap, there is always going to be a limit to our proper appraisal and consideration of much of the research to date. The author recommends that future research address this gap.

Consider other courtroom participants/actors. If we take the judge and the official court personnel, they are always seated at the top of the courtroom and facing everyone else. Consider further that some of the literature commentary has suggested that there may be effects of television cameras in the courtroom, but the judges will not be affected or will be the least affected. The basis of this suggestion is that the judges are professionally trained (and one might add experienced). However, if we now interpose the camera location issue, we note that regardless of where the television camera is located, the judge will be facing the camera (and the camera operator, if present). Is it not the case, therefore, that they are the courtroom actors whose cone-of-vision is most frequently going to contain the camera and who have the opportunity to be distracted by the television camera (and operator). Let us leave the issue of professional training aside for the moment, an issue that has not in any event been empirically researched. Can we still say that judges are the least likely courtroom participants/actors to be distracted by in-court TCB? The location issue suggests not. Admittedly, many other issues arise, such as training, professional experience, media experience, psychology, etc. A judge will have his or her professional training. Depending on the jurisdiction, they may or may not have additional specific judicial training. Even where such additional and express judicial training exists, the literature and research do not address how many judges are trained in camera issues. It is clear that the judicial distraction issue needs far more in-depth consideration than any of the literature and research has to date afforded.

The official courtroom personnel have been mentioned only briefly in the literature. However, the same concerns arise. Indeed, one might argue that the concerns are somewhat escalated given that they may have less professional training than a judge. From a location perspective, their cone-of-vision is more likely directed towards the camera than any other courtroom actor – with the exception of judges.

Without going into distraction issues and concerns in detail, the location issue and the recoding of the camera location is also relevant to a review of distraction issues and effects.

Audience effects/camera perspective bias

The research in relation to camera perspective bias and confessions highlights how important it is to record camera and media issues, which impact upon the legal process, and which may have effects. Only by recording and examining the data and carrying out research in relation to such data can we properly assess effects. Where adverse effects are identified, we can then factor this into policy decisions to ameliorate such adverse effects.

In terms of the camera perspective bias effect, as was already highlighted, G. Daniel Lassiter and Audrey A. Irvine showed the same interview recorded on different camera locations showing (1) suspect-only, (2) police officer only, and (3) both equally focused (Lassiter and Irvine 1986: 268–276; Schmidt above: 26). The people viewing who saw the suspect-only video believed that there to be less coercion (Lassiter and Irvine 1986: 268–276; Schmidt 2006: 26).

In any proper assessment of audience effects, and more importantly in comparing effect as between different forms of TCB, we need to be aware of the layout of the courtroom, the location of the courtroom actors/personnel and the location of the television camera(s). Potentially different locations can mean different audience effects, as different locations and frames can have different biases and effects in the context of video confessions. We need to expand our research knowledge of relevant research avenues.

Cone-of-vision

The concept of a cone-of-vision of courtroom actors/personnel needs to be researched. It is important, the author argues, for all research of TCB and TCB effects to accurately record where each individual courtroom actor is located, and to indicate and record where the television camera is located. If the television camera moves and is in more than one location, the exercise of recording location is obviously more difficult, but nonetheless necessary. Only when these two specifics are recorded, can we then consider the direction and cone of vision of the individual courtroom actor in question.

That enables us to research and examine whether the television camera is feasibly within the cone-of-vision, whether it is proximate-central or proximate-peripheral. When such information is recordable, it allows us to then consider research and distraction-effect issues properly and methodically. We are also better able to begin designing particular experiments with eye-trackers. There is no point, for example, introducing an eye-tracker to a mock barrister subject (real or otherwise) standing at the front of the courtroom if the fixed tripod television camera is located at the back of the courtroom or on a balcony at the back of the courtroom. It is not within their cone of vision. That is not to say that there can be no other effects other than visual distraction.

In designing experiments for distraction and eye-tracking in actual court settings, we need to respect the actual use of a normal courtroom. We need to be cognizant of cones-of-vision and location issues. We need to record these and we need to incorporate this knowledge into our distraction effects eye-tracking experiments in future.

Observer locations

Few studies, whether general or empirical, have sought to use trained independent observers in court to watch for actual in-court camera effects, and to seek to gauge and measure these effects. The Short report is one of the few studies that used observers for part of its research (Short 1981) (see Appendix 1 – full details not recorded, however).

However, no research, including the Short report, records where the observers were located in each of the courtrooms being examined. The Short report does provide some diagrams of courts and where the television cameras was located, though it is important that any parties looking at the Short report subsequently should also be able to consider and assess where the observers were, vis-à-vis, the cameras and the respective courtroom actors/personnel.

As pointed out elsewhere, the Short report and most studies do not begin the data collection process prior to the cameras entering the court. The baseline for recording effects again is absent.

It is noted elsewhere that there is increasing research in relation to camera perspective bias. This field of research has found that the camera focus, and who is in the focus of the camera, can influence viewers' perceptions of recorded confession interviews. In terms of TCB effects, we need to consider camera focus and camera location.

There is further research separate from the camera perspective bias research (for instance, Koyama 1982), which may be relevant to TCB. There is also research that suggests that fixed versus moving cameras can have different effects on perception (for example, see, Kipper and Mills 1986: 295–307). This is something that is not considered in terms of the wide disparity of camera footage shown in TCB.

These issues are also extremely relevant to the author's suggestion that eye-trackers should be used for TCB effects research, in particular distraction effects. There is also related research other than eye-tracking research (see for example, Mourant and Donaghue 1977: 39–46). Certain research also used television cameras to measure movements (Rudell 1979: 339–341). While not directly considered presently, even this research should be investigated further to see if it could be applicable to TCB research. Helen L. Westcott found that variations in production factors and type/length of camera shot lead to different results and effects (Westcott 1991: 254–265).

One early non-TCB study used the term "field of view," and incidentally found effects and decision errors relating to the television camera field of view and the size of the research targets in the view (Rusis and Snyder 1965: 493–501).

The "design consideration" (to use the words of Baker et al. in another context (Baker et al. 2010). Note also The Courtroom Design and Research Centre project (available at http://coweb.cc.gatech.edu/courtnext/3 and related pages. This project does not appear to consider design, location and layout issues in terms of the influence and effects of TCB.) and its relationship with in-court and out-of-court effects and potential effects is entirely lacking in the experiments and examples of TCB to date. The author recommends that this is a significant area for future research. In addition, it is suggested that a framework of design considerations should be developed for future TCB experiments, pilots and rollouts – if and where permitted, of course (the author makes no recommendation whether for or against TCB *per se*).

Eye-tracking and location

Generally neither the general nor empirical research of TCB effects refers to the importance of the layout of the courtroom or the recording of where the television camera is located in the courtroom. These are critical flaws in the research to date. These flaws need to be addressed. Just one of the implications of this gap is that it is not possible to compare the results of one study with another.

It is also not possible to assess the effects of the camera on any of the courtroom participants/actors.

The research does not refer to or record the layout of the courtroom and the location of the television cameras. None of the empirical and general research reviewed includes a diagram addressing the layout and location issues. The relevant research such that it is, and the implications for future research are referred to below.

One exception is the Short report. It does record the layout of some, but not all, of the courtrooms where research was undertaken. It included diagrams of seven courtrooms and the camera locations (Short 1981: 57–63) (see Appendix 1).

However, even this empirical research is flawed as it does not do so for all cases researched. It is also typical of the general and empirical research to not appreciate the importance of recording details of the courtroom and cameras for comparative purposes. One of the remits of the report was also in relation to effects research.

Yet, the Short report fails to appreciate that one cannot research and assess effects in court without factoring in the location of the courtroom actors/personnel and the location of the television camera. This is the first research to identify this important point. In terms of communications in the courtroom, Tuula-Riitta Valikoski notes that the communicative situation is formed by the purpose of the activity and the environment (Valikoski 2004: 116).

Let us consider an example of this point.

Distraction effects

If we wish to research distraction effects, we need to incorporate the courtroom actor location and camera location. The Short report refers to location issues in seven cases. Diagrams for the seven cases below were included,

- *Burnett v National Enquirer*;
- *People v Bittaker* (Sentencing);
- *People v Parnell*;
- *People v Robbins* (Opening and closing arguments only);
- *People v McDermand*;
- *People v Snyder*;
- *Michel v Dillard* (EMC Layout).

(Short report 1981: 57–63; *see drawings in* Appendix 1)

Let us assume that we wish to research for distraction effects on the lawyers in the respective cases. If we look at the diagram for the case of *Burnett v National Enquirer*, we note that the single television camera is located behind the rail, which itself is located behind the counsel table. The lawyers will be (generally) looking forward. Their cone of vision is forward. Therefore, the lawyers do not have the television camera within their cone-of-vision. They cannot be distracted visually by the television camera. While there can be other effects, there is no visual distraction effects. The situation is similar in *People v Parnell* and *People v Snyder*.

The situation is different in the case of *People v Bittaker*, where we note that the television camera is located before the lawyers, to the left. While it is not in the core of the cone-of-vision, it is still visible in the peripheral cone-of-vision.

In *People v Robbins* the courtroom layout means that the television camera is central in the cone-of-vision of the lawyers. The courtroom layout and camera location in *Michel v Dillard* also means that (one of) the television camera(s) is directly in the lawyers' cones-of-vision.

Therefore, only in three of the Short cases can we say that there is potential visual distraction effects on the lawyers causes by the television camera (and/or operator) in the courtroom. Without the courtroom layout and the location of the cameras and courtroom actors/personnel being recorded, we would not know this. We would not know that we should be focusing on these three cases for distraction effects on lawyers, and seeking to compare these cases with the distraction research in other studies. Unfortunately, the research is currently not sufficient to allow us to do this. If we are considering eye-tracking technology for researching distraction effects on lawyers, our research of the courtroom layout, courtroom actor location, and the location of the television cameras would tell us to focus on these three cases and/or courtrooms. A further point is that eye-tracking research of in-court distraction effects on lawyers may be less applicable to courts with the layout in the other cases referred to above.

However, we may wish to research other in-court distraction effects. Take witnesses for example. If we examine the courtroom layouts and locations, we can see that there is a television camera in the cone-of-vision of the witness in all seven cases referred to above (albeit in *People v Bittaker*, *People v Robbins* and *Michel v Dillard* the camera is in the peripheral cone of vision). Therefore, distraction effects and effects research are live issues in each of these cases. Eye-tracking technology as a research tool is applicable in all of the cases to examine witness distraction effects.

Though we only refer to lawyers and witnesses above, the layout and location issues are important in relation to all courtroom participants/actors.

The eye-tracking demonstration and location

It is important to realise that courtroom actors/personnel can be distracted by cameras. The issue is to research this and also to see the extent of this. This may then have implications for the legal, popular and policy arguments in relation to TCB. (Indeed, there may be potential implications for other forms of courtroom broadcasting, for example, radio).

In terms of distraction effects, a given courtroom actor may be looking at the television camera and/or camera operator directly. This is direct line of sight distraction/attraction.

However, there is also another important potential form of distraction. All individuals have a wide cone-of-vision. They can see things directly *and* peripherally. Many items can be seen within the field of vision of an individual.

The implication for TCB distraction effects research is that we must consider not just whether a courtroom actor is looking directly at the television camera in the courtroom, but also whether they see and are distracted by a television camera or television camera and operator in their peripheral cone-of-vision.

The cone-of-vision of the courtroom actors/personnel in the drawing below are represented in an angle field of vision of 120 degrees.

It is understood that normally people with good eyesight would have 20-20 vision, meaning a field of 140 degrees. It was chosen to show 120 degrees to allow for impairment, etc. and to remain conservative.

Location 1: ET1.1

This is a drawing of the courtroom, included in a whole longitudinal exterior section, of the court building in question.

The courtroom was located on the ground floor. There were two public entrances and two for the judge (see below).

Location 2: ET1.2

This drawing is similar to the Image ET1.1, with various courtroom participants/actors imposed. They are located in their normal or usual locations.

Seated at the left-hand side (top of the courtroom) is the judge (J). Sitting below the judge is the court clerk (C). Below the clerk one sees a solicitor or lawyer seated (S). (In this longitudinal drawing we do not see the witness box, nor the seated witness).

Images ET1.1–ET1.2

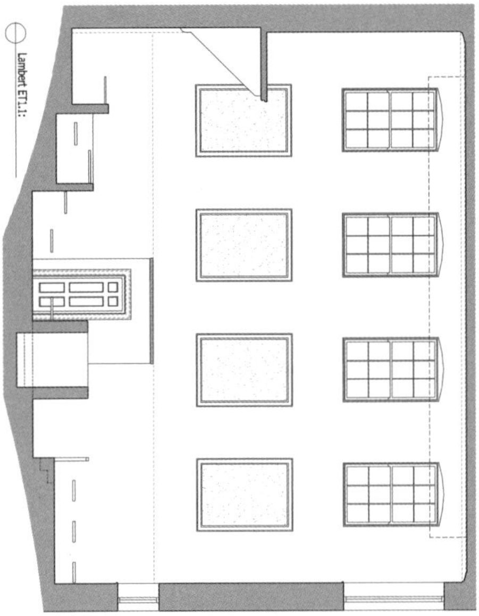

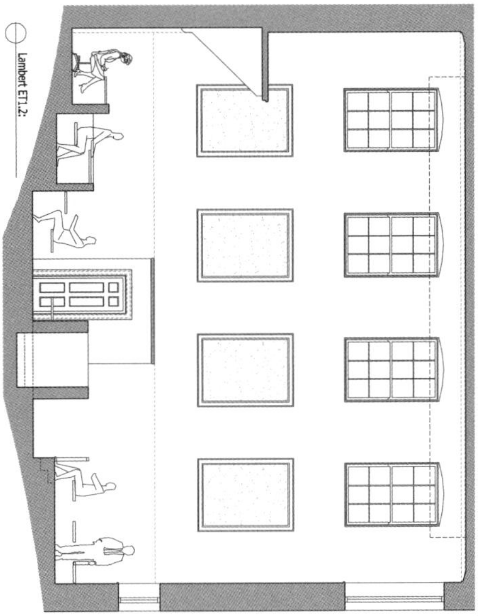

To the rear of the court, on the right-hand side of the longitudinal drawings, we see two members of the public, one seated and one standing. (In the demonstration there were no members of the public present.)

Location 3: ET1.3

Image ET1.3 is a topographical drawing of the courtroom. We see the two public entrances on the left- and right-hand sides. At the top of the courtroom we see two entrances on either side of the judge's bench (J).

The square seat on the raised area at the top of the drawing is the judge's seat and judge's raised bench (J).

Directly below the judge's seating area (J), there are two seats for the court clerk and assistant or alternatively a court transcriber (C).

To the immediate left and right of the court clerk's seating area, there are two separate witness boxes containing seats.

Directly below the judge's and court clerk's seats, there is a solicitors' or lawyers' bench (S) for sitting. On the left and right, there are two further benches for lawyers and/or police prosecutors to sit.

There is a stairwell area in the centre of the courtroom, which leads down to prisoner holding areas.

Images ET1.3–ET1.4

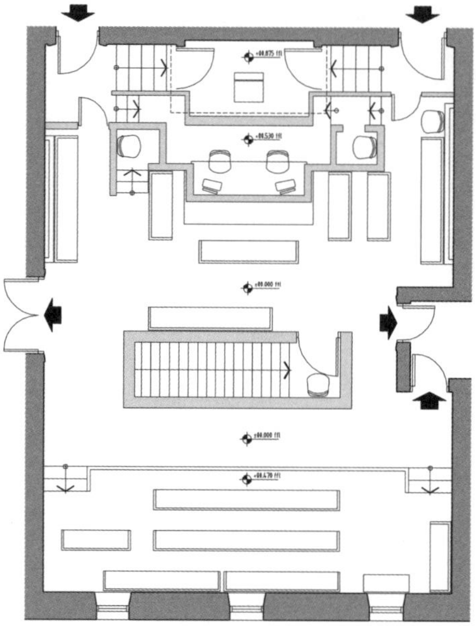

Lambert ET1.3:

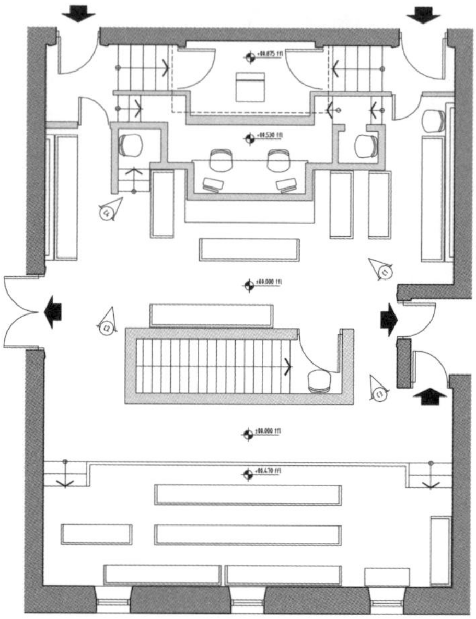

Lambert ET1.4: TV Camera Locations

Location 4: ET1.4 TV camera locations

Image ET1.4 shows the courtroom topography with the different tripod-television-camera locations marked (circle pointers).

These are locations C1, C2, C3 and C4. They are represented in a circle, with an arrow pointing in the direction that the camera is pointing and focusing.

Bear in mind, however, that the camera can tilt left and right and up and down, so the direction in which the camera is facing can change greatly. The directions marked are for the illustrative direction representation. However, they would be some of the most common directions.

Location 5: ET1.5 lawyer 2 to witness

This drawing shows the courtroom topography, the seats of the judge (J), court clerk (C), witness (W) and lawyers (S/L).

It also shows the four camera location positions C1–C4.

Image ET1.5

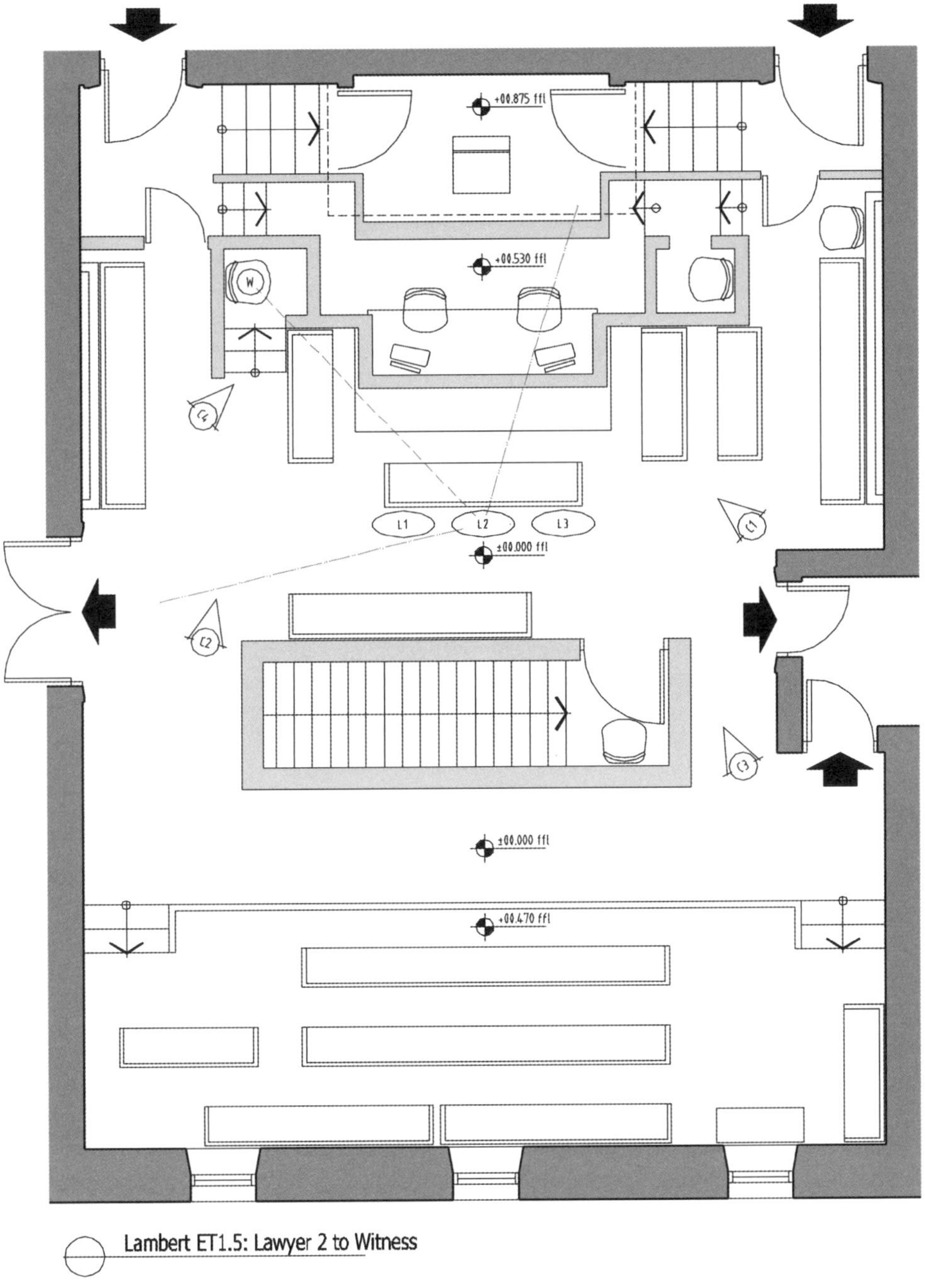
+00.875 ffl
+00.530 ffl
W
C4
L1
L2
L3
C1
±00.000 ffl
C2
C3
±00.000 ffl
+00.470 ffl
Lambert ET1.5: Lawyer 2 to Witness

In terms of the lawyer standing position (L), there are three lawyer standing positions represented, namely L1, L2 and L3. The reason is that standing lawyers can be located at any of these three potential standing locations.

In Image ET1.5 we also see a representation of Lawyer 2 (L2) looking at the witness (W). A cross-examination or examination could be in process. The broken centre line indicates the lawyer's direct line of sight (L2 to W). The non-broken lines left and right of the direct central line of sight represent the complete cone-of-vision of the lawyer.

It is evident that the cone-of-vision, looking directly at the witness, indicates that lawyer 2 (L2) can easily see camera position 4 (C4). Without a significant movement forward towards camera position 2 (C2), it also would come into the cone-of-vision of lawyer 2 (L2).

Location 6: ET1.6 witness to lawyer 1

In this courtroom topography the witness (W) is looking at lawyer 1 (L1). It is clear from the witness' cone-of-vision that camera positions 1, 2, 3 and 4 are *all* within the witness' cone-of-vision view.

Location 7: ET1.7 witness to lawyer 3

This courtroom topography also shows the witness (W), but this time looking at lawyer 3 (L3). In this cone-of-vision camera position 4 (C4) is (just) excluded. However, the witness can see in their cone-of-vision cameras position 1, 2 and 3 (C1, C2 and C3).

Location 8: ET1.8 judge to witness

The courtroom topography here indicates that the judge (J) is looking at the witness (W). The cone-of-vision indicates that the Judge can see camera position 4 (C4) and camera position 2 (C2).

Location 9: ET1.9 judge to lawyer 1

The courtroom topography shows that the judge (J) is looking at lawyer 1 (L1).

The cone of vision shows that all four camera positions are evident to the judge (C1, C2, C3 and C4). The judge can see all four cameras.

It is noted, therefore, that contrary to what might otherwise have been assumed, the judge is logically the person potentially most likely to be affected by distraction effects of television cameras in the courtroom.

Image ET1.6

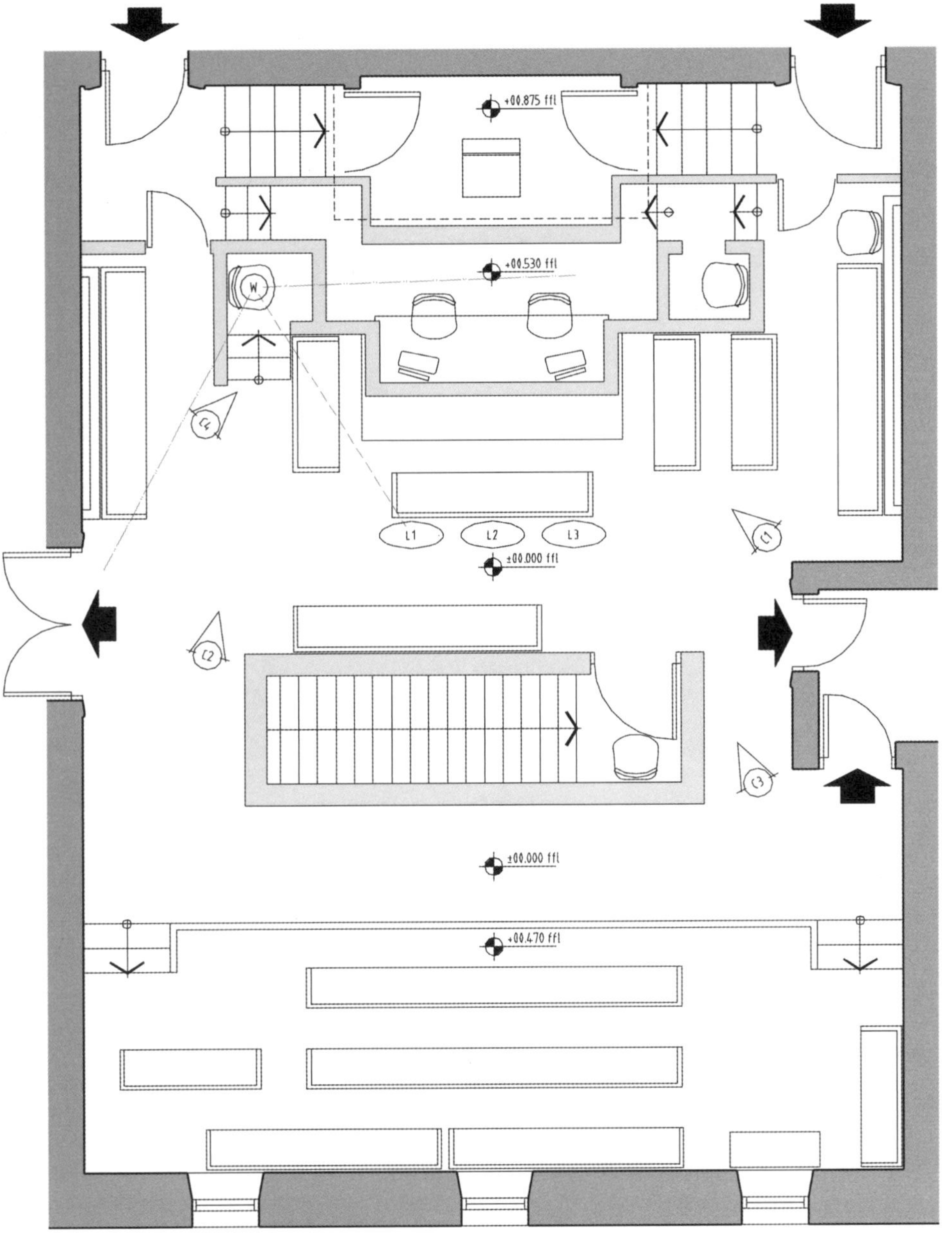

Lambert ET1.6: Witness to Lawyer 1

Image ET1.7

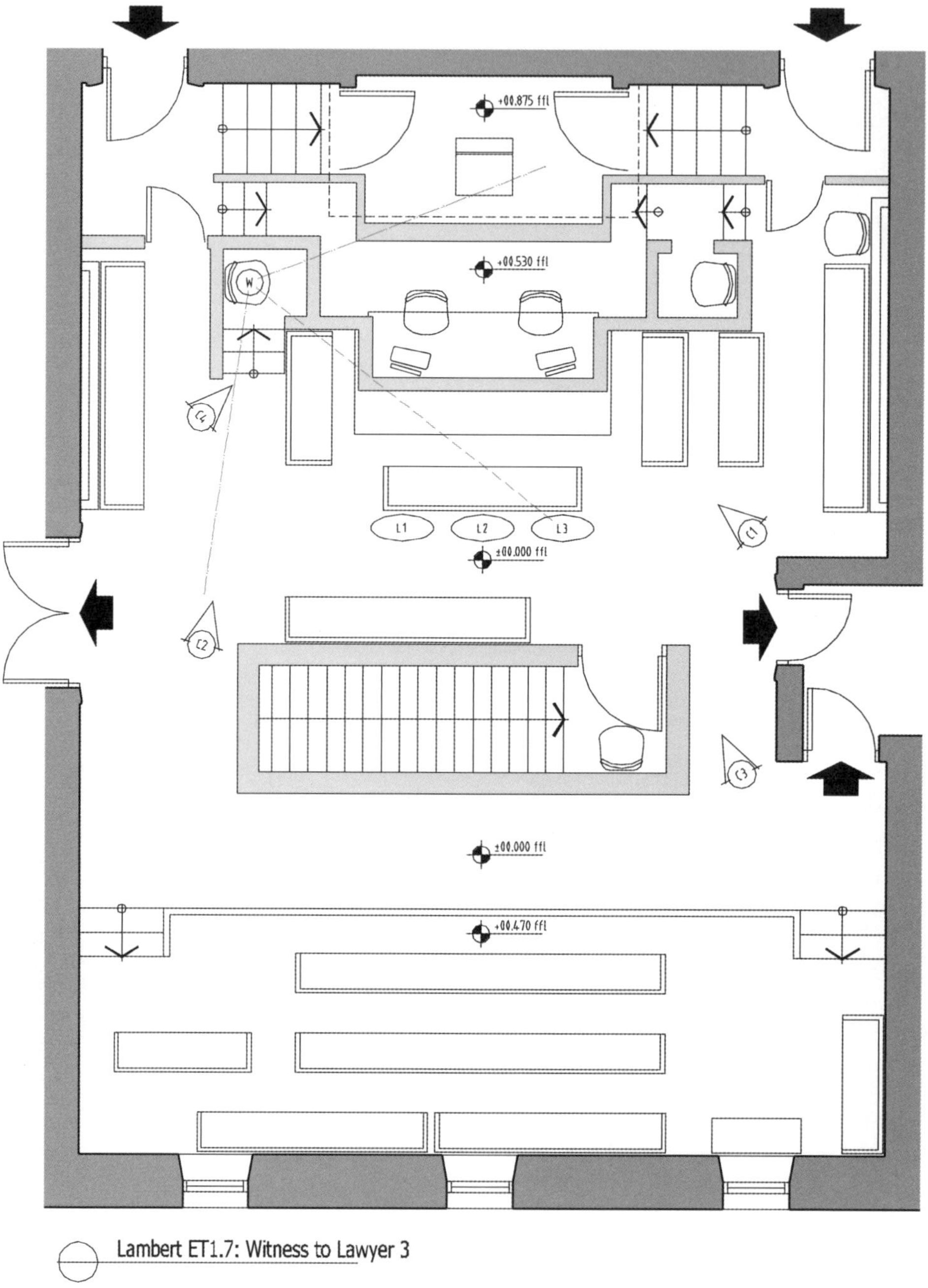
+00.875 ffl
+00.530 ffl
W
C4
C1
C2
C3
L1
L2
L3
±00.000 ffl
±00.000 ffl
+00.470 ffl
Lambert ET1.7: Witness to Lawyer 3

Image ET1.8

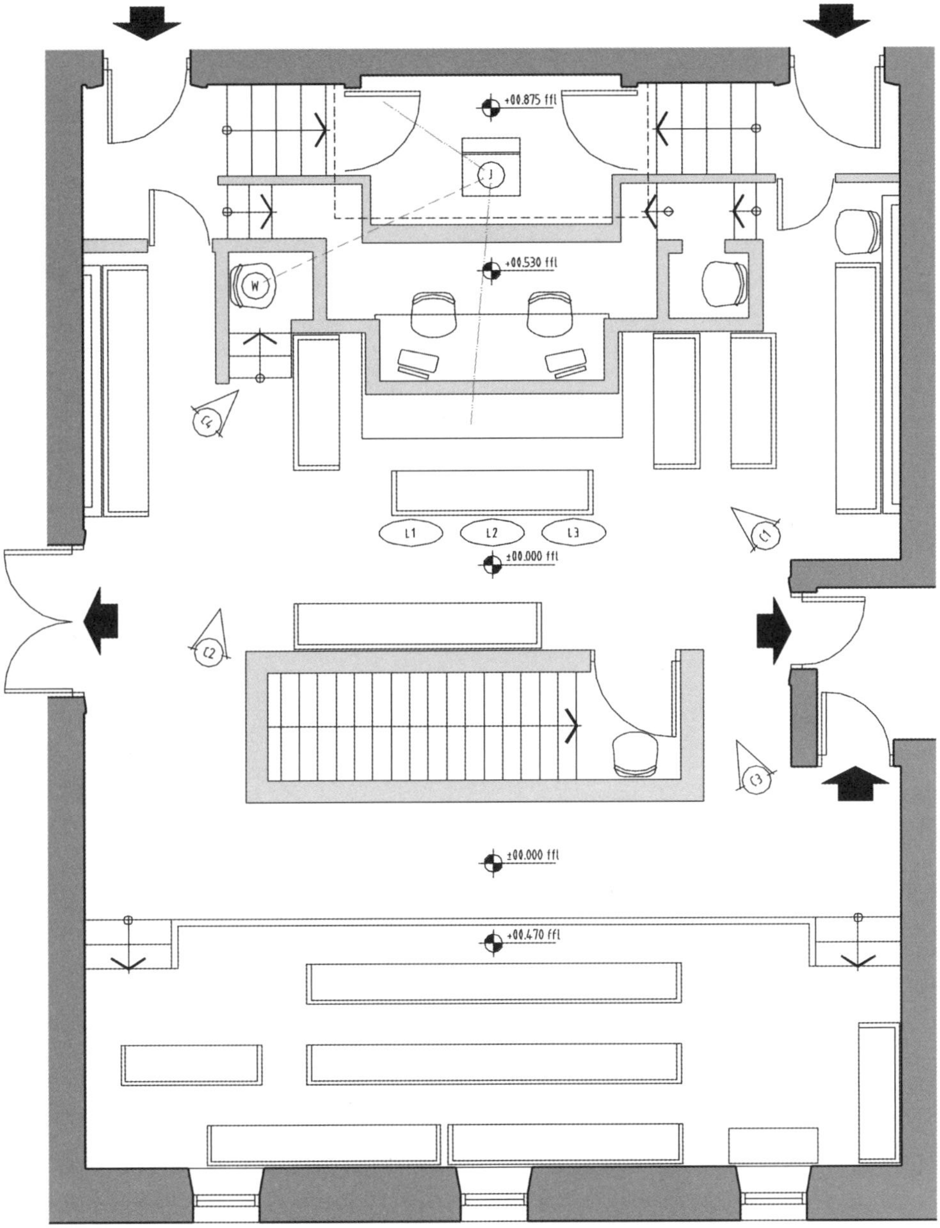

Lambert ET1.8: Judge to Witness

Image ET1.9

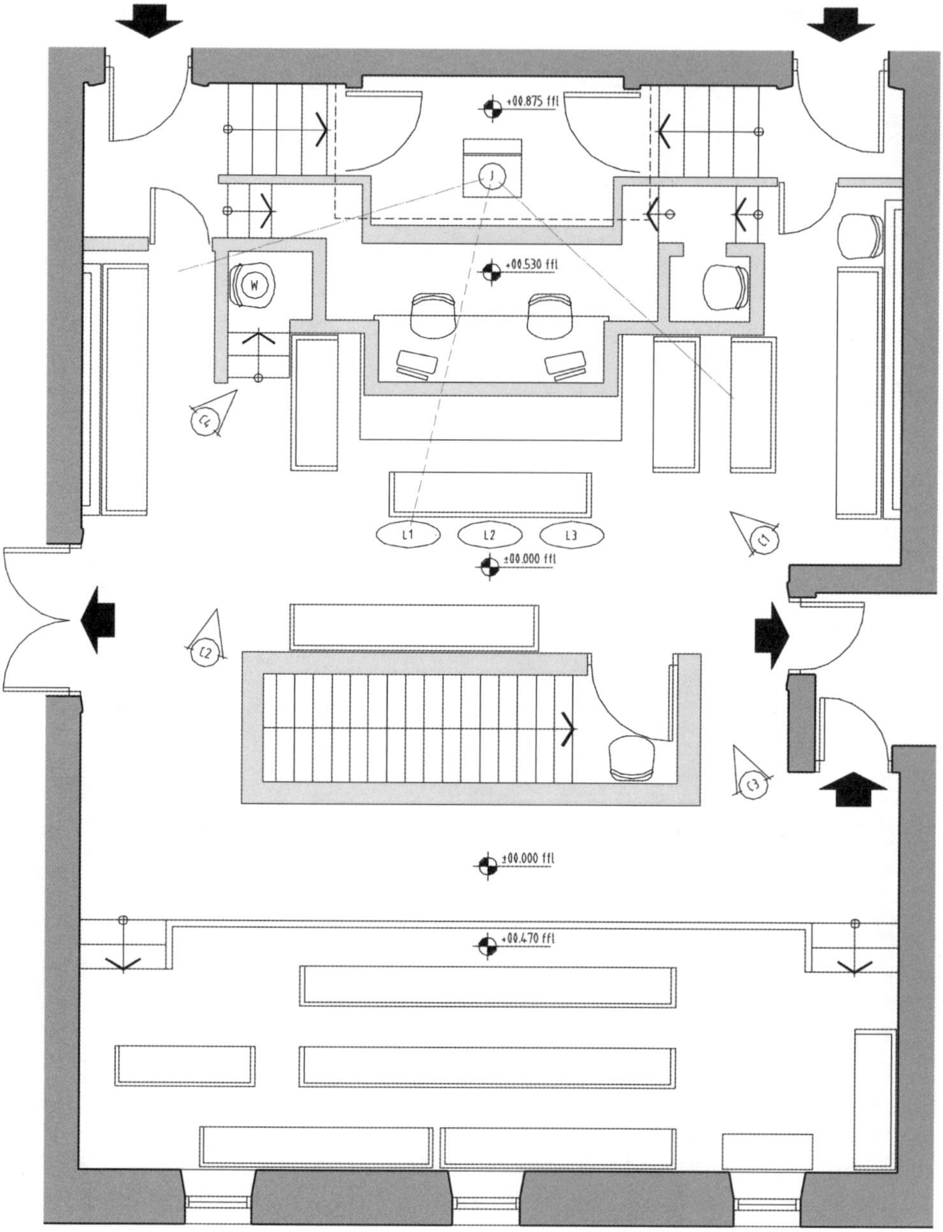

Lambert ET1.9: Judge to Lawyer 1

Of course, judges are experienced, professionally trained and in many instances judicially trained (albeit not always media trained). Traditionally these points are similar to the points raised in cases and policy discussion in terms of judges being not affected – or less affected – by media pre-trial publicity.

However, in light of the above finding, it is suggested that this is an issue deserving of more research and deeper consideration. This applies in terms of TCB *per se*, and also in terms of particular forms of such broadcasting where permitted.

Location 10: ET1.10 judge to lawyer 3

In this instance the courtroom topography indicates that the judge (J) is looking at lawyer 3 (L3).

The cone-of-vision for the judge in this instance reveals that the judge can easily see camera positions 1, 2 and 3 (C1, C2 and C3). Possibly camera position 4 (C4) in whole or in part is also visible. Even if it is not, even a small adjustment of the camera would bring it into focus in the judge's cone-of-vision.

We also see that the judge is looking directly at lawyer 3 (L3); camera position 3 (C3) is almost directly behind the lawyer.

Camera 1 (C1) is only slightly to the judge's left as s/he looks directly at lawyer position 3 (L3).

Future considerations

The location issue is clearly important. The author appears to be the first researcher to fully identify this. Recording the camera and courtroom actor location is also very important. We need to address this in order to be satisfied we are undertaking proper research. It is also critical as it is one of the markers that allows us to compare research results.

Future research also needs to cross-reference location issues and eye-tracking research.

A complicating issue for research is the suggestion that American courtrooms are increasingly changing their layout to place the jury in more strategic locations (as referred to in Netteburg 1980: 167. Also, Hall and Sales 2008). This would appear relevant to research on courtroom design, courtroom processes as well as TCB effects issues.

It is recommended that all effects research in future must record and document the courtroom layout, and in the case of research studies conducted in locations other than actual courtrooms, the layout of the research environment. Taking cognizance of the layout and location issues is also a prerequisite in planning any effects research. Without taking these issues into account, the research remains flawed individually. It is also flawed in that it precludes comparison and the build-up of a useful body of effects research in respect of each of the effects issues being examined in similar studies.

Image ET1.10

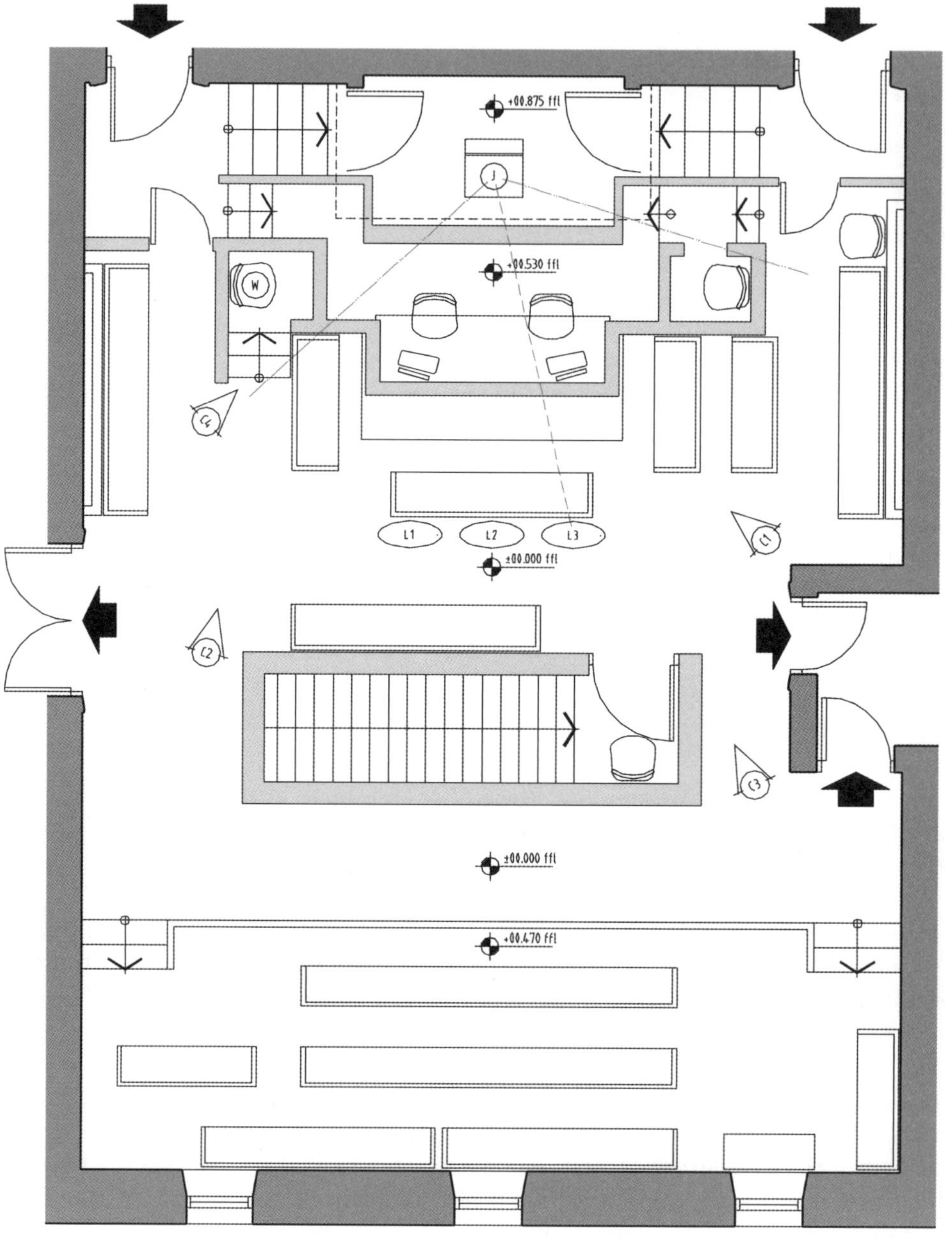

Lambert ET1.10: Judge to Lawyer 3

The television camera location and the cone-of-vision research have implications for the location of television cameras in experiments, pilots and in real courtrooms, which policymakers, judges and lawyers must consider. These issues have dimensions that are new legal, constitutional, ethical and research related. The above research emphasises the importance of further research and how important it is that the US Supreme Court research-challenge is properly addressed.

Chapter 13

Conclusion

Introduction

The book focuses on effects research issues with television courtroom broadcasting (TCB). Generally, it advocates that significant TCB definition, scoping and research be undertaken to address the effects concerns, gaps and challenges. In particular one of the Supreme Court's research-challenges, TCB distraction-effects, has never been properly researched. This includes using modern research methods and technology. Eye-tracking has now been demonstrated to be eminently capable of assisting us in undertaking eye-tracking distraction effects studies.

The research effort to date of the distraction effects of TCB (and by implication the legal, policy and arguments discussion) is not sufficient. The results fall far short of what we should expect. The literature also notes the lack of empirical research. Only by critically examining the research to date is it possible to fully appreciate this, and to look at how we might address it.

There are many and varied problems with the existing effects research, including distraction research. Most research is not defined or scoped. No body of sustained research currently validates any of the arguments whatsoever or any of the prior effects research. This includes distraction effects. Empirical studies are typically the most rigorous and more considered of effects-research studies. Unfortunately, these are the studies least frequently undertaken by those concerned. The issues of the location of the television cameras and the location of the courtroom actors/personnel, and its importance for effects research, are identified by the author for the very first time. Distraction and location research needs to be advanced.

Eye-tracking and distraction

This is the first in-court demonstration of eye-tracking anywhere. It was a success and proved the concept of eye-tracking for TCB effects research. Yet, this is only the first step. The next stage is to design and undertake an actual eye-tracking TCB effects experiment (and ultimately experiments). It is important to note, however, that as with previous research problems, one experiment on its own is not sufficient to prove or decide any individual effect. A body of TCB eye-tracking research and experiments must be built up. Only at that stage would we begin to seriously address the Supreme Court challenge. (Of course, eye-tracking is only one of many methods for researching TCB effects. Many methods need to be used in conjunction in order to build up the body of research knowledge required.)

We can be optimistic, however, in that the insights of the author and the eye-tracking demonstration offer a bright future for TCB effects research, which has thus far been lacking.

"If we don't like the way courtrooms look on camera, the solution is to change the courtrooms, not toss out the cameras. At least that's how a free and open society ought to work" (Kozinski and Johnson 2010: 1119). However, with respect, should it not be that if we decide to have TCB, and we do not like some aspect of it, we can alter and change the *form of* TCB where necessary? (This is not to suggest that we experiment willy nilly, or that we make and remake rules on the hoof. Separately, the wide disparity between the length and consent of the rules that do exist is also illuminating on the disparity of forms of TCB.)

H. C. Schmidt states that the current research in legal-psychology into videotaped confessions is motivated by the Supreme Court treatment of confession evidence cases (Schmidt 2006: 74). It is surprising that more research has not been undertaken into the effects of TCB, given that the Supreme Court first called for empirical research studies as far back as the *Estes* case (*Estes*: 532–616).

Judge Kozinski concluded with the suggestion that "[w]e must consider the issue [of TCB] again, in light of the world today" (Kozinski and Johnson 2010: 112). However, the present author suggests that we must also do so in light of our recognition of current research and current research methods. Indeed, we should not be blinkered in our approach. If other research is relevant, whether comparative or even unrelated, we must still embrace it. This includes technologies such as eye-tracking and fields such as legal-psychology.

Researchers use eye-tracking for research across a wide variety of fields and applications. Why should we not use eye-tracking in addressing the many TCB effects gaps and the Supreme Court challenge? The author recommends eye-tracking to examine some of the effects of TCB. Eye-tracking provides a direct measure of eye focus (Armstrong and Olatunji 2009). It permits testing and direct observation of eye fixation, focus and attention (see Ware 2006: 11). Eye-tracking research also has the advantage that is tracks and records exactly what people see (see www.prsresearch.com/prs-tools/). It also overcomes the limits of opinion-reports and self-reports. It can also test, and validate, opinion-reports and self-reports. "[E]ye movements are a direct indicator of overt attention" and provides "a highly direct measure of visual attention, eye systems also allow continuous measurement of eye movements" (www.prsresearch.com/prs-tools/). Eye-tracking is the future of TCB distraction- (and attraction-) effects research.

The time has come to address the research-challenge set by the Supreme Court and also to ensure that the research effort into the effects of TCB advances beyond the criticism that "[s]ocial scientists measure the intelligence of monkeys more effectively than courts have attempted to ascertain the effects of television in the courtroom" (Hirschhorn 1980: 7 and 9). It is time to move beyond limited self-reports and opinion-reports and embrace modern empirical research, including eye-tracking technology.

The author commends eye-tracking research to examine the distraction of witnesses, etc., in TCB. Quite simply, eye-tracking research is the future of TCB research.

The author recommends that research be undertaken culminating in a body of eye-tracking TCB effects research. Eye-tracking has been demonstrated to be possible for in-court research, and in particular in-court TCB distraction effects. It is recommended that the next stage, an actual eye-tracking effects experiment, be undertaken. The present demonstration (and the Supreme Court) can form the basis for planning and designing such an experiment.

Such an experiment could involve any one of the courtroom participants/actors referred to above in a single TCB eye-tracking experiment. In addition, a mock trial could be conducted, or the relevant portion of the trial, relevant to the particular courtroom actor being tested. We could take the example of a witness. Other actor subjects would act as actor facilitators for the experiment, acting as normal. The same test case could be re-run for test subjects who would attend and act as the witness in the case. It would be re-run for each test subject. The group of test witness subjects could, for example, be split into one group with no television camera present, and a second group with a television camera present. Each group of test subjects would wear an eye-tracker. Thus, in this briefly described experiment, we are able to test via eye-tracking whether (subject) witnesses are distracted or change their cone-of-vision or what they look at and or for how long when a television camera is present.

Variations of this type of experiment could include, for example, varying the camera location, varying the type and size and camera, varying between camera only and camera plus camera operator.

Further variation and experiment can be designed for all of the courtroom participants/ actors.

A further layer of experimentation involves carrying out self-reports and eye-tracking, and comparing the results. Are the self-reports verified or are there discrepancies between them? If there are differences, and significant differences, what are the implications for the general research previously conducted?

There is also a further issue to be considered. Obviously the individual actor wearing the eye-tracker is aware that they are wearing it, and may also have to have it individually calibrated to their eyes. However, there are different types of eye-trackers, which may not have to be so calibrated and/or which do not have to be "worn" by the subject courtroom actor. It may be possible to design an experiment where a non-conspicuous non-wearable eye-tracker and subsequently a wearable eye-tracker are used. If such an experiment is possible, this would go some way to measuring eye-tracker effects separate from the television camera distraction effect.

Eye-tracking experiments such as those above could be used to test for distraction-effect of television cameras. Fundamentally, they can also be used to research and measure location issues and camera size/type issues. These are important issues and issues that have never been researched to date.

Eye-tracking and the Supreme Court

Neither the Supreme Court, nor commentators, have recognised that as broadcasting technology may change, so too can the research tools available. One example of an advanced research tool is an eye-tracker. Eye-tracking (the study of eye movement and gaze) was not considered in the Supreme Court decisions. Neither has it been considered in the general literature in relation to TCB. Eye-tracking will assist in conducting research of effects of TCB, and in such way as the Supreme Court may not have even considered possible. Eye-tracking can greatly assist in addressing the research-challenge set by the Supreme Court.

The Supreme Court is not aware of eye-trackers and did not refer to eye-tracking in any way whatsoever. Eye-tracking can be used for conducting in-court effects research, in particular research of distraction effects. There are also many advantages of eye-tracking, including being able to track distraction effectively and being able to record the results.

The author undertook the world's first in-court proof of concept demonstration of eye-tracking technology for in-court distraction effects caused by TCB. This demands to be taken to the next level of research in future.

Distraction, cone-of-vision, actor and observer locations need to be incorporated into eye-tracking and location research.

Camera perspective bias research offers support for TCB research. It is also an example of eye-tracking research. Similarly the case with camera focus issues. It also exemplifies multidisciplinary legal-psychology research. Eye-trackers have also been used in another novel legal context, namely tobacco effects litigation and forms of court-mandated health advertisements. An important legal article in the *Harvard Law Review* (Kahan, Hoffman and Braman 2008–2009: 837–906) also undertook empirical interdisciplinary research.

Eye-tracking to address the Supreme Court

Identifying this challenge for the first time is significant, but the author goes further. Issues that the US Supreme Court has not yet identified as research-challenges are also dealt with by the author. Further still, the author identifies some specific research-challenges and how we might go about researching them with proper and empirical research. The distraction-research challenge referred to by the Supreme Court case law can be tackled with the use of eye-tracking technology. This requires both legal and technical expertise. As the Supreme Court appears to implicitly acknowledge, addressing the challenges is not solely a legal issue or solely an empirical issue. The research solutions are multidisciplinary. Addressing effects concerns via legal arguments alone is inadequate. The Supreme Court's appreciation of this point needs to be reflected in discussion and considerations in both Ireland and the United Kingdom in future. The solution proposed by the author to the distraction-research problem referred to by the Supreme Court (and yet to be considered in Irish or UK case law) is highly significant both here and internationally.

The author's research and recommendations and the linking of multidisciplinary research is supported by the Supreme Court; the effects research to date – such that it exists; and also related legal multidisciplinary research, for example, recent research published in the eminent *Harvard Law Review* (Kahan, Hoffman and Braman 2008–2009: 837–906). Legal research in family law, criminology and recently sentencing also rely increasingly upon empirical research. The eye-tracking propositions are equally valid.

Important research data points

TCB research generally ignores the gathering of important baseline and parameters data in effects research. Generally, the research where it exists tends be during or after the experiment, and gathers no baseline data before cameras are introduced. If a policy decision is made to experiment or introduce TCB, then the exercise of establishing the baselines and parameters should be commenced *prior to* the cameras being introduced.

Baseline and parameter research is essential as a prerequisite for any properly considered experimentation with (television) courtroom broadcasting. It is essential that this research and data gathering be undertaken over an extended period before television cameras are introduced into courtrooms. The author's research ensures that Ireland has started *some* of the baseline parameter research process, which has been missed by other jurisdictions.

Genres and formats research also helps us to recognise and distinguish different programmes. TCB research is criticised for involving only basic and cursory research methodologies, in particular self-reports and opinion-reports. We should not rely on self-reports and opinion studies alone. Research possibilities exist to deal with this.

Studies also need to be compared to each other, replicated and verified. Longitudinal research needs to be undertaken also. This does not occur to date. We need more research, and in particular using psychology, media, communications, camera perspective bias, eye-tracking distraction research and baseline research. Live courtroom broadcasting effects and implications need to be researched. Research needs to examine what occurs in courts normally and then how TCB uses and portrays this. We need a more robust and scientifically based research following the lead of other fields of research, such as psychology. No explicit definitions and forms are properly distinguished in the research literature. The location issues identified need to be incorporated in the effects research in future. We also need to begin detailed comparative research. These provide an abundance of relevant research opportunities.

In New Zealand what was broadcast was a mix of courtroom footage, out-of-court footage and re-cut file footage. What are the implications? There can be a significant difference between what is filmed and what may be broadcast. The TCB process needs to be researched and documented.

Conclusion

The author advances the international discussion and policy considerations of the often mooted adverse distraction effects of TCB, by identifying the Supreme Court TCB effects-research challenge and demonstrating eye-tracking technology to address the challenge. This requires significant research – and more than one study. It is also important to the United States, United Kingdom and elsewhere.

The research efforts and the sophistication of the research needs to be developed.

Eye-tracking has never been considered in any courtroom on any issue. Certainly it has not been addressed, nor considered, in any of the Supreme Court TCB cases nor the related TCB effects research. The literature on (television) courtroom broadcasting has not considered or referred to the utility of eye-tracking technology. The time has come to address TCB distraction research with eye-tracking.

Appendix 1

Diagrams from Short Report Study, September 1981

TABLE III-8A

EMC LAYOUT IN

BURNETT V. NATIONAL ENQUIRER

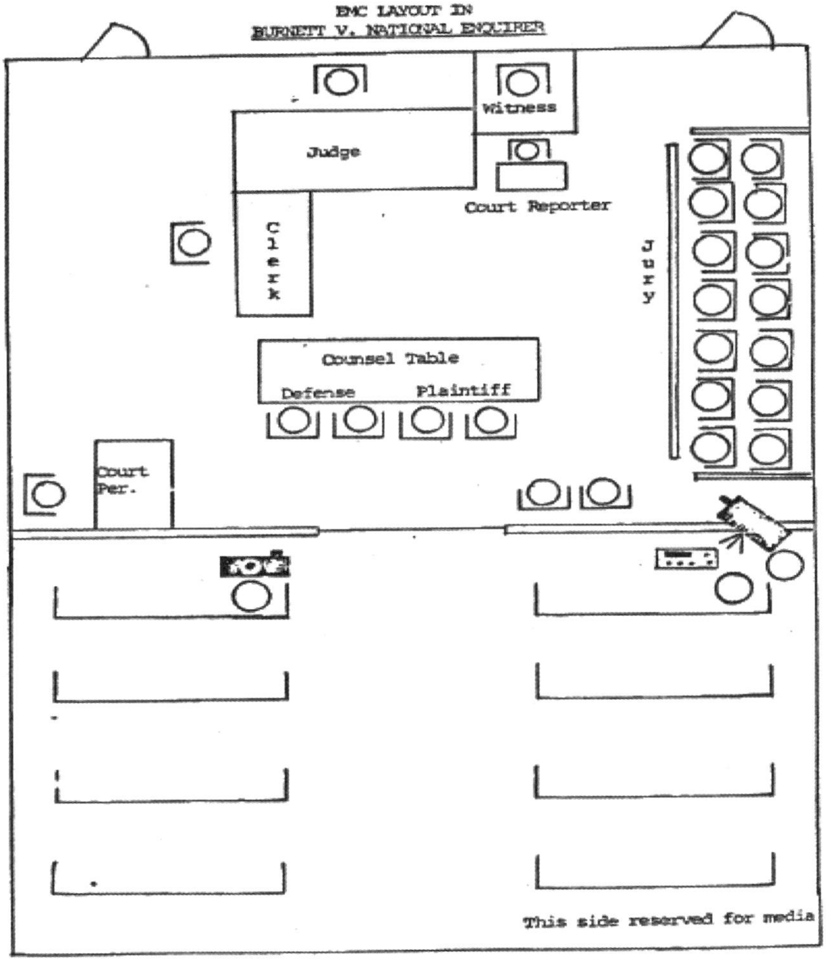

Los Angeles Superior Court

TABLE III-8B

EMC LAYOUT IN
PEOPLE V. BITTAKER SENTENCING

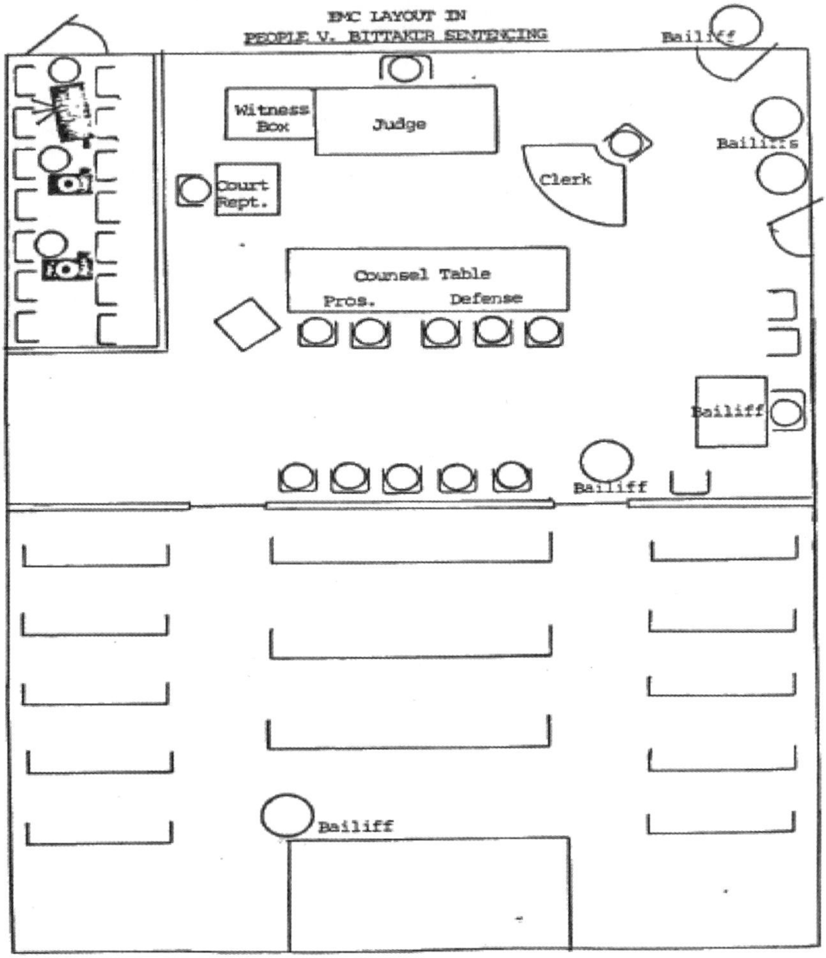

Los Angeles Superior Court
Torrance Branch
-58-

TABLE III-8C

EMC LAYOUT IN
PEOPLE V. PARNELL

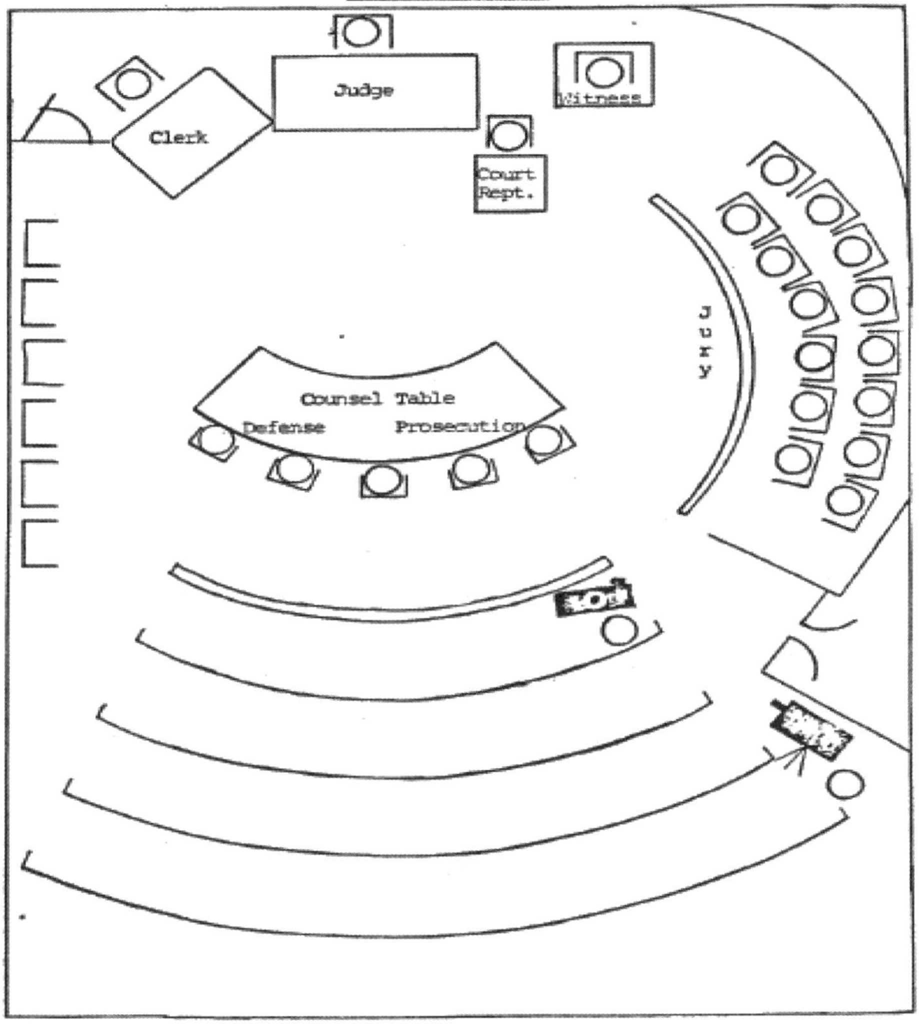

Alameda County Superior Court
Hayward Branch
-59-

TABLE III-8D

EMC LAYOUT IN

PEOPLE V. ROBBINS

(Opening and Closing Arguemnts Only)

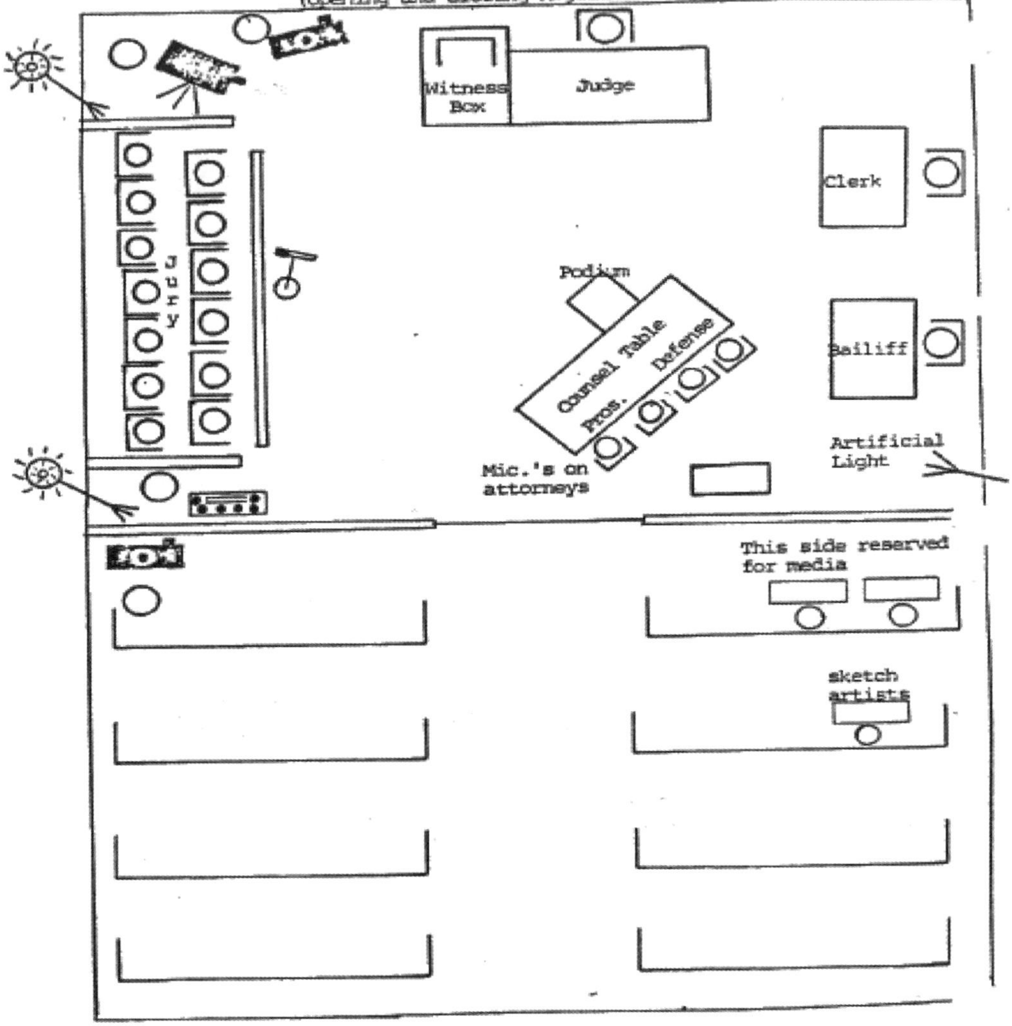

Sacramento Superior Court

-60-

TABLE III-8E

EMC LAYOUT IN
<u>PEOPLE V. McDERMOND</u>

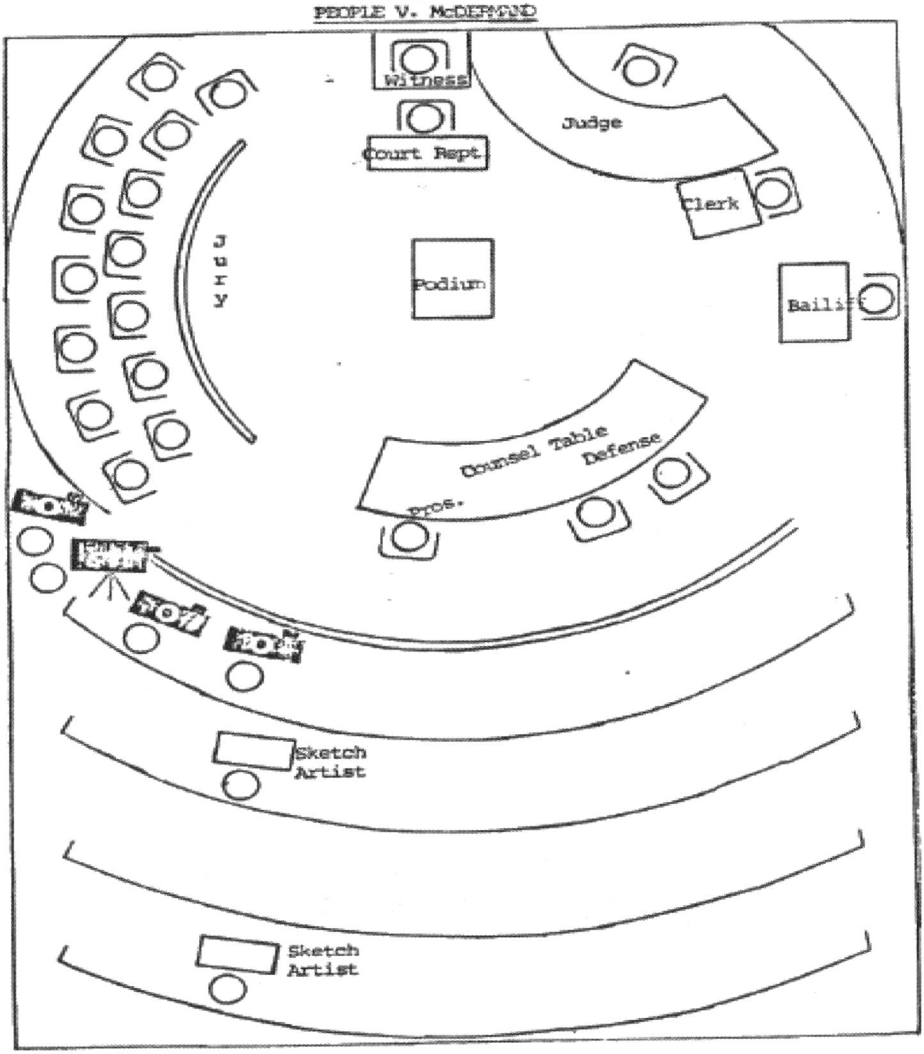

Marin County Superior Court

-61-

TABLE III-8F

EMC LAYOUT IN
PEOPLE V. SNYDER

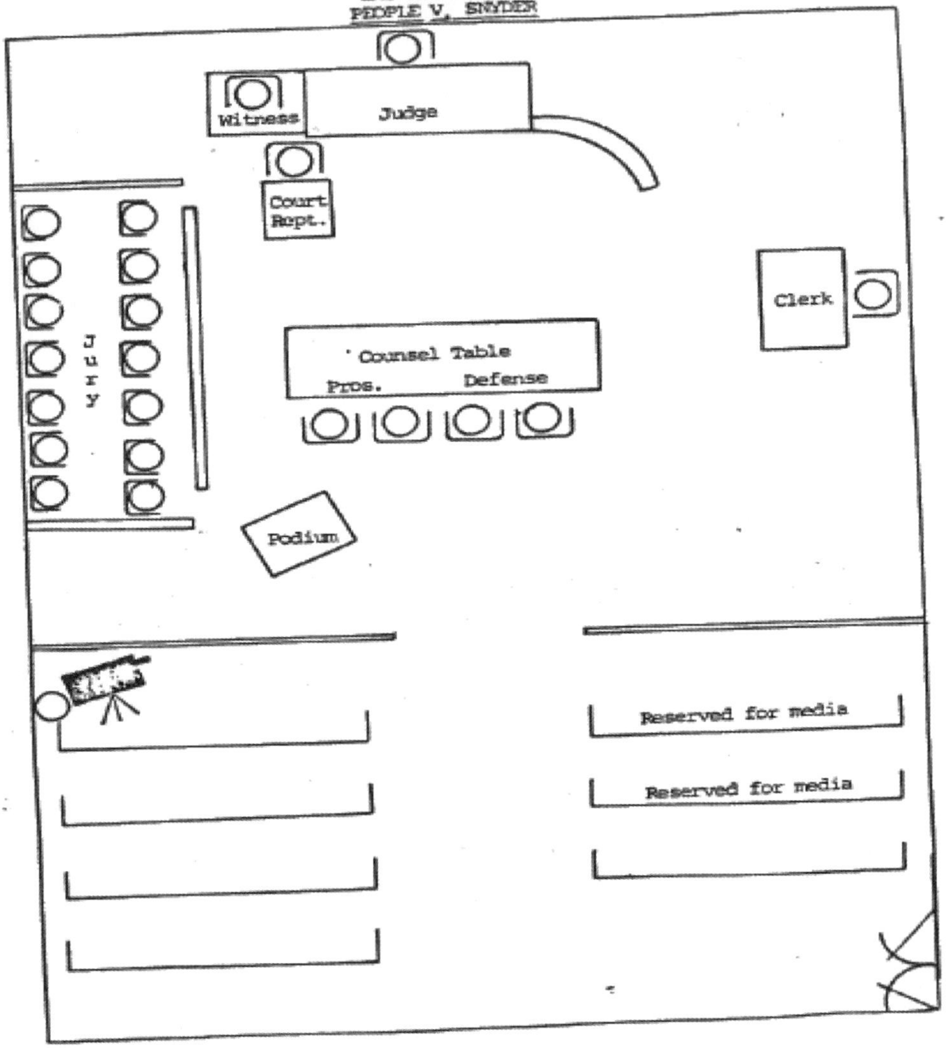

Los Angeles Municipal Court

-62-

TABLE III-8G

EMC LAYOUT IN
MICHEL V. DILLARD

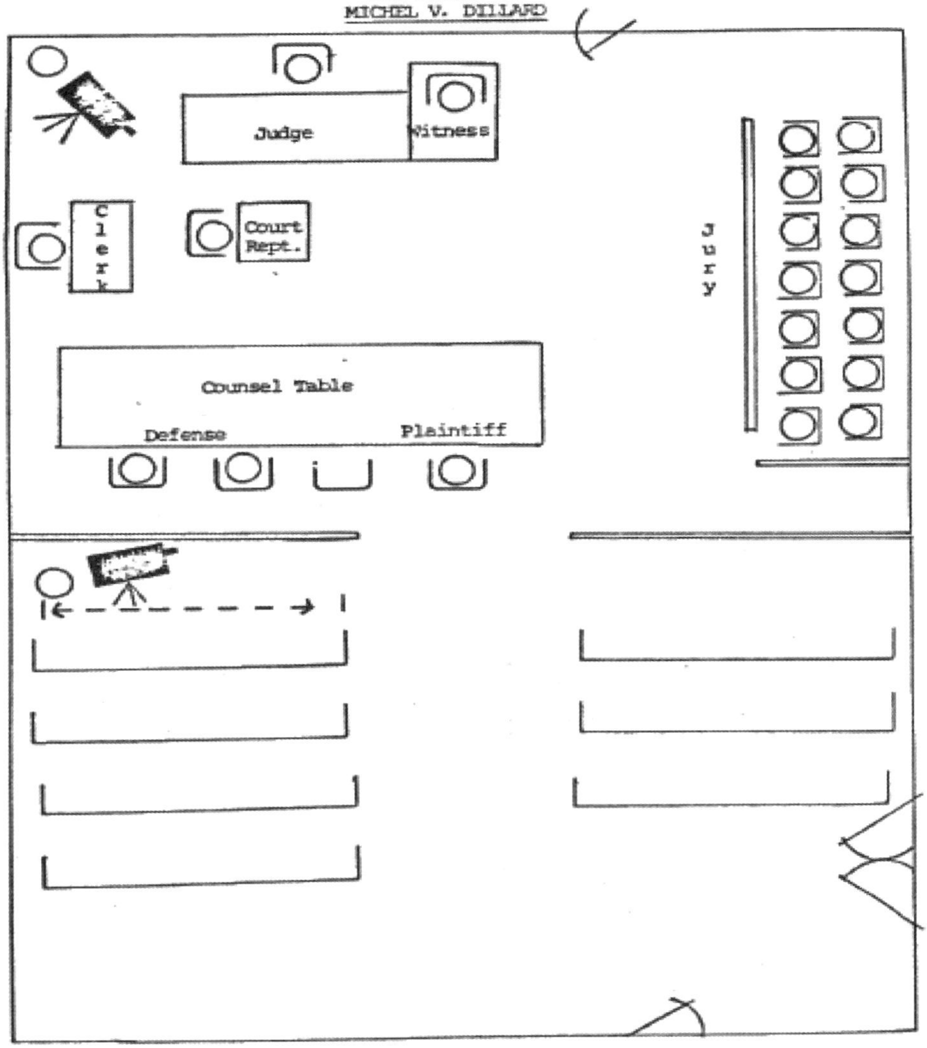

Yolo County Superior Court

-67-

Bibliography

Cases

Billy Eugene Manley, Oklahoma City, 1953, referred to in Barber (1987), 10–11.
Chandler v Florida 449 US (1981), 560–589.
Craig v The King, High Court, Australia; *Craig v R* (1933), HCA 41; (1933) 49 *CRL* (1933) (49) (29 August, 1933), www.austlii.edu.au, accessed 30 June 2012.
Decision on Application by Cable News Network (CNN), 25 October, 2001.
Estes v Texas 381 US (1965, 532–616.
*E*Trade Financial Corporation* v *Deutsche Bank AG* 582 F. Supp. 2d 528, 535 (SDNY 2008).
Hollingsworth v Perry 558 US _ 2010, http://www.supremecourt.gov/opinions/09pdf/09A648.pdf, accessed 30 June 2012.
In re Murchison 349 US (1955), 133.
In re Petition of Post-Week Stations, Florida, Inc., 370 So. 2d (1979), 764, 781.
Katzman v Victoria's Secret Catalogue, 923 F. Supp. 580 (SDNY 1996), 586–587.
Marisol A. v Giuliani 929 F. Supp. 660 (SDNY 1996), 661.
Nebraska Press Association v Stuart 427 US (1976), 539.
News Release, Federal Courthouses to Offer Remote Viewing of Pro-position 8 Trial (8 January, 2010), http://www.ca9.uscourts.gov/datastore/general/2010/01/08/Prop8_Remote_Viewing_Locations.pdf (accessed 13 January, 2010, and available in Clerk of Court's case file).
People (AG) v Casey (No 2) (1963), IR 33.
People (AG) v Stafford (1983), IR 165.
Petition of WMUR Channel 9, New Hampshire Supreme Court (13 December, 2002), www.courts.state.nh.us/opinions/2002/0212/wmur156.htm. Also http://www.courts.state.nh.us/supreme/opinions/2002/0212/wmur156.htm, accessed 30 June 2012.
Post-Newsweek Stations, Florida, Inc. v US 370 So2d 764 (Fla., 1979).
R v Dunne (English Court of Appeal) 4 October 1976 (unreported), referred to in Re (1984 :516).
R v Turnbull (1976), 3 All ER 549.
Rideau v Louisiana 373 US (1963), 723.
Schoeps v Museum of Modern Art, 599 F. Supp. 2d 532 (SDNY 2009), 534.
Sony, Warner, Atlantic, Arista and UMG, Court of Appeals For the First Circuit, No. 09-1090, Amicus Brief, 29 January, 2009, www.eff.org/files/filenode/inresonybmgetal/CVNMotionOralArgument.pdf, accessed 30 June 2012.
Tumey v Ohio 273 US (1927), 510.
Turner v Louisiana 379 US (1965), 466.
US v Amaral 488 F.2d (1973), 1148.
White Motor Co. v United States 372 US 253.

General

A Sample Survey of the Attitudes of Individuals Associated with Trials Involving Electronic Media and Still Photography Coverage in Selected Florida Courts between July 5, 1977 and June 30, 1978, available from the Florida Supreme Court, as referred to in Netteburg, K., "Does Research Support the Estes Ban on Cameras in the Courtroom," *Judicature* (1980) (63), 467–475, at 472.

"An Affordable Future for Eye-tracking in Sight," Phys Org, www.physorg.com/news63294534.html, 3 April 2006, accessed 29 June 2012.

Judicial Council of California Administrative Office of the Courts, *Cameras in the Courtroom, Report on Rule 980*, Administrative Office of the Courts, Research and Planning Unit, (San Francisco, May, 2000).

Administrative Office of the Courts of California, *Task Force on Photographing, Recording and Broadcasting in the Courtroom, Report Summary* (1996), referred to in Stepniak (2008), 114 et seq.

Administrative Office of the Courts, *Cameras in the Courtroom: Report on Rule 980* (May, 2000), referred to in Stepniak (2008), 114 et seq.

Agustin, J. S., as referred to in the eye-tracking blog of Martin Tall, Martin Tall on Gaze Interaction, A Blog on Research and Developments in Eye-tracking and Gaze Interaction, http://gazeinteraction.blogspot.com/2009/04/research-paper-on-itu-gaze-tracker-that.html, accessed 30 June 2012.

Alexander, S. L., *"Mischievous Potentialities": A Case Study of Courtroom Camera Guidelines, Eight Judicial Circuit, Florida, 1989*, Ph. D (University of Florida, 1990).

Allan, K., McGregor, J., and Professor, Fountaine, S. (Massey University), *The Impact of Television, Radio and Still Photography Coverage of Court Proceedings, Final Report, A Report for the Department for Courts* (April 1998) (New Zealand).

Alves, Hon. Nathan Braverman, Chaor, Baron, Hon. Jean Szekeres, Groton, Hon. Thomas C. III, Leasure, Hon. Diane O., Plitt, Hon. Emory A., Jr, *Report of the Committee to Study Extended Media Coverage of Criminal Trial Proceedings in Maryland,* Submitted by the Committee to Study Extended Media Coverage, a Subcommittee of the Legislation Committee of the Maryland Judicial Conference (Maryland, 2008).

Armstrong, T., and Olatunji, B. O., "What They See Is What You Get: Eye-tracking of Attention in the Anxiety Disorders," American Psychological Society, March, 2009, www.apa.org/science/about/psa/2009/03/science-briefs.aspx, accessed 30 June 2012.

Arrington Research, www.arringtonresearch.com/, accessed 30 June 2012.

Asl Eye-tracking, www.asleyetracking.com/Site/, accessed 30 June 2012.

Baker, P., Fairchild, A., Pater, J., and Seavey, A., "Community, Participation and Virtual Spaces: Design Considerations for Inclusivity," 10th European Conference on eGovernment, University of Limerick, 17–18 June, 2010.

Barber, S., *News Cameras in the Courtroom: A Free Press – Fair Trial Debate* (Norwood, New Jersey: Ablex, 1987).

Barrios, V. M. G., Manuel, V., Gütl, C., Preis, A., Andrews, K, Pivec, M, Mödritscher, F. and Trummer, C., "AdELE: A Framework for Adaptive E-Learning Through Eye-tracking," www.

iicm.tu-graz.ac.at/home/cguetl/publications/2004/Garcia%20et%20al.%202004%20-%20 IKNOW.pdf, accessed 30 June 2012.

Bell, B. E., and Loftus, E. F., "Trivial Persuasion in the Courtroom: The Power of (a Few) Minor Details," *Journal of Personality and Social Psychology* (1989) (56:5), 669–679.

Bingemann, M., "Eye-tracking Device Watches You Watching Ads," *PC World Business*, 10 May, 2007, http://www.pcworld.idg.com.au/article/182716/eye-tracking_device_watches_watching_ads/, accessed 30 June 2012.

Blashfield, A. E., "The Case of the Controversial Canon," *American Bar Association Journal* (1962) (48), 429–434.

Boggs, C. M., *Television Cameras in the Courtroom: An Examination of Studies and Their Value to Court Policy-Making*, MA (University of Pennsylvania, 1981).

Boies, Schiller and Flexner, L. L. P., *Memorandum, Prepared for the Committee on Court Administration and Case Management (Hon. John R Tunheim, Chair), The Judicial Conference of the United States, Submitted on Behalf of Courtroom View Network*, 6 June, 2009, www.google.ie/url?sa=t&source=web&cd=1&ved=0CBMQFjAA&url=http%3A%2F%2Fwww.courtroomview.com%2Fnews%2FCVN%2520White%2520Paper%2520(6%25206%252009)%2520(with%2520exhibits).pdf&ei=Gb2MTOuSFMOV4gbL2uWnCg&usg=AFQjCNEdysCcE_qaIlKgbw3EvomZW_7DTg&sig2=UJyaEtrpo493UfAhGO9kSw, accessed 30 June 2012.

Borgida, E., DeBona, K., and Buckman, L. A., "Cameras in the Courtroom: The Effects of Media Coverage on Witness Testimony and Juror Perceptions," *Law and Human Behaviour* (1990) (14:5), 489–508, at 491. [Minnesota].

Bowlin G. and Wnek, G., *Encyclopedia of Biomaterials and Biomedical Engineering*, Marcel Dekker, Inc, NY, 31 August, 2004.

Broomhall, B., *International Justice and the International Criminal Court: Between Sovereignty and the Rule of Law* (Oxford: OUP, 2003).

Bukoff, A., *The Effects of Video Camera Techniques on the Pre-Deliberation Judgements and Perceptions of Role-Playing Jurors*, Ph.D. (Kent State University, 1984).

Bundesen, C., and Habekost, T., *Principles of Visual Attention: Linking Mind and Brain* (Oxford: Oxford University Press, 2008).

Calvo-Goller, K. N., *The Trial Proceedings of the International Criminal Court, ICTY and ICTR Precedents* (Leiden: Martinus Nijhoff, 2006).

Caplan, J., Kalisher, M., and Speaight, A., *Televising the Courts: Report of a Working Party of the Public Affairs Committee of the General Council of the Bar* [of England and Wales] (London: Bar Council of England and Wales, 1989).

Carney, Hon. Mr Justice, "Restrictions on the Media Other Than Defamation," Dublin University, n.d..

Chandler, P., and Sweller, J., "Cognitive Load Theory and the Format of Instruction," *Cognition and Instruction* (1991) (8), 293–332.

Cherif Bassiouni, M., *The Legislative History of the International Criminal Court* (New York: Transnational Publishers, 2005).

Cohn, M., and Dow, D., *Cameras in the Courtroom: Television and the Pursuit of Justice* (New York: Rowman & Little, 1998, and 2002).

Comstock, G., S. and Katzman, N.*Television and Human Behaviour* (New York: Columbia University Press, 1978).

Coulter, C., "Judiciary Signals Support for Setting Up Judicial Council," *Irish Times*, 10 May, 2010.

Cranston, R., "The Rational Study of Law: Social Research and Access to Justice," in A. A. S. Zuckerman and R. Cranston (1995), 31–59.

Crosson, M., chief administrator of the courts in New York State, Public Report, as referred to in P. Thaler (1990), 30–31.

Culter., B., and Penrod, S., *Mistaken Identification: The Eyewitness, Psychology, and the Law* (New York: Cambridge University Press, 1985).

Cutler, B. L., Penrod, S. D., and Martens, T. K., "The Reliability of Eyewitness Identifications: The Role of System and Estimator Variables," *Law and Human Behavior*, (1987) (11), 223–258.

Davies, G., and Griffiths, L., "Eyewitness Identification and the English High Courts: A Century of Trial and Error," *Psychiatry, Psychology and Law* (2008) (15:3), 435–449.

Davies, G. M., Smith, S., and Blincoe, C., "A 'Weapon Focus' Effect in Children," *Psychology, Crime and Law* (2008) (14:4), 19–28.

Davis, N., "Television in Our Courts: The Proven Advantages, The Unproven Dangers," *Judicature* (1980) (64), 85–92.

Davis, S. F., *Handbook of Research Methods in Experimental Psychology* (Oxford: Blackwell, 2003), 367, 378.

DeBenedictis, D. J., "Cameras Banned, Pens Allowed: San Francisco Judge Refuses TV Station's Request to Tape Inmate Execution," *ABA Journal* (August, 1991), 16.

Department for Constitutional Affairs in Great Britain (DCA), consultation, "Broadcasting Courts," *Consultation Paper*, CP 28/04, November 2004, www.dca.gov.uk/consult/courts/broadcasting-cp28-04.pdf, accessed 30 June 2012.

Department of Constitutional Affairs, Broadcasting Courts, Response to Consultation, CP(R) 28/04, 30/06/2005, *Response to Consultation Carried Out by the Department for Constitutional Affairs (UK).*

Dershowitz, A., *Reasonable Doubts: The Criminal Justice System and the O. J. Simpson Case* (New York: Touchstone, 1996, 1997).

Duchowski, A., *Eye-tracking Methodology, Theory and Practice* (London: Springer, 2007).

Durant, A. and Lambrou, M., *Language and Media* (London: Routledge, 2009).

Einsiedel, E., "Television in the Courtroom: An Ohio Experiment," Association for Education in Journalism, Seattle (1978).

Egeilko, B., "Let Cameras in Courts, Chief Judge Says," *San Francisco Chronicle*, 8 October, 2010, at section C-3.

Entner, R., *The Image of the Judiciary: A Semiotic Analysis of Broadcast Trials to Ascertain Its Definition of the Court System*, Ph.D. (New York University, 1993).

Ergoneers, www.ergoneers.com, accessed 30 June 2012.

Esposito, S. A., *OJ TV: A Narrative Analysis of Television's Pretrial Coverage of the O. J. Simpson Case*, Ph.D. (Graduate School of Wayne State University, Detroit, Michigan, 1996).

ETRA, http://etra.cs.uta.fi/, accessed 30 June 2012.

EyeCam, *Dikabil Manual*, Section 2.1, at 5.

EyeLock, www.setcan.com/eyelock.html, accessed 30 June 2012.

Eye Tracker, www.eyetracker.co.uk/, accessed 30 June 2012.

Eye-tracking, www.eyetracking.com, accessed 30 June 2012 .

Eye-tracking, at the blog http://jeffnolan.com/wp/2010/03/25/eye-tracking/, accessed 30 June 2012.

Evans, A., "Lawyers' Perceptions of Their Values: An Empirical Assessment of Monash University Graduates in Law, 1980–1998," *Legal Education Review* (2001) (12), 209–266.

Ewing, L., Rhodes, G., and Pellicano, E., "Have You Got the Look? Gaze Direction Affects Judgements of Facial Attractiveness," *Visual Cognition* (2010) (18:3), 321–330.

Fatzer, J., former Chief Justice of Kansas Supreme Court, in Fatzer, H. R., "Cameras in the Courtroom: The Kansas Opposition," *Washburn Law Journal* (1978) (18), 230–243.

Federal Judicial Centre, Pilot Program Involving Electronic Coverage in Six US District Courts and Two Appeal Courts (1994).

Fisher, M. A., Memorandum to Members of the Court Management Committee from Administrative Office of the Courts, , with subject title "'Cameras in Court' Experiment (Rule 980.2)", 11, dated 28 October 1981, available from California courts service. The memorandum heading is The Judicial Council of California, Administrative office of the Courts.

Fixational Eye Movements and Visual Stabilisation and Eye-tracking Research and Applications (ETRA),http://etra.cs.uta.fi/, accessed 30 June 2012.

Fixation 2010, Stockholm, Sweden, 21–22 June, 2010, www.fixation2010.se/, accessed 30 June 2012.

Folker, S., Sichelschmidt, L. and Ritter, H., "Processing and Integrating Multimodal Material: The influence of Color-coding," in B. G. Bara, Barsalou, L. and Bucciarelli, M., eds, *Proceedings of the 27th Annual Conference of the Cognitive Science Society* (Mahwah, MJ: Erlbaum), 690–695.

Freedman, W., *Press and Media Access to a Criminal Courtroom* (New York: Quorum Books, 1988).

Gardner, N. T., "Cameras in the Courtroom: Guidelines for State Criminal Trials," *Michigan Law Review* (1985) (84:3), 475–516.

Geller, W. A., *Police Videotaping of Suspect Interrogations and Confessions: A Preliminary Examination of Issues and Practices* (A Report to the National Institute of Justice, Washington, DC: US Department of Justice, 1992).

Gerbner, G, "Trial by Television: Are We at the Point of No Return?," *Judicature* (1980) (63), 416–426, at 426.

Glatt, D. M., "Trial by Docudrama: Fact or Fiction?" *Cardoza Arts and Entertainment Law Journal* (1990) (9), 201–230.

Goldfarb, R. L., *TV or Not TV: Television, Justice, and the Courts* (New York: New York University Press, 1998).

Goldman, P. and Larson, R., "News Cameras in the Courtroom During *State v Solorzano*: End to the Estes Mandate?" *Southwestern-Nevada Law Review* (1978) (10), 2001–2061.

Goodenough, O. R., "Retheorising Privacy and Publicity," *Intellectual Property Quarterly* (1997) (1), 37–70.

Goodman, G. S., and Hahn, A., "Evaluating Eyewitness Testimony," in I. Weiner and A. Hess, *Handbook of Forensic Psychology* (New York: Wiley, 1987), 258–283.

Gould, J., *New York Times*, 11 March, 1956, S2, at X 11, col. 2.

Grady, S. "Cameras in Courtrooms Would Lead to a More Educated Public," in A. Hiber (2008), 61.

Graham, R., Friesen, C. K., Fichtenholtz, H. M. and LaBar, K. S., "Modulation of Reflexive Orienting to Gaze Direction by Facial Expressions," *Visual Cognition* (2010) (18:3), 331–368.

Granhad, P. A., Stromwall, L. A. and Hartwig, M., "Eyewitness Testimony: Tracing the Beliefs of Swedish Legal Professionals," *Behavioral Sciences and the Law* (2005) (23), 709–727.

Hall, S. R., and Sales, B. D., *Courtroom Modifications for Child Witnesses: Law and Science in Forensic Evaluations* (Washington, DC: American Psychological Association, 2008).

Harris, D. A., "The Appearance of Justice: Court TV, Conventional Television, and the Public Understanding of the Criminal Justice System," *Arizona Law Review* (1993) (35), 785–827.

Hatfield, G., *Perception and Cognition: Essays in the Philosophy of Psychology* (Oxford: Clarendon Press, 2009).

Heaton-Armstrong, A., Shepard, E., Gudjonsson, G. H., and Wolchover, D., eds, *Witness Testimony: Psychological, Investigative and Evidential Perspectives* (Oxford: OUP, 2006).

Heffernan, L., *Evidence: Cases and Materials* (Dublin: Thomson Round Hall, 2005).

Henderson, J. M., ed., *Real-world Scene Perception* (New York: Psychology Press, Taylor and Francis, 2005).

Henderson, J. M., and Ferreira, F., "Scene Perception for Psycholinguists," in J. M. Henderson, and F. Ferreira (2004), 1–58.

Henderson, J. M., and Ferreira, F., eds, *The Interface of Language, Vision and Action: Eye Movements and the Visual World* (New York: Psychology Press, 2004), 1–58.

Hiber, A., ed., *Should Cameras be Allowed in Courtrooms?* (New York: Gale, 2008).

Hirschhorn, J., "Cameras in the Courtroom? No," *Barrister* (1980) (7:3), 7, 9.

Hogan, G., and Whyte, G., *JM Kelly: The Irish Constitution* (Dublin: Lexis Nexis, Butterworths, 2003).

Hollin, C., *Psychology and Crime: An Introduction to Criminological Psychology* (London: Routledge, 1989).

Holmqvist, K., Holsanova, J., Barthelson, M., and Lundqvist, D., "Reading or Scanning? A Study of Newspaper and Net Paper Reading," in J. Hyona, R. Radach, and H. Duebel (2003), 657–670.

Holsanova, J., Holmberg, N., and Holmqvist, K., "Reading Information Graphics: The Role of Spatial Contiguity and Dual Attention Guidance," *Applied Cognitive Psychology* (2008) (22), 1–12.

Holsanova, J., Rahm, H., and Holmqvist, K., "Entry Points and Reading Paths on the Newspaper Spread: Comparing Semiotic Analysis with Eye-Tracking Measurements," *Visual Communication* (2005) (5), 65–93.

Holtenson, O. P., "The Admission of Expert Evidence of Opinion as to the Potential Unreliability of Evidence of Visual Identification," *Melbourne University Law Review* (1988) (16), 521–547.

Hope, L., and Wright, D., "Beyond Unusual? Examining the Role of Attention in the Weapon Focus Effect," *Applied Cognitive Psychology* (2007) (21), 951–961.

Hoyt, J. L., "Courtroom Coverage: The Effects of Being Televised," *Journal of Broadcasting* (1977), 487–495. [Wisconsin].

Hulse, L. M., and Memon, A., "Fatal Impact? The Effect of Emotional Arousal and Weapon Focus on Police Officer's Memories for a Simulated Crime," *Legal and Criminal Psychology* (2006) (11), 313–325.

Hyona, J., Radach, R., and Duebel, H., eds, *The Mind's Eye: Cognitive and Applied Aspects of Eye Movement Research* (Amsterdam: Elsevier Science, 2003).

Innocence Project, www.innocenceproject.org, accessed 30 June 2012.

Irvine, Lord, of Lairg, "Reporting the Courts: The Media's Rights and Responsibilities," 4th RTE/UCD Media Lecture, University College Dublin, 14 April, 1999.

Jacob, R. J. K., and Karn K. S., *Eye-tracking in Human-Computer Interaction and Usability Research: Ready to Deliver the Promises*, in J. Hyona, R. Radach and H. Deubel (2003), 573–605.

Jacoby, J., "Survey and Field Experimental Evidence," in S. Kassin and L. Wrightsman *The Psychology Of Evidence And Courtroom Procedure.* Beverly Hills, CA: Sage. (1985), 175–200.

Jeung, H. –J., Chandler, P., and Sweller, J., "The Role of Visual Indocators in Dual Sensory Mode Instruction," *Educational Psychology* (1997) (17), 329–343.

Ji, Q., and Yang, X., "Real-Time Eye, Gaze, and Face Pose Tracking for Monitoring Driver Vigilance," *Real-Time Imaging* (2002) (8:5), 357–377.

Johnson, M. T., and Krafka, C., *Pilot Program Involving Electronic Coverage in Six US District Courts and Two Appeal Courts* (Federal Judicial Centre, 1994).

Josephson, S., and Holmes, M., *Have You Seen Any of These Men? Looking at Whether Eyewitnesses Use Scanpaths to Recognize Suspects in Photo Lineups*, ETRA, Proceedings of the 2010 Symposium on Eye-Tracking Research & Applications, Austin, Texas, 22–24 March, 2010.

Joy, P. A., and McMunigal, K. C., "Clients, Lawyers, and the Media," *Criminal Justice* (2004–2005) (19), 77.

"Judiciary Approves Pilot Project for Cameras in District Court," www.uscourts.gov, accessed 30 June 2012.

Kahan, D. M., Hoffman, D. A., and Braman, D., "Whose Eyes Are You Going to Believe? *Scott v Harris* and the Perils of Cognitive Illiberalism," *Harvard Law Review* (2008–2009) (122), 837–906.

Kassin, S. M., "TV Cameras, Public Self-Consciousness, and Mock Juror Performance," *Journal of Experimental Social Psychology* (1984), 337–349.

Kassin, S. M., "The Psychology of Confession Evidence," *American Psychologist* (1997) (52), 221–233.

Kassin, S. and Wrightsman, L. *The Psychology Of Evidence And Courtroom Procedure.* Beverly Hills, CA: Sage 1985

Katz, J., "What Makes Crime 'News'?" *Media Culture and Society* (1987) (9), 47–75.

Keane, A., *The Modern Law of Evidence* (Oxford: OUP, 2008).

Keating, "Not 'Bananas,' Not 'Peyton Place,' But the U.S. Senate," *NY Times Magazine*, 25 April, 1965, 67, 72.

Keller, T. D., *Cameras in Courtrooms: An Analysis of Television Court Coverage in Virginia*, Ph. D. (The University of Tennessee, 1992).

Khosla, R., Simola, J., Salojarvi, J and Kojo, I., "Using Hidden Markov Model to Uncover Processing States from Eye Movements in Information Search Tasks," *Cognitive Systems Research* (2008) (9), 237–251.

Killian, D. P., "The Propriety of Restrictive Guidelines for Cameras in the Court," *Communications and the Law* (1987) (9), 27–43.

Kipper, P., and Mills, C., "Television Camera Movement as a Source of Perceptual Information," *Journal of Broadcasting and Electronic Media* (1986) (30), 295–307.

Kohm, S. A., *I'm Not a Judge But I Play One On TV: American Reality Based Courtroom Television*, Ph.D. (Simon Fraser University, 2004).

Kowler, E., ed., *Eye Movements and Their Role in Visual and Cognitive Processes* (Amsterdam, The Netherlands: Elsevier, 1990).

Koyama, S. A., *Effects of Television Camera Angle, Locus of Control, and Two-sided/One-sides Persuasive Messages Upon Attitudes Toward Disabled People* (University of Washington, Seattle,1982).

Kozinski, A., and Johnson, R., "Of Cameras and Courtrooms," *Fordham Intellectual Property Media & Entertainment L. J.* (2010) (20), 1107.

Kramer, T. H., Buckhout, R., and Eugenio, P., "Weapons Focus, Arousal, and Eyewitness Memory, Attention Must be Paid," *Law and Human Behaviour* (1990) (14:2), 167–184.

Kwak, J. Y., *Remembering Faces: Using Eye Movement Measures to Investigate Differences Between True and False Memory*, Ph.D. (University of California, 2009).

Lambert, P., "Courtroom Television Cameras and the Media," *Journal of Media Law and Practice* (1995) (16:4), 139–144.

Lambert, P., "Courtroom Television Broadcasting," *Communications Law* (1997) (2:5), 180–187.

——— "Effects-research Issues in Television Courtroom Broadcasting: Getting Past Monkey," 10thEuropean Conference on eGovernment, University of Limerick, 17–18 June, 2010.

——— "Eye-tracking Technology and Television Courtroom Broadcasting," *Computers and Law*, 11 August, 2010, at www.scl.org/site.aspx?i=ed16965, accessed 30 June 2012.

——— "Monkey Magic: Problems With Effects-research of Television Courtroom Broadcasting," *Irish Law Times* (2010) (18), 278–280.

——— "Time to Leave the Monkey Behind?: How Eye-tracking and Psychology Can Contribute to Television Courtroom Broadcasting Effects-research," British Psychological Society, BPS Cognitive Psychology Section Annual Conference, 27th Annual Cognitive Psychology Section Conference, Cardiff University, 6–8 September, 2010.

——— "TCB Effects: Eye-tracking and Camera Distraction in Court," Irish Association of Law Teachers Annual Conference, Strand Hotel, Limerick, 26–28 November, 2010.

——— "A Candid Camera, Eye-tracking Technology Could Transform Courtroom Broadcasting," *New Law Journal*, 10 December, 2010, 1699–1700.

——— "Confessions and Camera Perspective Bias," *Bar Review* (December, 2010), 128–130.

——— "Eyeing the Supreme Court's Challenge, A Proposal to Use Eye-tracking to Determine the Effects of Television Courtroom Broadcasting," *Reynolds Courts and Media Law Journal* (2011) (1:3), 277.

Landstrom, S., Hjelmsater, E., and Granhag, P., "The Camera Perspective Bias: A Case Study," *Journal of Investigative Psychology and Offender Profiling* (2007) (4), 199–208.

Lassiter, G. D., "Illusory Causation in the Courtroom," *Current Directions in Psychological Science* (2002) (11), 204–208.

Lassiter, G. D., Munhall, P. J., Ploutz-Snyder, R. J., and Breitbecher, D. L., "Illusory Causation: Why It Occurs," *Psychological Science* (2002) (13), 299–305.

Lassiter, G. J and Irvine, A. A., "Videotaped Confessions: The Impact of Camera Point of View on Judgements of Coercion," *Journal of Applied Social Psychology* (1986) (16), 286.

Lassiter, G., Geers, A., Munhall, P., Handley, I., and Beers, M., "Videotaped Confessions: Is Guilt in the Eye of the Camera?" in M. Zanna (2001), 189–253.

Law Reform Commission, *Consultation Paper on Contempt of Court* (Dublin: Government Publications, 1991).

Law Reform Commission, *Report on Contempt of Court* (Dublin: Government Publications, 1994).

Lee, D. E., "Cameras in the Courtroom," First Amendment Centre, 13 September 2002, www.firstamendmentcenter.org/Press/topic.aspx?topic=cameras_courtroom. Also http://www.firstamendmentcenter.org/cameras-in-the-courtroom, accessed 30 June 2012.

Lillington, K., "IBM Plots the Future at Tech Summer Camp," *Irish Times*, 29 July, 2005.

Lindsay, R. C. L., Ross, D. F., Read, J. D., and Toglia, M. P., eds, *The Handbook of Eyewitness Psychology* (Mahwah, NJ: Erlbaum, 2007).

Lloyd-Bostock, S., and Clifford, B. R., eds, *Evaluating Eyewitness Testimony* (New York: Wiley, 1985).

Loftus, E., *Eyewitness Testimony* (Cambridge, MA: Harvard University Press, 1979, 1996).

Loftus, E. "A 30-year Investigation of the Malleability of Memory," *Learning and Memory* (2005) (12), 361–366.

Loftus, E. F., and Doyle, J. M., *Eyewitness Testimony: Civil and Criminal* (New York: Kluwer, 1987, second edition/supplement published in 1994 by Lex Law Publishing).

Loftus., E. F., and Ketcham, K., "The Malleability of Eyewitness Accounts," in S. Lloyd-Bostock and B. R. Clifford (1985).

Loftus, E., Loftus, G., and Messo, J., "Some Facts About 'Weapon Focus,'" *Law and Human Behaviour* (1987) (11:1), 55–62.

Loftus, G. R., and Mackworth, N. H., "Cognitive Determinants of Fixation Location During Picture Viewing," *Journal of Experimental Psychology* (1978) (4:4), 565–572.

Maass, A., and Kohnken, G., "Eyewitness Identification: Simulating the Weapon Effect," *Law and Human Behavior* (1989) (13), 379–408.

Mannheim, K., *Ideology and Utopia* (London: Routledge and Keegan Paul, 1936).

Martin, D., and Macrae, C. N., "Processing Style and Person Recognition: Exploring the Face Inversion Effect," *Visual Cognition* (2010) (18:2), 161–170.

Marxist Institute for Public Opinion Poll (1996), in *An Open Courtroom, Cameras in New York Courts*, New York State Committee to Review Audio-Visual Coverage of Courts Proceedings (New York: Fordham University Press, 1997).

Mason, P., "Court on Camera: Electronic Broadcast Coverage of the Legal Proceedings," www.usfca.edu/pj/camera-mason.htm.

Mayer, R. E., *Multimedia Learning* (Cambridge: Cambridge University Press, 2001).
——— ed., *Cambridge Handbook of Multimedia Learning* (New York: Cambridge University Press, 2005).
——— "Principles for Managing Essential Processing in Multimedia Learning: Coherence, Signalling, Redundancy, Spatial Continuity and Temporal Contiguity Principles," in R. E. Mayer (2005), 183–200.
——— "Multimedia Learning: Guiding Visuospatial Thinking with Instructional Animation," in R. E. Mayer (2005), 477–508.
McCraty, R. T., Atkinson, M., and Sundram, J., *Impact of the HeartMath Self-Management Skills Program on Physiological and Psychological Stress in Police Officers* (Boulder Creek, CO: Institute of HeartMath, HeartMath Research Centre Publications No. 99-075, 1999).
McGonagle, M., *A Textbook on Media Law* (Dublin: Gill and MacMillan, 1997).
——— *Media Law* (Dublin: Sweet and Maxwell, 2006).
McQuail, D., and Windahl, S., *Communications Models: For the Study of Mass Communication* (London: Longman, 1993), 47.
McQueen, R. A. and Knussen, C., *Introduction to Research Methods and Statistics in Psychology*, (2006), 347.
Mitchell, M., and Jolley, J., *Research Design Explained* (London: Wadsworth, Thomson Learning, 2001), C-13.
Morimoto, C., and Mimica, M. R. M., "Eye Gaze Tracking Techniques for Interactive Applications," *Computer Vision and Image Understanding* (2005) (98:1), 4–24.
Mourant, R. R., and Donaghue, R. J., "Acquisition of Indirect Vision Information by Novice, Experienced, and Mature Drivers," *Journal of Safety Research* (1977) (9), 39–46.
Netteburg, K. L., *Cameras in the Courtroom: Is a Picture Worth a Thousand Words?*, Ph.D. (University of Minnesota, 1980).
Netteburg, K., "Does Research Support the *Estes* Ban on Cameras in the Courtroom," *Judicature* (1980) (63), 467–475.
New Law Journal (30 November, 1987) at 13 et seq., as referred to in Freedman W. (1988), 46.
New York State Committee to Review Audio-Visual Coverage of Court Proceedings, *An Open Courtroom: Cameras in New York Courts* (New York: Fordham University Press, 1997).
Nielsen, J., and Pernice, K., *Eyetracking Web Usablility* (Berkely, CA: New Riders, 2009).
O'Brien, R. J., Mattson, E. S. and Healey, B. J.., "Chapter Eight: Cameras in the Courts," *Media Law Handbook*, www.isba.org/newscenter/medialawhandbook/CHAPTER%2008%20-%20Cameras%20in%20the%20Courtroom.pdf. Also http://www.isba.org/sites/default/ files/Media%20Law%20Handbook%20Chapter%2008%20-%20Cameras%20in%20the%20Courtroom.pdf, accessed 30 June 2012.
O'Regan, J. K., "Eye Movements and Reading," in Kowler E., (1990), 395–453.
——— "Optimal Viewing Position in Words and the Strategy-tactics Theory of Eye Movements in Reading," in Rayner K., (1992), 333–354.
O'Scannlain, D. F., "Some Reflections on Cameras in the Appellate Courtroom," *Journal of Appellate Practice and Process* (2007), 323–330.
Ossinger, J., *Electronic Access to Courtrooms: Television as an Educational Socializing Agent on the Judiciary*, MA (The University of Maine, 2006).

Oue, W., Hakoda, Y., and Onuma, N., "The Effects of Visual Features of a Weapon on Eyewitnesses' Cognitive Processing," *Japanese Journal of Psychology* (2006) (77:5), 443–451.

Overview, http://www.fixation2010.se/overview, accessed 30 June 2012.

Paddon, A. R., *Television Coverage of Criminal Trials with Cameras and Microphones: A Laboratory Experiment of Audience Effects*, Ph.D. (University of Tennessee, Knoxville, 1985).

Paddon, A. R., "Television Coverage of Criminal Trials with Cameras and Microphones: A Controlled Experiment of Audience Effects," Radio-television Journalism Division, AEJMC Montreal, Que, Canada, August 7, 1992, 14.

Parker, C., "What Do They Learn When They Learn Legal Ethics?" *Legal Education Review* (2001) (12), 175–208.

Pasternack, S. R., *The Effects of Perceived Community Pressure on Simulated Juror Guilt Attributions: An Experimental Study*, Ph.D. (The University of Tennessee, Knoxville, 1982).

Petkanas, W., *Cameras on Trial: An Assessment of the Educational Affects of News Cameras in Trial Courts*, Ph.D. (New York University, 1990).

Pickel, K. L., "Unusualness and Threat as Possible Causes of Weapon Focus," *Memory* (1998) (6), 277–295.

Pickel, K. L., French, T. A., and Betts, J. M., "A Cross-modal Weapon Focus Effect: The Influence of a Weapon's Presence on Memory for Auditory Information," *Memory* (2003) (11), 277–292.

Pickel, K. L., Narter, D. B., Jameson, M. M., and Lenhardt, T. T., "The Weapon Focus Effect in Child Eyewitnesses," *Psychology, Crime and Law* (2008) (14:1), 61–72.

Pickel, K. L., Ross, S. J., and Truelove, R. S., "Do Weapons Automatically Capture Attention?" *Applied Cognitive Psychology* (2006) (20), 871–893.

Podlas, K., "Please Adjust Your Signal: How Television's Syndicated Courtrooms Bias Our Juror Citizenry," *American Business Law Review* (2001) (39), 1–24.

Polhemus, www.polhemus.com, accessed 30 June 2012.

Pryor, B., Strawn, D., Buchanan, R., and Meeske, M., "The Florida Experiment: An Analysis of the On-the-Scene Responses to Cameras in the Courtrooms," *Southern Speech Communications Journal* (1979) (45), 12–26.

"Project Expanded: More Courts Offering Digital Audio Recordings Online," US Courts, The Federal Judiciary, www.uscourts.gov/newsroom/2009/digitalAudio.cfm. Also http://www.uscourts.gov/news/NewsView/09-04-15/More_Courts_Offer_Online_Digital_Audio_Recordings.aspx, accessed 30 June 2012.

Pros and Cons of Courtroom Cameras Set Out, 15 November, 2004, www.number10.gov.uk/Page6578, accessed 30 June 2012.

PRS Research, www.prsresearch.com/prs-tools/, accessed 30 June 2012.

Punches, A. D., *The Cognitive Effects of Camera Presence on the Recall of Testimony in a Simulated Courtroom Setting*, Ph.D. (Colorado State University, Fort Collins, 1991).

Re, L., "Eyewitness Identification: Why So Many Mistakes?" *Australian Law Journal* (1984), 517.

Rayner, K., ed., *Eye Movements and Visual Cognition: Scene Perception and Reading* (New York: Springer-Verlag, 1992).

Reith, M., "Viewing of Crime Drama and Authoritarian Aggression: An Investigation of the Relationship Between Crime Viewing, Fear, and Aggression," *Journal of Broadcasting & Electronic Media* (1999) (43), 211–221.

Richardson, D., and Spivey, M., "Eye-tracking: Research Areas and Applications," in G. Bowlin and G. Wnek (2004).

Rimmer, T., *Electronic Media in the Courtroom: Legal and Social Science Perspectives* (Portland, OR: American Association for Education in Journalism and Mass Communication, 1988).

Roberts, A., "Eyewitness Identification and Expert Insight: *R v Forbes*," *International Journal of Evidence & Proof* (2010) (14), 57–62.

Rotunda, R. D., "Reporting Sensational Trials: Free Press, a Responsible Press, and Cameras in the Courts," *Communications Law and Policy* (1998) (3), 295–313.

Rudell, A. P., "The Television Camera Used to Measure Movement," *Behaviour Research Methods and Instrumentation* (1979) (11), 339–341.

Rusis, G., and Snyder, H. L., "The Effects of TV Camera Field of View and Size of Targets Upon Air-to-ground Target Recognition," *Human Factors/personnel* (1965) (7), 493–501.

Ryley, J., "Justice Must Be Televised, Allowing TV Cameras in Court Would Greatly Help to Restore Public Faith in Criminal Proceedings," *Guardian* online, 5 December, 2010, www.guardian.co.uk/commentisfree/2010/dec/05/justice-television-cameras-court-mps-expenses, accessed 30 June 2012.

RTNDA, Radio Television Digital News Association (RTDNA), http://www.rtnda.org/pages/media_items/cameras-in-the-court-a-state-by-state-guide55.php, accessed 30 June 2012.

Rutherford, H., and Raymond, J., "Effects of Spatial Cues on Locating Emotional Targets," *Visual Cognition* (2010) (18:3), 389–412.

Safer, M., Christianson, S.-A., Autry, M., and Osterlund, K., "Tunnel Memory for Traumatic Events," *Applied Cognitive Psychology* (1998) (12), 99–117.

Sato, W., and Yoshikawa, S., "Detection of Emotional Facial Expressions and Anti-Expressions," *Visual Cognition* (2010) (18:3), 369–388.

Saunders, J., "Memory Impairment in Weapon Focus Effect," *Memory and Cognition* (2009) (37:3), 326–335.

Scheiter, K., Wiebe, E., and Holsanova, J., "Theoretical and Instructional Aspects of Learning with Visualizations," in R. Zheng (2009).

Schmidt, H. C., *Effects of Interrogator Tactics and Camera Perspective Bias on Evaluations of Confession Evidence*, MSc thesis (Ohio University, 2006).

Setcan, www.setcan.com/eyelock.html, accessed 30 June 2012.

Shah, P., Freedman, E., and Vekiri, I., "The Comprehension of Quantitative Information in Graphical Displays," in P. Shah and A. Miyake (2005), 426–476.

Shah, P., and Miyake, A., *The Cambridge Handbook of Visuospatial Thinking* (Cambridge: Cambridge University Press, 2005).

Sherwin, R. K., *When Law Goes Pop: The Vanishing Line Between Law and Popular Culture* (Chicago: The University of Chicago Press, 2000).

——— "The Jurisprudence of Appearances," *New York Law School Law Review* (1999–2000) (43), 821–842.

Shores, D., *The Effects of Courtroom Camera on Verbal Behavior: An Analysis of Simulated Trial Witness Testimony in Courtrooms Using Television Cameras*, Ph.D. (The University of Florida, 1981), 59.

Short Report; Short, E. H., and Associates, *Evaluation of California's Experiment with Extended Media Coverage of Courts, Submitted to The Administrative Office for the Courts, The Chief Justice's Special Committee on the Courts and the Media and The California Judicial Council*, September 1981.

Silver, D. and Biggs, A., "Keystroke and Eye-Tracking Biometrics for User Identification," (2008), http://citeseerx.ist.psu.edu/viewdoc/summary?doi=10.1.1.88.4306, accessed 30 June 2012.

Slater, D. and Hans, V. P., "Methodological Issues in the Evaluation of 'Experiments' with Cameras in the Courts," *Communications Quarterly* (1982) (30:4), 376.

Slotnick, E. E., and Segal, J. A., *Television News and the Supreme Court: All the News That's Fit to Air?* (Cambridge: Cambridge University Press, 1998).

SMI, www.smi.com, accessed 30 June 2012.

——— www.smivision.com/en/gaze-and-eye-tracking-systems/home.html, accessed 30 June 2012.

Smith, C. E., *Courts and Trials: A Reference Handbook* (Santa Barbara, CA: ABC-CLIO, 2003).

Smith, P., *Evaluating the Corrective Statements Proposed in the Court Case US Department of Justice vs Philip Morris U.S.A. Inc., et al.*, MS (State University of New York at Buffalo, 2009).

Spector, J. M., *Handbook of Research on Educational Communications and Technology* (New York: Lawrence Erlbaum Associates, Taylor and Francis, 2008).

Sporer, S., Penrod, S., Read, D., and Cutler, B., "Choosing, Confidence and Accuracy: A Meta-analysis of the Confidence-Accuracy Relation in Eyewitness Identification Studies," *Psychological Bulletin* (1995) (118), 315–327.

Steblay, N., "A Meta-analytic Review of Weapon Focus Effect," *Law and Human Behavior* (1992) (16), 413–424.

Stepniak, D., *Audio-Visual Coverage of Courts* (Cambridge: Cambridge University Press, 2008).

Stewart, R. E. R., *The Changing Relationship Between Camera and the Courts*, MA (Florida Atlantic University, 1998).

Strickland, R. A., and Moore, R. H., "Cameras in State Courts: A Historical Perspective," *Judicature* (1994) (78), 128–135.

Stuart, R. E. R., *The Changing Relationship Between Camera and the Courts*, MA (Florida Atlantic University, 1998).

Study by Journalism Department at the University of Arizona, *New Law Journal*, 30 November, 1987, 13.

Sundstedt, V., *Eye-tracking in User Studies*, SIGGRAPH 2009, New Orleans, http://www.siggraph.org/s2009/, accessed 30 June 2012, and also http://www.scss.tcd.ie/Veronica.Sundstedt/ (link now broken).

"Sunshine in the Courtroom" bill. Introduced for the first time in 105th Congress (1997–1998), reintroduced in 109th (2005–2006), 110th (2007–2008) and 111th Congress (2009–2010). See H.R. 1280 (105th Congress), S. 829 (109th Congress), H.R. 2128, S. 352 (110th Congress), H.R. 3054 and S. 657 (111th Congress), www.govtrack.us/congress.

Tapper, C., *Cross and Tapper on Evidence* (Oxford: OUP, 2007).

TerBeek, C., "A Call or Precedential Heads: Why the Supreme Court's Eyewitness Identification Jurisprudence is Anachronistic and Out-of-Step with the Empirical Evidence," *Law & Psychology Review* (2007) (31), 21–51.

Terry, H. B., "Electronic Journalism in the Colorado Courts," *Journalism Quarterly* (1957) (34), 341–348.

Thaler, P., *The Impact of the Television Camera on Courtroom Participants: A Case Study of the Joel Stenberg Murder Trial*, Ph.D. (New York University, 1990).

The Courtroom Design and Research Centre, http://coweb.cc.gatech.edu/courtnext/3 and related pages, accessed 30 June 2012.

The Impact of Television, Radio and Still Photography on Coverage of Court Proceedings – Final Report, A Report Prepared for the Department of Courts by a research team from the Department of Human Management, Massey University (April, 1998) (New Zealand research).

The Special Committee on Radio and Television of the Association of the Bar of the City of New York, *Radio, Television, and the Administration of Justice: A Documented Survey of Materials* (New York and London: Columbia University Press, 1965), 99–100.

Tinkham, R. P., "Should Canon 35 be Amended? A Question of Proper Judicial Administration," *ABA Journal* (1956) (42), 843–845.

Tobii, at www.tobii.com, accessed 30 June 2012.

Tuggle, C. A., and Huffman, S., "Live Reporting in Television News: Breaking News or Black Holes?" *Journal of Broadcasting & Electronic Media* (2001) (45), 335–344.

Twining, W., *Rethinking Evidence, Exploratory Essays* (Oxford: Blackwell, 1990).

——— "Identification and Misidentification in Legal Processes: Redefining the Problem," in S. Lloyd-Bostock and B. R. Clifford (1985), 255–280.

UMR Insight Ltd., *Media Coverage of Court Proceedings: Summary Report* (February, 1998) (New Zealand research).

"US Judge Overturns Gay Marriage Ban," *Irish Times* online, 5 August, 2010, www.irishtimes.com, accessed 30 June 2012.

VAB Assessment Report to the [Virginia] Supreme Court, 1989, as referred to in T. D. Keller (1992), 12.

Valentine, T., Pickering, A., and Darling, S., "Characteristics of Eyewitness Identification that Predict the Outcome of Real Lineups," *Applied Cognitive Psychology* (2003) (17), 969–993.

Valikoski, T.-R., *The Criminal Trial as a Speech Communication Situation* (Tampere, Finland: University of Tampere, 2004).

Vo, M. L-H., and Schneider, W., "A Glimpse is Not a Glimpse: Differential Processing of Flashed Scene Previews Leads to Differential Target Search Benefits," *Visual Cognition* (2010) (18:2), 171–200.

Warden, K. P., "Canon 35: Is There Room for Objectivity?," *Washburn Law Journal* (1965) (4), 211.

Ware, L. J., *Monitoring Visual Attention in Videotaped Interrogations: An Investigation of the Camera Perspective Bias*, MSc thesis (Ohio University, 2006), 34–35.

Wedel, M., and Pieters, R., *"Eye-tracking for Visual Marketing" Foundations and Trends in Marketing* (2008), 4.

Weisberger, J. R., "Cameras in the Courtroom: The Rhode Island Experience," *Suffolk University Law Review* (1983), 299–311.

Wells, G., "Applied Eyewitness-testimony Research: System Variables and Estimator Variables," *Journal of Personality and Social Psychology* (1978) (12), 1546–1557.

Wells, G. L, and Bradfield, A. L, "'Good, You Identified the Suspect': Feedback to Eyewitnesses Distorts Their Reports of Witnessing Experience," *Applied Psychology* (1998) (83), 360–376.
Wells, G. L., Lindsay, R.C.L and Ferguson, T.J., "Accuracy, Confidence, and Juror Perceptions in Eyewitness Identification," *Journal of Applied Psychology* (1979) (64:4), 440–448.
Westcott, H. L., "Children's Credibility on Camera: The Influence of Age and Production Factors/ Personnel," *Children and Society* (1991) (5), 254–265.
Wickens, C. D., Vincow, M., and Yeh, M., "Design Applications of Visual Spatial Thinking: The Importance of Frame of Reference," in P. Shah and A. Miyake (2005).
Williams, C. C., "Not all Visual Memories Are Created Equal," *Visual Cognition* (2010) (18:2), 201–228.
Wisenand, J., "Florida's Experiment," *American Bar Association Journal* (1978) (64), 1860–1863.
Wood, K., "Calls for Live TV of Tribunals," *Sunday Business Post*, 30 April, 2000.
——— *Televising the Courts: A Radio Telefis Eireann Discussion Paper* (Dublin: RTE, 1995).
Woolnough, P. and MacLoud, M., "Watching the Birdie Watching You: Eyewitness Memory for Actions Using CCTV Recordings of Actual Crimes," *Applied Cognitive Psychology* (2001) (15), 395–411.Yuille, J., and Cutshall, J., "A Case Study of Eyewitness Memory of a Crime," *Journal of Applied Psychology* (1986) (71), 291–301.
Yuille, J., Davies, G., Gibling, F., Marxsen, D., and Porter, S., "Eyewitness Memory of Police Trainees for Realistic Role Plays," *Journal of Applied Psychology* (1994) (79), 931–936.
Zanna, M., ed., *Advances, in Experimental Social Psychology*, Vol. 20 (San Diego, CA: Academic Press, 2001), 189–253.
Zheng, R., ed., *Cognitive Effects of Multimedia Learning* (Hershey, PA: IGI Global, 2009).
Zuckerman, A. A. S., and Cranston, R., *Reform of Civil Procedure: Essays on Access to Justice* (Oxford: Clarendon, 1995).